ARTS IN THE RELIGIONS OF THE PACIFIC

RELIGION AND THE ARTS SERIES

Also published in the series:

Art and Religion in Africa by Rosalind I.J. Hackett

Frontispiece. Mask for harvest dance, wood, 57cm high. Torres Strait
islands. Otago Museum (photo).

ARTS IN THE RELIGIONS OF THE PACIFIC

SYMBOLS OF LIFE

Albert C. Moore

CASSELL

London and Washington

Cassell

Wellington House, 125 Strand, London WC2R 0BB, England
PO Box 605, Herndon, Virginia 20172-0605, USA

First published in hardback by Pinter 1995
First published in paperback 1997

British Library Cataloguing in Publication Data
A catalogue record for this book is available from the British Library.

ISBN 0-304-70058-4 (paperback)

Library of Congress Cataloging-in-Publication Data
Moore, Albert C.
    Arts in the religions of the Pacific: symbols of life/Albert C.
Moore.
      p. cm. – (Religion and the arts series)
    Originally published: London : New York : Pinter, 1995.
    Includes bibliographical references and index.
    ISBN 0-304-70058-4 (pbk.)
    1. Arts and religion – Oceania. 2. Arts – Oceania. 3. Symbolism in
art – Oceania. I. Title. II. Series.
NX180.R4M66 1997
704.9'48992 – dc21   97-36168
                                                   CIP

Typeset by Mayhew Typesetting, Rhayader, Powys
Printed and bound in Great Britain by SRP Ltd, Exeter

CONTENTS

vii

LIST OF ILLUSTRATIONS

ABBREVIATIONS

BCE Before Common or Christian Era (BC)
CE   Common Era (AD in Christian chronology)
Chap./ch. Chapter
Edn   Edition
ER   *Encyclopedia of Religion* (ed. M. Eliade) 1987
EWA *Encyclopaedia of World Art*
LMS   London Missionary Society
NZ   New Zealand (Aotearoa New Zealand)
PAN *Pacific Arts Newsletter*, 1975–89
PAJ   *Pacific Arts, Journal of Pacific Arts Association*, 1990–
PNG   Papua New Guinea.

PREFACE

Like the Pacific Ocean itself, the subject of the arts in religions of this area may seem impossibly large for one book. It can be frustrating to have to cover so much in a short space and for the writer this means constantly summarizing and selecting. Despite this, I have found the research rewarding as new material and new ideas are opened up on this vast canvas.

My hope is that the book will communicate some of my excitement and provoke readers to do their own exploring by travel to the Pacific both intellectually and geographically.

Aim, scope and approach

The focus of this book is on the religions of the Pacific and on their expression in art forms. As an introductory book it does not seek to impose or prove a theory but to draw on a variety of theories and methods which may prove illuminating for the great variety of religious cultures in the Pacific, each with its own pattern of events, observers and records. Hence a variety of methods and disciplines may be drawn on throughout this book. These derive first from the wide 'subject-field' of religious studies, based on the history of religions and the phenomenology of religion. Among the associated disciplines, prominence is given to anthropology and art history, with reference to music and dance as well as to the visual arts. If there is a dominant approach here it is the readiness to use these various disciplines wherever they help to reveal something of the life experience in the art and religion. In the concrete examples of the arts cited throughout the book we seek to place them in the context first of the local life-setting of religion and the arts, then of the wider context of the geographical and cultural region (such as Polynesia) and then the historical setting where this can be known. Specifically, this involves us in looking at the arts as ways of understanding the life and soul of the people who practise them, which means an alertness to their religious forms of experience.

In writing about each region of the Pacific my concern has been to outline the history and connections with the past, as a museum seeks to do for viewers. But arts and religions are not static and we must consider the changes which have affected them throughout the past and continue at a faster pace in the 20th century. In the case of the Pacific we see the changes drawing the hitherto isolated regions and cultures into relations with others. Since 1993 was publicized as the 'year of indigenous peoples', it is fitting to study the peoples of the Pacific with awareness of these changes.

Further use of this book

The emphasis of this book is on the particular forms of religion and art in the context of life in the Pacific regions. There is a great diversity of themes and these are not manifested equally in the regions; this makes it difficult to generalize about the Pacific as a whole. Nevertheless, it is worthwhile to compare on a wider canvas some important recurring themes such as the following:

'Art' and 'Craft' in the Pacific
Artists and their relation to the sacred
Ancestors and skulls
Animal life and the sacred
Body-painting, tattooing, 'personal art'
Magic in art and religion
Masks as mediators of the sacred
Patrons and clan ownership of the arts
Roles of men and women in the arts
Sacred materials, paints and ochres
Sacred space and places
Sacred times in use of the arts
Water and other natural symbols

Readers and students are encouraged to follow up some of these themes, first by referring to the index of this book and then by following up the themes from encyclopedia articles (Eliade 1987, *ER*) and from larger works listed in the references. For instance, the theme of 'sacred place' could be compared on the wider scene of major religions of the world covered in the volume of that title in the recent series of 'Themes in Religious Studies' (Holm and Bowker 1994). Similarly, the theme of 'picturing God' relates to sacred images and the iconography of religions (Moore 1977). While the present book is limited in the detail that can be offered in its pages, it seeks to offer a comprehensive introduction to the Pacific arts and religions; it is intended as a stimulus to making further connections and opening up further research on such themes.

The sources and authors cited in the text of each chapter are listed in full in the concluding list of references. It is important that readers become aware of the new and often excellent material which is available but not well known, especially if published in a corner of the Pacific. Increasingly this may include films and video recordings which convey the 'happening' and living quality of Pacific arts; it is worth the effort of hunting these out from educational film libraries.

The living quality of these Pacific arts is central to this book and is summed up in the sub-title *Symbols of Life*. Several threads from this lead through the Pacific arts described here to have relevance for arts in Western and other cultures. One is the power of symbols drawn from nature and materials in local life to find universal and cosmic significance. Another thread is the variety of Pacific arts which transcends formal distinctions between 'art' and 'craft' and between 'high' and 'popular' arts. These distinctions are now to be questioned in Western arts, as the philosopher David Novitz argues well in his book *The Boundaries of Art* (1992); he views art as integral to life and explores their intersectings in ways which can relate to our understanding of Pacific arts. Another thread is that of the imagination working on everyday life experience to bring a 'magical transformation' as I call it. A further thread is the focus on the human body, not only in visual depictions but in the bodily postures and movements evoked in the viewer by music, dance and ritual. These will raise questions for readers to apply to their own experiences of the arts. For my part, I intend to pursue them further in my own experience, study and writing in the arts.

For further reading of accessible books with colour illustrations (which this book does not supply) a short list of 'recommended reading' of books and also journals is given at the end. A glossary is included to explain some key terms used in the various regions.

Finally, in my view, the index should be much more than a handy short-cut or a perfunctory conclusion to the book. It is meant to help the reader to cross-reference and to make fruitful connections, contrasts and comparisons across the regions of the Pacific.

Albert C. Moore
Dunedin, New Zealand
August 1994

ACKNOWLEDGEMENTS

More than one writer has experienced the labour of completing a book as a process of giving birth. Amid all the labour pains one is grateful for the support and encouragement given by others.

This book owes its birth to the originating vision of Professor John Hinnells (formerly of Manchester and now at SOAS, University of London) and to the organization of Pinter Publishers. For their work and suggestions I express my gratitude – spanning the world by communications from Britain to the antipodes in New Zealand, we have found it possible to produce the present book. For immediate practical assistance here in Dunedin I have relied on the work of Trudie Aicken in typing the manuscript. I also appreciate the work of the illustrator, Mark Lawson, as well as the photography by the University Photographic Unit and by François Leurquin, conservator at the Otago Museum.

I wish to thank those individuals and institutions providing photographs as acknowledged in the captions to the illustrations – the Otago Museum; Dr. Erich Kolig of the Anthropology department, University of Otago; the National Gallery of Victoria, Melbourne; and the Aboriginal Artists Agency, Sydney. For the cover painting I am glad to have 'Pacific Solar', the work of a New Zealand artist, Nigel Brown of Auckland; this is by courtesy of Milford Galleries, Dunedin.

Much of my interest in the subject of arts in the religions of the Pacific has emerged from my 25 years of teaching and research in Religious Studies at the University of Otago. I am grateful for the facilities and encouragement offered by the University. Of special importance for research is the availability in Dunedin of excellent library resources and the help of staff of the University Library, the Hocken Library and the Hewitson (Knox College) Library. As for the Otago Museum, there is visual evidence in this book of the value of its collections and the stimulus given by its fine displays of Pacific material, especially in the Melanesian and Maori halls.

I must also acknowledge my debt to colleagues in the university who have shared their knowledge, ideas and criticisms. Some of the material in this book came to light through seminars with my colleagues in Religious Studies. I have gained much from contacts with the departments of History, Anthropology and Art History and Theory, as well as the Theology Faculty research group on 'Christianity in Asia and the Pacific'. This sharing of information and ideas is surely what a university should be for. Whether from staff, students or fellow-researchers, such criticisms and suggestions have made a welcome contribution to my writing. In covering such a wide range of material I acknowledge my vulnerability to errors and misinterpretations; the responsibility for these is mine.

Further afield I have been helped by researchers of similar interests in the Pacific area – especially my colleagues in Religious Studies at Massey University, Palmerston North, as well as others whom I have met at conferences of the Religious Studies associations in New Zealand and Australia. I have sought to acknowledge my specific sources in the lists of references and illustrations for this book. However, some of the help received is not so easy to categorize because it is in the form of personal example and inspiration. When my wife Alexa and I spent several weeks in mid-1992 in the Pacific (at Suva, Fiji, then the Solomon Islands and Papua New Guinea) we felt we had met some great people who were dedicated to life in the Pacific, religion and the arts. To them this book is dedicated.

A.C.M.

CHAPTER I

INTRODUCTION: THE PACIFIC — UNDERSTANDING ITS RELIGIONS AND ARTS

'The Pacific Ocean is the greatest single geographical feature of our planet . . . .' (Douglas Newton, in Gathercole et al. 1979: 27)

'Of all the parts of the world, Oceania is the emptiest of land and people. Water is the commonest element by far, and fire is rarely absent.' (Jean Guiart 1963: 1)

The Pacific region: Oceania

Many books dealing with the Pacific region and its cultures and religions begin by stressing the vastness of the area — and justly so. We do well to realize the sheer courage of those original peoples who settled the Pacific Islands by sailing vast distances into the unknown, like 'Vikings of the Pacific' (Buck 1959). When we look at European maps from the great Renaissance age of exploration in the 16th century we may be chilled by their labelling of the mysterious southern continent as 'Terra Australis incognita'. We realize again the achievement of Europeans such as the Dutch explorer Abel Tasman in the 17th century and the British James Cook in the 18th century.

This book is not attempting to cover either the prehistory of the Pacific (Bellwood 1978a) or the European 'discovery' and response to it (Badger 1988). But it can be said that the term 'Pacific Ocean' is a result of such European exploration (and exploitation). The indigenous inhabitants were unaware of being part of some pan-Pacific family. It was the Portuguese Magellan whose round-the-world voyage took him through the straits that bear his name at the southern tip of the Americas to traverse the vast but comparatively calm waters which he called the Pacific in 1521 CE; he died in the Philippines before completing the journey home. In the following centuries it was due to European exploration and navigation that labels came to be given to the major geographical–cultural regions within the Ocean. These are shown on the accompanying map (figure 1). There is a certain artificiality about the demarcation of such regions which have had waves of

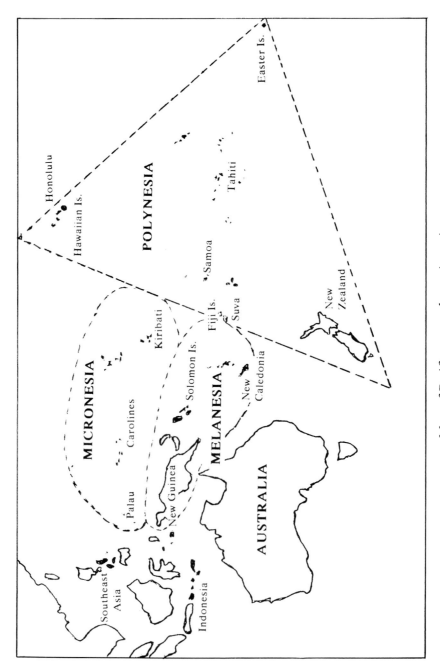

1.   Map of Pacific area and 4 main regions.

migration and degrees of cultural overlap. The labels were given by outsiders voyaging in the Pacific and have neither uniform logic nor relation to the inhabitants' own views. 'Melanesia' (literally 'black islands') refers to the black colour of the people. 'Polynesia' ('many islands') refers to the number of islands scattered over the vast area. 'Micronesia' ('small islands') refers to their size. Nevertheless, the terms are convenient groupings for our purposes and will be explained further in the relevant chapters which follow.

In recent years there has been much interest in the development of links between countries of the 'Pacific rim'. The term 'Pacific basin' can be used to include six major zones in an extended sense. These are: 1. the South and Centre ('Island Pacific'); 2. Southeast Asia; 3. China; 4. Japan and 'fringe East Asia'; 5. North America; 6. Latin America. While modern communications have brought these zones into much closer contact with each other, there is little chance of making sense of the Pacific area from such an array of disparate peoples and nations. Since these include over half of the world's population they have to be related to the yet wider global context of politics and modern economics (Segal 1990: 1–13).

However, it does make good sense to focus on the first of these zones in our study of the arts of religions. The South and Centre ('Island Pacific') includes Australia and New Zealand, Polynesia, Micronesia and Melanesia. Apart from Australia, the indigenous peoples belonged to the East Austronesian language family (Bellwood 1978a: 116, ch. 5). They can be understood as linked by prehistoric migration patterns, from antiquity to the last millennium. They developed their primal cultures and religions virtually without any contact from Asia and Europe until the 19th century. Since then Christianity has replaced the traditional religions as the dominant religion, in its various forms, within the Pacific. In the 20th century the peoples have become increasingly conscious of participating in the region of the Pacific Ocean, often being included under the term 'Oceania'. The Pacific Arts Association refers to the art and artists of 'Oceania' in the titles of its conference symposium volumes (Mead 1979, 1983; Hanson 1990). Within this framework we shall be following the major divisions listed above.

Some practical adjustments have been made here, such as the inclusion of Micronesia as a section in the chapter on Polynesia. Also a decision has been made to include Fiji in the chapter on Polynesia. Although the Fijians, as the original population, are Melanesian in physical type and in aspects of their religion, culture and social organization, they have also had Polynesian influences and admixtures. On the map of the Pacific the boundaries of Polynesia can be shown as a triangle from Easter Island to Hawaii and down to New Zealand. The western side of the triangle would run through the Fiji Islands, which is appropriate enough. Of course there are no such boundary-lines in reality and we must keep in mind the overlapping of influences in culture, religion and the arts.

One further area adjoining Australia and Melanesia is Indonesia, referring to the former 'East Indies' with its heritage of Hinduized culture from Southeast Asia. On the evidence assembled in Bellwood's masterly and comprehensive survey of the prehistory of the Pacific, it is essential to relate this to prehistoric origins in Southeast Asia (Bellwood 1978a). Links to the Pacific are still to be seen in some indigenous cultures such as the Batak in Sumatra, the Dayak in Borneo and the Toraja in Sulawesi (Barbier and Newton 1988). However, present-day Indonesia as a whole represents a cultural area and a large population that do not fit easily with our study of the 'Island Pacific'. With some reluctance, therefore, we shall keep within the lines of division as stated, while recognizing their limitations.

Why be interested in the Pacific?

Confronted by the vast spread of Oceania and the comparatively small population scattered over its islands, one might well ask why anyone beyond its inhabitants would be interested in studying such a remote area. Continents with long-established cultures and religions as in Europe, Asia and Africa have massive populations and a wealth of artistic forms to claim our attention, so what can we expect to gain from studying the arts of the religions of the Pacific? Our own expectations probably follow those of the European discoverers and explorers of the Pacific who brought back information to the western world and aroused the interest of many. It should therefore prove helpful to follow through their interests.

First there is the challenge of the unknown which elicits the desire to explore, to find new lands and travel-routes and to make contact with peoples of strange languages and customs. This is not confined to the great explorations of the Pacific in the 18th and 19th centuries. In the mid-20th century remote areas and tribes in New Guinea were still being opened up for the first time to contact with the 'outside world'. Knowledge of the Pacific area is still thinly spread in the world and when 'discovered' can awaken intense interest and the desire to visit the Pacific. At the lower levels this may be little more than curiosity, the longing for adventure and the hope of making money by exploiting the people and resources of the area. These motives guided many early explorers and adventurers, as they do their more sophisticated modern representatives. But it is also fair to recognize as a motivation the desire to gain information about the world and to spread understanding of the peoples and their cultures. As Bernard Smith points out, a European vision of the Pacific arts developed from interest in 'curiosities': 'To say that an object was "curious" was to express an interest in it without passing an aesthetic judgment', as for instance in noting that Maoris were 'curiously tattooed' (Smith 1985: 123). Here we can see the beginnings of a respect for another culture's ways, amounting even to admiration and wonder at its artistic achievements. This is apparent in the late Michael Rockefeller's anthropological observations in 1961 of the head-hunting Asmat people of Irian Jaya (see chapter 3 below). It is also found in the modern study of religions — for instance in the 'detached-within' approach of the phenomenology of religion which seeks first to understand the unknown 'other' without pre-judging it (King 1968: 6–8).

Another appeal of the Pacific for the European public lay in the idealized expectation of a Pacific paradise. This has ancient roots in the myth of a lost paradise and a nostalgia for recovering it. In the 18th century Jean-Jacques Rousseau voiced the idea of the 'noble savage' who was a child of nature, unspoilt by Western civilization. It is not surprising therefore that this expectation could feed on travellers' tales of idyllic ease and freedom from restraints in the Pacific. In fact, of course, such stereotypes were proved false by experience of the constraints of living in a 'savage' society; moreover, the proud warrior was also capable of treachery, avarice and cruelty, like people in other cultures. These idealized stereotypes of the Pacific continue to be employed in popular entertainment and in promoting commercial tourism for the Pacific. In this sense the appeal is a betrayal of Rousseau's Romanticism. But in its more profound sense the Romantic movement was a search for personal experience, emotion and spirituality in touch with nature. This search has provided an ideal by which to criticize Western exploitation of the environment, for instance. The Romantic ideal has also inspired researchers in anthropology and religion with the expectation that we have something to learn from primal cultures of the Pacific and that we can grow in understanding and empathy by sharing in their way of life at first hand.

A third avenue of appeal is through the application of this in the experience of the arts. When, in the later 19th century, so-called 'primitive' art became accessible through museums and travel, it began to have an impact on European artists. Its immediacy, simplicity and emotional power seemed to offer an alternative to the formal traditions of classical art. The example of Gauguin is well known: his 'romantic primitivism' led him in 1891 to abandon France for life in Tahiti and the Marquesas islands of Polynesia (Danielsson 1965; Amishai-Maisels 1985; Daws 1980). Following the post-impressionists, the 20th-century modern art movement was catalysed around 1905 by the impact of Negro and other 'primitive' art on Picasso and Matisse, leading to cubism and fauvism. Among the German expressionists, Emil Nolde was influenced by a visit to Southeast Asia and the western Pacific in 1913. The affinity of the tribal and the modern in the artists of the 20th-century movements has been well documented and critically discussed (Rubin 1984). In an earlier study of the 'primitivism' of modern painting and sculpture, Robert Goldwater concluded that it had little real similarity with primitive art understood in terms of its own background and aesthetics (Goldwater 1938, 1986). Some recent studies have found racist and colonialist assumptions underlying much of the fashionable interest in 'primitivism' in modern art (Hiller 1991; Torgovnick 1990). In the following chapters of this book we shall seek to understand the Pacific arts in the light of their own religious and associated concerns. Meanwhile, even the artistic fashions of the 'primitive' have brought to Western awareness some of the qualities of these works as art of a different sort with a living and potentially universal appeal.

A fourth area of interest in the Pacific, of relevance here, is the scholarly study of religions. Here, as in the field of the arts, travel and the contacts of colonialism and missionary work in the 19th century made available a rich collection of materials on the religions of the world. It is no surprise that with the experience of its Dutch East Indies the Netherlands gave an early lead, with scholars of comparative religion and university courses in the history of religions. In Melanesia and Polynesia British missionary teachers and ethnologists such as Codrington set the example of gathering data on religion for a more embracing view of the religions of humanity. One of the motivating questions behind such studies in the later 19th century was: 'How did religion begin?' This hardy perennial had been given mythologically based answers since antiquity; but now the empirical study of 'primitive' religions seemed to offer the possibility of scientific research on religions which were assumed to be survivals of religion from the 'childhood of mankind', from prehistory. We can now see that such an assumption is misguided and that indeed the whole search for origins in religion was misguided. (Probably the underlying motivation of this search was really to know the future of religion; once its truth or falsity could be exposed by seeing how religion began, humanity could evolve towards a more universal true religion or a replacement of religion.) Nevertheless, this search did stimulate scholarly and public interest in the religions of the Pacific. Did the concept of *mana* from Melanesia and Polynesia point to religious power as the basic concept for all religions? Was there after all a primordial belief in a High God preceding primitive animism? If the Australian Aborigines were the most primordial survivals from prehistory, would not totemism be the original source of religion? And could not the Polynesian sense of *tapu* indicate the force of social prohibitions at the root of all religion?

It is noteworthy that religions from the Pacific area provided a focus for many studies of these questions in the 19th and early 20th centuries. As scholarly research has moved on from these issues, Australia and Melanesia have continued to be important in studies of the nature of primal religion, of cargo cults and of other such new religious movements combining traditional features with modern expectations. Magic, ritual and the arts of a given culture are all important themes in recent anthropological studies of Pacific area peoples. Often they are able to delineate processes of change which have been observed over several decades, thus showing realistically the changing forms and interpretations of religion. At the more practical level the study of primal religions and arts has led to the revival of art forms in many parts of the Pacific, thus feeding back into the life of local cultures and artists. At the international level such studies have also re-awakened the search for myth, self and community; primal religions and arts, as evident in shamanism, are seen as an antidote to the decline of modern art in the West which is in need now of 're-enchantment' (Gablik 1991).

Not all of these expectations will be in the minds of those who study the Pacific; but the interests evident in the past continue to motivate people in the present. Whatever the initial interest may be, it will lead on to a more comprehensive view. In studying the arts of the Pacific one finds that they are interwoven with the religions of the Pacific region. In this book religion is the focus of our approach to the arts.

What does 'religion' mean?

Since religion can mean many things there is an urgent need to clarify the way in which it is understood here, so that the focus will do justice to the variety of the Pacific arts and religions and not unduly distort the data studied. Clearly, the many-sided nature of religion and the diversity of the world's religions render any single definition inadequate. It is misleading to expect to find an immutable 'essence' of religion in these. A more profitable beginning is to regard religions more as living organisms and to look for the component, inter-related, parts. In this way Ninian Smart suggests that we can discern patterns in the 'luxurious vegetation of the world's religions' by looking at the different aspects as seven 'dimensions' (Smart 1989: 12–21). These are: the practical and ritual dimension; the experiential and emotional; the narrative or mythic; the doctrinal and philosophical; the ethical and legal; the social and institutional; and the material (art, architecture and sacred places of religion). Although these dimensions will be manifested and related very differently within the various types of religion, the value of the list lies in ensuring a balanced description of religions. By contrast, for instance, a typical Western dictionary definition of religion such as 'belief in gods or supernatural powers' is quite inadequate for understanding the ritual celebration of an Australian Aboriginal initiation or the vivid use of Melanesian masks. On the other hand it does select one central dimension as the criterion of religion: 'the firm conviction on the believer's part (not the observer's) of the actual existence of a supernatural, supersensory order of being' and of its interplay through symbols with life in the world (Sharpe 1983: 48). More important than defining religion, says this scholar, is the ability to recognize it when we come across it.

A good definition must be comprehensive and free from tendentiousness while also bringing out crucial characteristics. It is a mark of responsibility to bring some order and consistency to usage of the term 'religion' and to show what features warrant our applying it to certain human activities and experiences (otherwise we are likely to be subjected to vagueness and bias from unexamined popular usage). Further, the definition(s) should relate to religion as it happens in the lives of people and not as an abstract analysis; for we know religion only through experiences, events and expressions in human lives. For this, two complementary definitions are illuminating.

From the standpoint of the sociology of religion, Peter Berger writes:

> Religion is the human attitude towards a sacred order that includes within it all being – human or otherwise – i.e. belief in a cosmos, the meaning of which both includes and transcends man. (Berger 1967: 338)

This definition focuses on the 'cosmos', meaning an ordered universe which includes in its space all things visible and invisible; it can apply to a monotheistic religion, based on worship of God the Creator, and also to the Aboriginal whose life is surrounded by the eternal 'Dreaming'.

If this definition presents a more static spatial image of a sacred cosmos, it is complemented by a more dynamic emphasis on transformation in time; this is the well worked out definition by Frederick Streng: 'Religion as a means toward ultimate transformation' (Streng et al. 1973: 6–15). Its concern is to understand the world of the believer as he or she experiences the world and moves through events and stages towards an ultimate goal beyond. Examples here would be religious festivals for the community and 'rites of passage' which progress from birth, through initiation and marriage and finally through death where one may join the ancestors. Life may be seen as a journey with a sacred destiny which is highlighted from time to time in life's crises.

Further definitions could be cited to describe the transformation as 'salvation', or to show how it is mediated by 'revelation' and a 'system of symbols'. To count as religious they must be understood as in some way related to what is sacred, transcendent, of ultimate value. In its most general form of expression this 'what' or object of religion has been referred to as power – for instance in the Melanesian term *mana* which is a dynamic happening (see chapter 3). In primal religions it is clear that people find themselves in a world full of mysterious powers, powers which they confront as 'a highly exceptional and extremely impressive "Other"' (Leeuw 1938:

ch. 1). From this experience of Other Power, religious worship (literally 'worth-ship') is the human response to the supreme power-worth, as sacred or holy.

Our emphasis here is on the human *response*, for it is the response to sacred powers in space and time which calls for the religious rituals and the expressions in the arts which we are studying. Here we must note an ambivalence in regard to the sacred. On the one hand the sacred is understood as something or some state opposed to the profane or ordinary, thus dividing the world into two domains (Durkheim 1915: 36–42). The sacred makes a break in the homogeneous space of the profane (Eliade 1959: 20–29). Yet the sacred is also manifested in the midst of the profane – for instance, in an otherwise ordinary-looking stone, or a house or person. There can be degrees of sacredness in the way sacred designs are kept secret or made available on everyday objects. Another ambivalence is emphasized in Rudolf Otto's study of 'the Holy'. On the one hand is the *mysterium tremendum,* the mysterious and overwhelming power of the 'Wholly Other' to which the response is amazement and shuddering awe. But the other side of this 'numinous experience' is the *fascinans,* to which one is drawn in positive wonder, joy and devotion (Otto 1923: chs 1–6). Both sides are part of religion.

Examples of such responses are readily to be found in the world's religions and in the arts of religions in the Pacific. Here we are not concerned to make a rigid distinction between the universal 'world religions' such as Christianity and the so-called 'primitive' religions of tribal, pre-literate peoples. The term 'primitive' is misleading because of its implications of inferiority and backwardness, as well as of misplaced evolutionism. Instead we prefer the term 'primal' to indicate that, while the religions of these smaller-scale societies anteceded the arrival of the great historic religions, they continue to show many of the basic or primary features of religion. Harold Turner analyses these as human kinship with nature and relations with transcendent powers in the universe; human weakness yet also destiny in afterlife; and above all the existence of a living cosmos within which physical acts are vehicles for the spiritual, in a sacramental universe (Turner 1977). The point is that these features can be discerned in varying degrees in the diverse primal religions; they also apply to universal religions. Therefore we can regard primal religions not as primitive, nor as elementary and peripheral, but as nuclear and elemental. The powerful appeal of their art-forms to Europeans, as already mentioned, is evidence in support of this judgment. This appeal, however, should not be linked to the term 'primitive'. Likewise, such terms as 'ethnographic', 'underdeveloped', 'Third World' and 'marginal' define their art as in contrast to dominant Western power and affluence. These terms should now be read 'in quotes' as being deeply problematic (Hiller 1991: 4).

Religion and art: common ground

Despite the difficulties raised by the task of defining religion amid the sea of diverse religions, there is value in comprehensive definitions which focus on the human response to the transcendent in terms of a sacred cosmos and ultimate transformation. These bring out a distinctively religious strain in the data studied from a wide range of cultures. But when we look at the rituals, myths and sacred objects and institutions, we find the religion to be expressed through familiar forms of the culture. This is inevitable in so far as culture depends on communication through symbols including language and visual images. Metaphor is built into human thought and we live by metaphors (Lakoff and Johnson 1980; Armstrong 1971: xix, 55–79). Religion points to and mediates the realm of the sacred by a system of symbols which become 'magic doorways' to the mysterious beyond; even the plainest symbols 'are magic portals into the other world where the truth of one's religion is visible, felt and far overshadows the inconsistent ordinary' (Ellwood 1983: 100). Religious rituals are like a drama involving actors and audience who are carried away in a story that stirs the emotions.

These and other parallels provide the grounds for a 'first attempt at a theory' in socio-psychological terms by Benjamin Beit-Hallahmi: that religion is a work of art. 'Religion, like art, is a form and a product of human labor . . . . It is (for believers and even for nonbelievers) beautiful, harmonious, pleasing and attractive . . . . Religion and art are both comforting illusions in a world which makes such illusions necessary' (Beit-Hallahmi 1989: 77). 'We go to church for the same reason that we go to the movies, because the fantasies presented at both places are gratifying' (1989: 104). Questions will be asked about this provocative argument. How then are art and religion different? The second part of this theory argues that religion and church-going express identity by sacralizing a group identity and involving the followers in claims to truth and behaviour based on this identity. This appears to be a distinguishing criterion of religion; yet the question must be asked whether art also involves identity.

Here we are looking at the complex issue of the relation – or interrelation – of art and religion. In much traditional art of past ages religions supplied the content and direction, while artists were their servants. But when in modern times the artist is given the status of a free creative agent, is it now art that swallows up religion? Is religion just aesthetic taste? The reality is surely much more subtle and complex. As David Chidester points out, 'in the lived reality of our experience we are caught up in an intricate network of judgments that are simultaneously religious and aesthetic' (Chidester 1983: 55). To show the common ground shared by religion and art we shall now refer to four concepts: identity, power, magic and imagination.

The concept of *identity* refers to a sense of belonging which an individual may experience as a member of a family, a tribal group, a religion and other communities. It relates the person to the social or cultural group; there is both a sense of being recognized as somebody in oneself and a sense of loyalty to the group. In the case of religion, identity is sacralized by being part of a given order of things, along with the ritual, myth and emotional commitment by which the religion continues to support the member's identity. In the case of the arts we find similar effects, as examples make clear from the Pacific Arts Association's 1984 symposium on 'Art and Identity in Oceania'. Among the questions raised was the political issue of the 'ownership' of arts by local Pacific cultures as against outsiders seeking to comment on what was part of local identity (Hanson 1990: 3–4). But the use of art as a political tool is only one aspect of identity, since there can be an unselfconscious traditional expression of it in art and also a more conscious reflection on changing values and lifestyles.

In Papua New Guinea a whole range of arts becomes focused at a high level around initiation and other ceremonies which relate the human and spiritual worlds via the sacred arts (E. Schwimmer, in Hanson 1990: 6–7). For the Australian Aboriginal, identity is deeply felt through the land and its features as hallowed by the 'Dreaming'; so even when modern styles of painting are borrowed from the white man the aim is to reflect a sense of separate identity (J.V.S. Megaw, in Hanson 1990: 282–92). Identity is at its strongest at the more local, sub-tribal or *hapu* level of New Zealand Maori art. This is not to overlook the strong sense of national pride in Maori art expressed both by Maori and pakeha (non-Maori) people in New Zealand as a whole, but the strength of local identity comes out in this account of reunion with cultural roots in the arts:

> After being away from the tribal heartlands for many years one of the greatest experiences for us is to stand before our tribal house and then to go inside it . . . . It is a proud moment when one can say: 'This is my house, these are my ancestors, and this artwork is part of my heritage'. (S.M. Mead, in Hanson 1990: 281)

In such experiences religious and cultural identities are embodied in the artworks, themselves often occasions combining a number of art forms.

The concept of *power* is one which is likewise significant for both religion and art. This is in spite of a common attitude in modern Western society to see them as relatively powerless and to classify them together as marginal 'leisure-time' activities. If the 'real world' is a matter of politics and the market-place, arts and religious gatherings are seen from that standpoint as useless or at best as decorative luxuries. But this is far from the traditional assessment of them. As we have seen, religion has meant tapping the spiritual

source of power and the modern study of primal religions has led to a focus on cosmic and transformative power as important for a definition of religion. When it comes to the arts these again are efficacious, suffused with power from the gods or supernatural sources. The tendency of Western art history and criticism has been to classify such traditional attitudes as 'popular and superstitious' in their expectation of magic; art instead has 'aesthetic' functions which are the proper concern of a cultivated appreciation of art. However this opposition has been strongly challenged recently by David Freedberg, an art historian who deals with 'the power of images' and religious and other responses to them. It is not enough to discuss images in terms of the formal qualities of high art criticism nor to view them in their historical context alone. We must be prepared to consider the use and function of images and of responses to them. This applies not only to 'primitive magic' but to the psychological arousal and behavioural responses we can observe in ourselves as 'civilized' people. Freedberg considers, with abundant examples, such themes as death, sex and religious devotion. Artworks can have a 'presence' which moves us 'beyond words, even to tears' (Freedberg 1989: 432).

His case is concerned to prepare for a theory of response; this is meant to cover the outwardly markable responses of beholders along with their motivating beliefs. This leads on to consideration of the effectiveness and vitality of the images and what they are expected to do. For instance, when images are consecrated there is a transition to a sacredly endowed object; and when people garland, wash or crown images, these acts 'are symptoms of a relationship between image and respondent that is clearly predicated on the attribution of powers which transcend the purely material aspect of the object' (Freedberg 1989: 91). The emphasis here on the response of the beholder is vital for the understanding of art and religion, as well as for art in general. Although Freedberg's study is in the area of Western art, its implications relate to all art and particularly to examples from primal and modern religion in the Pacific.

The concept of power has already involved the concept of *magic*, understood as the drawing on special supernatural powers to change the course of events or to affect people for good or ill. 'Magic' is a controversial term with a number of dimensions and applications (O'Keefe 1982). It has traditionally been seen as opposed to established religions, although the history of religions shows magical ideas and practices to be at work within and around religions through the ages, as well as in the arts. It can be fairly argued in this light that in its prehistoric origins art was involved in the magic of power for society; art was a magic tool and the artist was society's supreme sorcerer (Fischer 1963: ch. 2). But leaving aside speculations about the past, one can find the common source of religion and art in the human potential for a type of magical experience. This is not the literal use of magic through spells and

charms but the experience of 'enchantment' by which our imagination is switched to a different plane, thereby transforming our vision of ourselves and our everyday world. The skilled artist – painter, dancer, musician – is able to evoke in us this alternation to other worlds which we are able to enter imaginatively. Religious devotion and ritual also evoke this alternation to what is perceived as a sacred cosmos. The experience linking magic, religion and the arts in this way I have called 'magical transformation', seeking to relate it to responses in religion and art which can change the vision of the person for moments which may prove to have life-changing effects over longer periods (Moore 1983; Moore 1989a).

Imagination is the channel by means of which these magical transformations occur. By blurring the distinction between what is real and unreal it enables us to stand off from our actual situation and envisage different situations. Developing the ideas of Sartre on this point, the philosopher Mary Warnock describes the function of the imagination for the artist and spectator as being 'to detach themselves from the world in order to think of certain objects in the world in a new way, as signifying something else' (Warnock 1976: 197). All human beings, she says, have a capacity to go beyond what is immediately in front of their noses and to sense that there is more to experience and more in what we experience than we can predict. From this comes a whole range of expressions of human creativity in culture, religion and the arts. It was the Italian philosopher Vico whose theory saw art as imagination. It was the German Feuerbach (1841) who saw religion, God and Heaven as projections of the imagination: 'The imagination is the original organ of religion' (Feuerbach 1957: 214). Others, however, do not draw his sceptical conclusion that religion is illusion but find the air cleared for the theologian's 'faithful imagination' (Green 1989: ch. 7) and a rediscovery of the 'religious imagination' (Greeley 1981). From many modern studies of the role of imagination in philosophy, psychology, religion and the arts, its central importance has become clear and its implications are being reconsidered.

To turn from Western academic discussions to the experience of primal societies is to discover a different view from that in modern usage which sees imagination as a capacity to form a mental image of something which is not present to the senses or not real. In contrast, the 'primitive imagination' is concerned with what is believed to be present but invisible; the singer does not invent his subjects out of nothing but assumes that they exist and have a character and actions to be shown forth (Bowra 1963: 192). Here the singer expresses the beliefs and assumptions of his tribal culture. But this is true also for the modern individual. The sea of images which each of us has within is shaped and patterned with the support of the surrounding culture which has nurtured us. Ours is a 'tutored imagination'.

This last phrase comes from the writings of Paul Pruyser, a Dutch-

American who (up to his death in 1987) worked as a clinical psychologist at the Menninger Foundation, Kansas. His argument and programme are of great importance for the issues just raised. First, Pruyser makes the imagination his starting-point. The assertions of religion are imaginative assertions (Pruyser 1983: chs 1, 8). He also draws on many examples from the arts in his psychological study of the dynamics of religion (Pruyser 1968). He can draw on the thought of Feuerbach and Freud and speak of the 'delicate illusionism of religion' (Pruyser 1987: 101). But he does not follow their naturalistic conclusions to the point of dissolving the transcendence and mystery of religion into the self-projection of the believer. He rejects the two-valued orientation of positivism's view of reason and empirical reality versus the fantasy-based illusions of religion. There is a more positive sense of illusion (in distinction from delusion) that Freud himself was reaching out for in his free use of analogies from mythical themes, literature and the humanities. It is the symbolic dimension of religion, the arts and indeed of the world of culture which people share most of the time. Pruyser finds a psychological basis for this normal and healthy sense of illusion in D.W. Winnicott's 'transitional sphere' of infants' ritual play objects which are handled with reverence and love to bridge the child's inner and outer worlds. This is continued into subsequent stages of life in play and culture. Pruyser proceeds to apply these insights systematically to the various domains of culture – the visual arts, literature, music, religion and the sciences (Pruyser 1983). He emphasizes that in each area the imagination needs 'tutoring', for instance, to induct students into the world of scientific symbols and formulae. In each field he shows the creative significance of play and illusion in furthering the work of the artist or participant in that field.

The crucial aspect of Pruyser's argument lies in his diagrammatic comparison of the 'three worlds'. At one extreme is the 'realistic' world of sense-perception. At the other is the 'autistic' world of fantasy and delusion. But in between is the 'illusionist' world of the imagination covering all the fields of culture which need 'illusion processing' and tutoring. This involves space and time to play – hence Pruyser's 1983 title: *The Play of the Imagination*. Play allows for creativity but also presupposes guidance through rules from the culture. The illusionistic world is not one of whimsical fantasy but of 'tutored fantasy' which encourages an orderly imagination and cultural creativity.

Pruyser's argument suggests further applications and questions (Moore 1990). Its importance for the understanding of religion and the arts comes out in two ways. First is the ambiguity that pervades all experience of the arts and religion. This derives from the very nature of the illusionistic world, at once public and private and open to belief and unbelief. Religion, like the arts, cannot be finally proved true or false; it remains an area of commitment,

rejection and reinterpretation and is therefore precarious. For this reason also it is a precious area of human freedom and personal response. Secondly, this precious area of imagination is threatened by the ever present dangers of slipping over to the worlds on either side. The religious imagination, for instance, can run riot with destructive fantasies, or it can lose its symbolic quality to be channelled into rigid institutions and doctrines of literal realism. In life we are required to move in and out of these worlds. It is the task of education in our culture to tutor the imagination to do this appropriately. It may be that primal cultures are more skilled and relaxed in this.

If Pruyser's argument and warnings are important for the understanding of the relation of religion to the arts, they should be relevant to our more specific area of the Pacific. It is therefore of great interest that a group of anthropologists have recently explored the cross-cultural meaning of the religious imagination in New Guinea (Herdt and Stephen 1989). This involves such religio-cultural expressions as dreams and trances, altered states of consciousness, possession, spirit mediumship, witchcraft and sorcery, shamanism and cargo cults. Michele Stephen sees 'autonomous imagining' as a creative capacity of the shaman to relate to the healing of a patient and to be shared in the symbolism of group culture. Instead of the opposition posed by Freud between the interests of culture and the hidden desires of the individual's unconscious, the two are woven together. 'Religious rituals and symbols are not attempts to disguise, but rather to identify and bring into consciousness, subliminal fantasy – or imagination' (Herdt and Stephen 1989: 212). A sacred ethos involves a sense of cosmic order and emotions that it sustains; the religious realm consequently bridges the interior and exterior, the self and other. It may be due to the influence of Winnicott that these authors have a parallel view to Pruyser's of the intermediate realm, in this case between subject and object, a 'wilderness' of subtle and elusive inbetweenness. Thus Melanesian ancestors speak through a dialogue between self and other: 'It is a dialogue not contained purely within culture or within the individual's skin. It is inbetween these, a realm of personal perceptions and representations of cultural objects, the inbetweenness of imaginative/symbolic reality' (Herdt and Stephen 1989: 11).

Primal religions and their arts

On the basis of this understanding of the central place of imagination, we can expect works of art to communicate the imaginative worlds in which people live. What then does this mean for the art of primal societies, especially in the Pacific? Here expectations among Western viewers have been confused by the still-used term 'primitive art'. A survey conducted in Berkeley, California, in the 1970s concerning viewers' aesthetic judgments of Canadian Cree Indian

and Eskimo art showed they were based on prejudgements about the materials, artists and lifestyles behind these 'non-Western' works on display – some were disappointed that these were not authentically traditional works but made for sale (Nelson Graburn in Greenhalgh and Megaw 1978: 51–70). The very term 'primitive art' is a general category used by Westerners to cover a great variety of non-Western art forms which are characterized by their 'otherness' compared with familiar European art. Now it can be refreshing to come to terms with 'otherness' in cultures and religions, but this has often been misunderstood.

'Primitive art' was first seen and rejected by Westerners as barbaric, savage, crude and rude. However, under the influence of 19th-century colonialism, museums, especially in Germany, established large collections from Africa, Oceania and the Americas. By the beginning of the 20th century there was growing appreciation of these collections as art, especially by younger artists who admired the primitive vitality and the unselfconscious simplicity of vision. There was no doubt a certain 'romantic' idealization again of the noble savage, as pure and sincere, even naive. In reality the artists from primal societies were far from naive; nor were they lacking in artistic technique. From the Western outlook their art seemed lacking in the sophistication of realistic portraits and landscape, yet there are examples of such subject matter even though other priorities dominated their interests. In accordance with the values of the Western colonial period, 'natives' were seen as inferiors, as still at the stage of the childhood of man. Their art was often judged as 'child-like' – a term also applied to sophisticated modern European artists such as Paul Klee. The positive side of this judgement was the recognition of something direct and emotionally powerful, even uncanny and grotesque, as in the bold expression of sexuality, fertility and animal power. It was a partial recognition of the 'elemental' in nature and religion, which accords with our use of the term 'primal'. What then can be said more usefully about this art? We can bring out some general characteristics which relate to the Pacific traditions also.

First it is limited in *technology*, using tools but not machines. In introducing *Masterpieces of Primitive Art* from the Rockefeller Collection (now in the Metropolitan Museum, New York) Douglas Newton offers a minimal non-judgemental definition: 'It encompasses the art of those people who have remained until recent times at an early technological level' (Newton 1978: 27). The aesthetic significance of this is that it covers an enormous proportion of the earth's surface and past populations.

Secondly, it belongs to *non-literate* societies. The term 'non-literate' has been used as a more neutral alternative to 'primitive'. On the one hand, it indicates a reliance on oral tradition in conveying the content and instruction about art from one generation to another, in contrast to art of the universal religions

which could rely also on written texts of the Buddha's life and teaching or of the detailed iconography of icons for the Eastern Orthodox church. On the other hand, it means that, in the absence of writing, image-making and visual symbols such as pictographs were a preliminary form of writing. 'Pictures and letters are really blood-relations' (E.H. Gombrich 1955: 32). In his excellent short study Sam Gill goes 'beyond the "primitive"' to understand the religions of non-literate people (not 'pre-literate' or illiterate). This does not make them different from the rest of the religions of humankind, but non-literacy does shape conceptions of time and space as expressed in religious art and symbolism. Moreover it shapes relationships and orientations within time: 'It encourages the face-to-face, person-to-person transmission of culture in forms especially appropriate to the needs of such processes – stories, songs, prayers, and other aspects of oral tradition' (Gill 1982: 111, ch. 1).

Thirdly, it is the art of mainly *tribal* societies. Although this is by no means an adequate term it has been used by some as less patronizing than 'primitive'. David Attenborough's fine television series called *The Tribal Eye* sought to examine types of tribal art (including Melanesian cult houses in one of the seven programmes) in the context of the societies and landscapes that produced them (Attenborough 1976: 11–12). Tribal life is limited in the sense of marking off one tribe from its neighbour by custom and perhaps by language: separation can mean hostility and constant warfare, expressed in the prestige of battle and reverence for valued weapons and canoes. Tribalism means that there is little conception of a wider humanity including all peoples and no wider outreach for the religion, in contrast to that which occurs in 'universal religions'. On the more positive side, life in a small-scale society has closer bonds between the members and includes all aspects of the common life in its cultural and religious activities.

Fourthly, within the tribal life art is related to the whole range of experiences of people, both in everyday activities and special ceremonies. As a result of this, some Western commentators have classified the work of these artists as 'crafts' for *practical use*. One of the first to study 'primitive' art was the German scholar Gottfried Semper whose two volumes (1860–63) saw early art as derived from techniques for shelter and useful activities (Newton 1978: 34).

There is, however, much evidence from prehistoric and present-day tribal art for ornament and design which transcends the useful. It must be understood in different terms, as Leonhard Adam points out: 'In the simpler social structure of primitive tribes the word utilitarian has an altogether different meaning. There is no clear contrast between "art for art's sake" and art in the service of a practical purpose' (Adam 1948: 45).

Fifthly, primal societies are *conservative* in the sense of appealing to the traditions from the ancestors. If no other explanation of a practice is available, one can always say 'The ancestors did it this way'. For the arts, 'custom' lays

down the lines for artists and people to follow, although this does not mean that the artist has no freedom to develop the traditional style and exercise his creative imagination; tradition in fact is able to accommodate, to change. In an oral culture particular traditions – songs, stories and art works – are regarded as property which is treasured by the tribal, clan or family group owning the traditions. Again, this does not rule out transference by sale or exchange.

Sixthly, the ancestral traditions are overwhelmingly patriarchal and *male-dominated*. In her article surveying the role of women artists in Polynesia and Melanesia, Jehanne Teilhet observes that 'women uniformly have only limited access to the art arena'. They may be allotted the repetitive craftwork of weaving and pottery, or share in the important process of making colours, but the actual work of decoration, painting and carving is to be done by men. '. . . The hieratic visual arts in particular, reflect male behaviour and opinion, for it is the men who dominate the "important" arts' (Teilhet, in Mead and Kernot 1983: 45–56). Similar observations could be made about the art establishment in the Western world and most traditional societies.

Why then has this division of labour been so pervasive in the Pacific? Here, women have been associated with work in the home, garden and family; their work with soft materials of less enduring nature is said to reflect their femaleness, so they are forbidden to work with hard enduring materials and certain specialized tools. The latter need a male artist who has been initiated into the requisite ritual and magic; the tools are symbolic markers of their manhood and ritual prowess. Teilhet suggests that this may have derived from the almost universal division of labour where men have been the hunters and warriors, with magico–religious sanctions surrounding these activities and especially the weapons. There is also the felt 'balance' of the sexes. Women are believed to have greater innate powers than men through creating and controlling life; women are feared and respected for their creative powers, with protective prohibitions covering childbirth and menstruation. To match this, the art object enhances the importance of the male artist and leader. In Polynesian belief (Handy 1927: 295) 'the canoe, house or other object had a soul and a vital principle that needed strengthening'. The living art work is the nearest substitute for a newborn child which a male can create to restore the balance of the sexes.

This leads on to our seventh and final point which concerns the central place of *religion*. The arts of primal societies may exert a strong appeal for many modern observers through their expressive power and vivid imagination. But if we are to go beyond this and understand the works in terms of their symbolism and cultural purpose, a knowledge of religion is essential (Adam 1948: ch. 4). Examples of this have already been mentioned: the pervasive conception of *mana*, the depiction of the ancestors, and the influence of myth in everyday actions and objects. The ceremonial highlights of

religious life such as initiation provide the focus for much of the art. It is not, therefore, sufficient to admire or assess a mask as displayed in a collection, as it must be understood in its ritual setting where the mask-dancer sees through the eyes of the mask, re-living the myth of the ancestor or spirit. Since primal religions relate to the total culture they contribute to the wholeness within which the various art forms appear. To these we now turn.

Diversity and wholeness of the arts

'The problem of meaning in art' is the concern of the anthropologist Anthony Forge (in Mead 1979: 278–86). From his first-hand contact with art and artists in the Sepik area of Papua New Guinea (PNG) he was aware as an outsider of the array of patterns internalized by the insiders to convey and conceal the unspoken fundamental assumptions about society and the cosmos where men and women live. There are diverse forms of the arts – not only the visual but also music, song, dance and movement, costume and gesture, along with language forms such as myth, invocation and oratory. But it is in the ritual context that all these forms come together and reinforce each other to convey excitement and mystery in the experience of the participants.

A similar conclusion is to be drawn from the research of Philip Dark (also in the 1960s–70s) of the arts among Kilenge people, villagers of West New Britain, PNG. It is revealing just to list the headings from his detailed listing of their diverse art forms: architecture (domestic and ceremonial); cicatrization; containers; costume and ornament; dance paddles; flowers; hair combs and dyes; masks and headdresses; monuments of stone; musical instruments; nets for fishing; ornaments (carved animal forms); plants; tools and utensils; water transport; and weapons. The materials listed as used in their art are also varied, ranging from bamboo and bark, lianas and canes, wood and charcoal, to pig tusks, iron, plant fibres, juices and leaves, cotton, feathers, shells and stones. Techniques of woodworking, burning, grinding, painting, gluing and inlaying, teasing and plaiting are used faithfully. The satisfaction given to all by the artist producing a fitting piece of work is summed up in the phrase of one informant: 'Art is something which is well done' (Dark, in Mead and Kernot 1983: 25–44). This purposeful skill is related to the idea of dancing well; and further, master artists and 'big men' are believed to have magical power at their command.

Once again, these diverse skills and art forms come together in special moments such as are provided by the *agosang* festival of the Kilenge, vividly depicted in a series of ten photographs (Dark, in Greenhalgh and Megaw 1978: 31–50). Asking the question 'What is art for anthropologists?', Dark concludes that this must relate to the personnel – the artists who make the costumes and other decorations, the performers who put these into practice

and the audience who participate in the festival. It is the interaction of the personnel with art that results in aesthetic experience. This is rather different from the more isolated and rarefied Western view of art and the artist. Here among the Kilenge (and probably for most primal societies) the artist is subordinated to the social conventions and the art is a temporary vehicle for aesthetic expression, as required by the occasion. 'It is an interest focus for a brief period. Its iconography, its symbolism, is but to be seen in the light of the meaning it has or contributes when activated as art, rather than something which is always there as art' (Dark, in Greenhalgh and Megaw 1978: 38). Here we see the dynamic understanding of primal arts as focused in a process and a happening − a view to which we shall return.

It would be desirable, but impracticable, in this introduction to cover all the art forms listed by Dark above. Instead they will be referred to, where relevant, in the specific instances of Pacific arts in the following chapters. The visual arts predominate because of their being more readily available through museums and illustrations in books. Yet other forms which cannot be so presented in a book deserve our attention. We select two of these which are of special importance: dance and song.

Dance is central to the religious rituals and public ceremonies of primal societies. It was a saying of R.R. Marett, the British anthropologist of the early 20th century, that primitive religion is not thought out but danced out. (A similar attitude is reported from a Shinto priest in answer to a Western visitor to Japan: 'We have no theology. We dance'.) Writing in 1932 on the arts in religion and theology, the Dutch scholar van der Leeuw began with the dance as exemplifying 'beautiful motion'. It is the most universal of the arts, accompanying and stimulating all the processes of life, and in turn enables other arts to come into being. Yet it is also a simple unity: 'To dance, one needs nothing, not paint, nor stone, nor wood, nor musical instrument; nothing at all except one's own body. Man can produce for himself the rhythm which induces the body to dance (though, of course, others may do this); it is marked out by the stamping of feet and the clapping of hands' (Leeuw 1963: 12−13). To discover the dance has a twofold meaning. For the self it means stepping into a new dimension of one's existence where, by dancing to a fixed beat one finds a power that gives a new character to movement. This in turn is an ordered movement which reflects the heavenly dance, the harmony of divine movement in the cosmos and history.

In his interpretation of the dance and the other arts, van der Leeuw sees the primeval unity of art and religion being subsequently broken up, leading to opposition between religions and the body; the arts become separated, secularized and deprived of power and significance. Nevertheless his insights from the history and phenomenology of religion lead him to find ways

towards a new unity of the arts, religion and theology. In the field of the
social sciences there has also been awareness of the richness of the dance in
human culture and ritual action (Hanna 1979; Spencer 1985). In a dance the
body has the capacity to create patterns and moods that communicate
emotions and attitudes at a deep non-verbal level of symbolism. This can be
used by society in many ways. In the more specifically religious sense the
dance can express a cosmic world-view to the audience. As a form of worship
dancing can be offered to honour, entertain and placate the gods. In the form
of masked dancers it can bring the world of the spirits into visibly present
figures in the community. In the spectacular performance of a shamanic type
of ecstatic, the dance can display and mediate supernatural power to transform
the shaman and help the community.

Music is a ready ally to the dance. The drum is the most elemental form of
musical instrument and is typically used by shamans to drum themselves into
an ecstatic state on their journey to the spirit world. Drums and flutes are
often believed to 'speak' with voices of the spirits. These are among the many
sound-producing instruments which have been observed in Oceania in their
construction and playing-technique (Fischer 1983). With or without instruments, such as the *didjeridu* or drone pipe of the Australian aboriginal, singing
is a basic means of summoning up or activating supernatural powers and
becoming close to the ancestors. In the form of prayers and ritual incantations
to the gods, singing and chanting add a dimension of power to the words.
The rhythm and balance of a song lift the imagination of the singer to
another, more exalted, sphere. The 'enchantment' which we recognize, more
in metaphorical senses, in a song which takes hold of us, can be taken more
literally as magical: 'The primitive song-man feels within himself an eruptive,
domineering force which he must release on others' (Bowra 1963: 255). In
oral cultures, the usual way of presenting poetry of all types is through
singing, as can be illustrated from the 'unwritten song' in Oceania (Trask
1966–67).

Song and sound may be valued as more important religiously than the
visual arts. This is brought out and vividly and beautifully in the experience
recounted by Colin Turnbull with a Pygmy people in Zaire, Africa. Invited
by several men to enter the forest where they had a nightly ceremony of
'singing the forest' with the aid of a sacred *molimo* trumpet, he expected to see
an ornately carved object. He was shocked and disenchanted to find instead
two lengths of bent drainpipe which could be blown to produce a variety of
sounds both solemn and ridiculous. But this was not seen by the singers as
sacrilege, for the drainpipe filled the forest with animal sounds and mysterious
unapproachable sounds quite unlike the song of men. In citing this account,
Sam Gill points out that the physical trumpet is only instrumental; the real
values, religious and aesthetic, are placed on the song it produces. For without

the song the forest is dead. 'To sing to the forest awakens the forest so that it will maintain its responsibility to its children' (Gill 1982: 28–30). Art and religion are here working together to maintain the cosmos.

This example, along with others mentioned in this section, has much to say about the understanding of the arts in primal religions. 'Art objects' are destructible and disposable. The real thing is the act and not the object. It is the use to which the objects are put, the context, the relationships, that give life and make life possible. 'For the Pygmy and the Eskimo, sound and the power of speech are identified with life' and the vitality of breath and speech has a transient, dynamic quality (Gill 1982: 33). This leads Gill to conclude that sound, as communicated via the human voice, is a predominant and distinctive feature of non-literate cultures. Sound is their most central and common symbolic medium – especially as formed in song, prayer, story and poetry. He goes on to emphasize: 'Art is dynamic, not static. It is a process, not a product' (Gill 1982: 34–6). He suggests that a more fitting term than 'art' would be 'arting' to bring out this dynamic process and transformative effect. Whether it is carved or painted, danced out, sung or acted out, the art of primal religions is derived from the process of creating and maintaining life-giving relationships.

A further example of this emphasis on process comes from the actual making of art objects. In the Western world, the approach is to leave the artist to create art in privacy until the work is completed and ready to be exhibited and presented in public. At this point discussion, analysis and criticism can begin on the work. But the Oceanic tradition has not been to leave the artist in seclusion. The artist fetches the raw materials, prepares them and produces his artwork in communication with others of his clan group, if not the general public. 'Art production is usually open to the scrutiny of many people and every stage of manufacture is subject to discussion and criticism' (S.M. Mead in Mead and Kernot 1983: 15). In this way again relationships are an essential part of the art process.

Modern changes in religion and art

The integration of religion and the arts in the primal societies of the Pacific has been greatly altered by changes over the past two centuries. As a result of the missionary work by Christian churches, the majority of peoples have been converted to some form of Christianity which has now become indigenized in varying degrees (Garrett 1982; Forman 1982). The effect of Christian teaching, accompanied by educational and medical work and the pacification of previously warlike tribes, has led to the demise of the old religions or reduced them to remnants of 'folk religion'. The festivals and the arts so closely linked with them have undergone corresponding changes. Some

churches sought conversion by replacing the old order completely, banning traditional festivals, initiations and art forms of the 'heathen' religions. Churches from the more Catholic tradition sought to accommodate the best of the old by 'baptizing' some of the art forms into the church life and worship or by accepting them as cultural expressions.

At the same time the Pacific has undergone two centuries of European contact in the form of trade, colonial rule, education and communications. All these have been part of an overall process of 'modernization'. At the economic level this is part of the process of the Industrial Revolution over the past two centuries which has brought new technology to replace old patterns of work and transport. At the level of social and political organization, bureaucracy has introduced more impersonal forms of government administration and law, replacing some traditional authorities. The sociologist Peter Berger considers technology and bureaucracy to be the primary agents of modernization which lead on to secondary carriers such as urbanization, the 'private sphere' of life, mass education and the mass media of communication (Berger et al. 1974: ch. 4). The significance of these is not just that they are dominant social forces but that they affect the consciousness of people. In the Pacific area as elsewhere, for instance, modern transport has stimulated physical mobility; technology and education have stimulated social mobility; and, above all, mass media and communications have created an appetite for new forms of food, clothing, entertainment and the 'bright lights' of towns, thus stimulating the longings for progress and advancement, by means of 'psychic mobility' (Lerner 1958: ch. 2). In contrast to the world of village life bounded by cultural and religious tradition, this represents a move away from tradition towards secularization.

Cities and mass media bring new lifestyles and a variety of forms of religion, leading to increasing pluralism in society. This offers greater freedom of choice to the individual; but at the same time it takes away the social integration and sense of identity in belonging to a religious 'home'. In answer to the modern sense of 'homelessness' there have arisen various movements of nostalgia for the past traditions to reassert ethnic identity and religious certainty, a trend which can be seen as 'counter-modernization' (Berger et al. 1974: ch. 6–9). These tensions are evident in the new nations of the Pacific. Education, especially if it is in Western languages, may lead to biculturalism, which can be both confusing and enriching for those involved in the ambivalence of belonging to more than one culture.

Art forms in primal societies are vulnerable to these changes. European art has also undergone changes over the past two centuries since the French Revolution marked a breach with tradition. A similar pattern emerges when we look at four factors where we can discern changes from tradition to modernity in the visual arts. First of all, traditional subject-matter was often

based on religious themes which had to be followed by carefully prescribed patterns of iconography; but this now gives way to a much broader range of subject-matter chosen from everyday life, nature and urban living. Secondly, the location of artworks is diversified. They were traditionally housed in a sacred place if the concern was religious; this could be an ancient grove, a mediaeval cathedral or a cult house. But in modern times artworks, even of explicit religious themes, may be hung in art galleries or private homes, and reproduced in art books, calendars, colour-slides and documentary films. There is no need to go to a sacred or ritual place. Thirdly, the artist enjoys new freedom. In the past the artist served the community and its established tradition; his skill was recognized for this. But now the artist is comparatively free to explore and choose various themes and styles as a creative individual. Finally, patronage of art has changed from the established institutions of the church or the tribal community to private collectors and new secular institutions for art, education, government and banking.

Examples of these changes are readily seen in the arts of Oceania. Among the new forms of patronage tourism now has become dominant. In his survey of tourist arts in various ethnic communities of the modern world, Nelson Graburn distinguishes older 'primitive' art (based on one symbolic or aesthetic system) from 'arts of the Fourth World' where the people have become dependent part-societies or at least have to accommodate to the majority peoples around them (Graburn 1976: ch. 1). In tourist arts we see art being produced by one group for consumption by another; no longer is there just one tradition, but changing arts and identities. Once again there is a change of consciousness involved. The art is being made to sell on the tourist market. Tourism is a Western-style leisure activity which seeks something different overseas and expects to find a new experience of 'the other' in Oceania – the simple truth in a way of life related to nature and tribal traditions. Photographs and souvenirs help to satisfy the expectations. In the form of 'airport art' a simplified and easily identifiable theme is reproduced for tourists to pick up quickly at the airport as a memento of the visit. It signifies the abandoning of traditional forms to produce 'a slogan rather than a poem' (Attenborough 1976: 135–6). An illuminating analogy can be drawn here between art and language: airport art is the equivalent of pidgin with its restricted vocabulary and simplified grammar. Pidgin is nobody's mother-tongue but a secondary language developed for trade and other practical purposes for communication between people of different languages. It is primarily commercial and secular. However, in a setting of cultural meeting and change it can grow and be applied with greater enrichment to wider fields such as education in schools and religious worship and sermons in churches. Tourist arts are likewise able to serve wider purposes (Graburn, in Mead and Kernot 1983: 70–79).

Artistic change can take different directions, from extinction of indigenous

art forms at one end of the spectrum to renewal at the other (Graburn 1976: 5–9). In between, the tourist can find traditional or functional fine arts which may use modern tools and incorporate European-derived symbols yet retain the traditional form. This can lead to commercialized production of pseudo-traditional arts of lower standard. At the lowest level is the mere standardized souvenir, such as the native doll, which may be called 'ethno-kitsch'. These conform to the consumers' popular notions of the 'primitive' or to what is exotic and colourful. Examples of this unfortunately abound (T. Schneebaum, in *PAJ* Jan. 1991: 27–8). However, on the positive side it is possible for more creative new syntheses to emerge which may lead to reintegration of traditional arts with imported forms, avoiding mere stereotypes and grotesque distortions. European techniques may be used to express genuine feelings of the artists for the ancestral tradition as it lives on in changing times. Here the artists are less dependent on foreign consumers, making art more on their own terms. Fortunately, examples of this also are to be found in our account of the Pacific region.

In view of the pace of change affecting all parts of the world in the 20th century, it is unrealistic to expect that primal societies and 'Fourth World' arts can remain isolated from international influences and events. How then should we assess and accept the impact of tourism? Some light is thrown on this question by Phillip Lewis, a curator at the Field Museum of Chicago who visited three contexts of art during a visit to Papua New Guinea in 1981. These included the Sepik area with tourist art markets, New Ireland with traditional ceremonies, and the then newly founded National Museum of PNG at Port Moresby. He feared that the 'good' traditional art was being replaced by 'bad' inferior tourist art. But he discovered that the boundaries had shifted. While some traditional art objects were not being made because they were no longer useful, others were now being reproduced for a wider public because they were no longer under sacred restrictions if sold to tourists. Again, on the other hand, some traditional works gained in sanctity by being displayed in the quasi-sacred atmosphere of the Museum where they could not be sold nor touched; thus they could become revitalized as models for artists. Lewis concludes that there is an interrelation between the three contexts of traditional ritual use, museums and changing tourist settings. Therefore 'we should not turn up our noses at "tourist" arts and wait only for the chance to acquire traditional art . . . . We should collect and study them all' (Lewis, in Hanson 1990: 162).

Change is an important ingredient in the arts of religions in the Pacific because they come from dynamic living traditions. Even when they appear to be part of a dying order they can grow and change. A first-hand observation comes from Michael Gunn's research on the traditional *malagan* sculptures in New Ireland (see chapter 3):

Each time a malagan is made it is still the same as it was the first time because the rights to own it were directly descended from the original rights, but the malagan sculpture changes because the people who make and use it change. Things change yet stay the same, and things stay the same yet change. (Gunn 1992: iv)

Problems and resources in the study of Pacific arts

The changes we have just discussed create both problems and opportunities for indigenous artists. They create problems also for those who would study the arts of the Pacific in their religious and cultural context. This is because so much evidence has disappeared over the past two centuries. In the course of conversion to Christianity most of the art associated with the old religions was discarded or deliberately destroyed. In some cases Christian missionaries preserved materials from cult houses, masks and 'god-sticks' for historical purposes as museum exhibits or as evidence for missionary societies back home. Some teachers, administrators and early ethnologists recorded information from older informants about the ancient myths and ritual practices. Then, in the late-19th century and first part of the 20th century, collectors and museums competed in obtaining all the available older art objects. Unfortunately much of the material was collected at times when there was little communication between buyer and seller. As Douglas Newton pointed out from the Museum of Primitive Art in New York (1967) it is embarrassing to realize that we know so little about the original meaning and function of these works now in museums. It is difficult to know how much of the surviving information, fragmentary as it often is, has been misconstrued in the reporting.

Scholarly attempts to fill the gaps have often been inadequate or based on baseless speculation. Newton observes that until the mid-20th century anthropologists felt uneasy with the idea of 'art' except as a kind of ornamental frill to the concerns of social studies – it would appear at the end of an ethnographic report under headings such as 'Decorative Art' or 'Bildende Kunst', figurative and pictorial art, perhaps with its economic setting or an inventory of design motifs:

> Today, anthropologists are far more conscious of the integration of art into culture as a whole, and art historians understand that they cannot be ignorant of the elements of anthropology and remain effective. Released from attempts to isolate the arts . . . researchers have become engaged with the expansive roles of all the arts, including architecture and music. (Newton, in Lutkehaus et al. 1990: 467)

At the level of theoretical analysis and interpretation anthropology has explored a number of approaches which have contributed new insights: the

stylistic approach, the functionalist emphasis on the social framework of art, studies of cultural change; and studies of individual artists in a culture. The focus on signs and symbols has led to the structuralism of Lévi-Strauss and also to the comprehensive semiotic search for signification systems underlying all human communication, including the arts. The study of 'ethno-aesthetics' looks at the aesthetic judgments made by people of a single society on a sample of artworks, rather than imposing Western evaluations. The basic orientation and limitations of these approaches have been helpfully summarized by Roger Neich (1984). These recent developments in anthropology are not a major concern of the present book but the combination of theory and research is important to understand in the ongoing study of Pacific arts and religions. This combination is well represented in volumes including researchers of Australian and Pacific arts (Layton 1981). Alfred Gell draws from research in Melanesia on the 'carving-magic' of canoes in the Trobriand islands to assert provocatively an anti-aesthetic, even 'philistine', methodology for anthropological studies on art; the artist, like the Trobriand gardeners and carvers, engages in idealized forms of production, 'enchanted technology' (Gell, in Coote and Shelton 1992: 40–63).

At the more practical level of research, various new methods have been devised and applied by anthropologists and others. For instance, in order to elicit the meaning of traditional designs of the Abelam in PNG, Anthony Forge persuaded artists to record them by painting on sheets of paper; likewise Nancy Munn obtained paper drawings of the sand designs communicating the ideas of the cosmic order from the Walbiri of Central Australia (Forge 1973). George Corbin showed old photos to older informants in New Britain as part of a programme of 'salvage art history' to recover forgotten forms of ritual and art (Hanson 1990: 67). Revival of traditional crafts has been achieved in various parts of the Pacific. Canoes and traditional oceanic craft have been built for celebrations by NZ Maori; and on Gela, Florida, in the Solomon Islands, a Catholic priest who was the son of a canoe-builder coordinated the construction of a *binabina*, a war canoe which was subsequently sailed to the capital, Honiara, and presented to the nation. Such activities can also reactivate other neglected aspects of traditional culture such as dances and stories related to the canoes (B. Kernot, review in *PAN* June 1984: 21). Another expression of long-term concern for the effects of research is for an anthropologist to make a bargain with the people to record findings that they could understand and which would 'represent them as they portrayed themselves to me, not as Westerners portray Melanesians to other Westerners' (Gunn 1992: 171).

The above methods are those used by anthropologists and indigenous leaders or researchers from the new generation in the Pacific who adapt and innovate in the study of the arts. But for those who are not able to engage in

such full-scale research, what resources are available? We can conclude with an encouraging list.

First, as the references indicate in this book, there is a wealth of written material, beginning with early explorers, traders and missionaries and continuing with more thorough and sophisticated studies by scholars and administrators in government, education and religion. These are usually observers with a long-term commitment to understanding Pacific peoples; and now they are being supplemented or replaced by writers from the indigenous cultures. Techniques of oral history are being used to gather information from the older generation of a people.

Secondly, museums are a vital and accessible resource for 'exhibiting cultures' – to cite the title of a recent book of conference papers on museum display. The museum is no longer an antiquarian assemblage of curiosities in glass cases, but rather its object is to present objects in the living context of the culture so as to communicate with the viewer. The aim is to transform the experience of the viewer by the use of display and lighting to show the mystery and wonder of the objects. Taken to an extreme this could create a different sort of isolation and artificiality where 'the treasured object exists not principally to be owned but to be viewed' (Stephen Greenblatt, in Lavine and Karp 1991: 52). Another issue of growing interest and debate concerns the control over the way materials from ethnic arts and cultures are to be presented in museums. Instead of Western ways of organizing experience, experiments are being made in using the aesthetic categories of the culture itself and drawing on multiple perspectives. This relates to some of the new anthropological approaches already mentioned. In the widest sense of education the museum is concerned to conserve cultures and present them vividly to enhance our humanity.

Thirdly, modern technology has made available a wealth of films, sound recordings and programmes on television and video which bring the arts of the Pacific to life in a moving form. These are the next best thing to actually visiting the Pacific region and meeting artists and performers in the living context of the art forms. Live performances and travelling exhibitions provide occasional opportunities and they should not be missed. There is need for development in teaching the arts of the Pacific (Dark 1984: 93–132).

Finally, at the scholarly level there is the Pacific Arts Association which has, since the mid 1970s, held international symposium gatherings and provided a network of information (Dark, *PAJ* 1990: 1–3). The fine volumes of symposium papers constitute an up-to-date resource for readers of this book (Dark and Rose 1993).

It may still be felt that these resources are weighted very much with Western scholarship and expertise and that the study of arts of the Pacific and the religious and cultural context should be left now in the hands of the

indigenous peoples who 'own' the arts. To press this argument seems to be party to a confusion. Knowledge of Pacific cultures, like other knowledge, is available for all who are concerned to share in a partnership of research and understanding. Even if it were desirable to restrict such public knowledge it would be unrealistic in the modern age of international communication which has made these things accessible.

What is legitimate and important here is the protest against control of the production and sale of the Pacific arts by dominant Western consumerism. This control is part of the legacy of colonialism with its patronizing sense of ownership of the lands and their peoples. Traders saw them as potential markets to be owned and exploited. Missions engaged in counting the heads of converts owned by their churches. Anthropologists collected these people through research and classified them as primitive cultures. The time for such attitudes is now past. In the end the peoples themselves do have a say in the direction they wish to take and the selection they wish to make in such matters as the arts and religions. Phillip Lewis again offers a piece of timely wisdom (Lewis, in Hanson 1990: 162):

> Their art is going to change − some of it is going to be good, some of it bad . . . . They are going to do both wise and foolish things just as we Westerners do.

CHAPTER 2

AUSTRALIA

To have seen, felt and smelt the land is to already recognize something of the art.
(Rosemary Crumlin 1991: 17)

The vast Pacific Ocean is bounded at its south-west corner by the large land mass which is Australia. One hundred million years ago it was part of a continuous continental platform from Japan down to Australia and New Zealand. Subsequently it was separated by water, resulting in quite different zoogeographical zones in Asia with its elephants and monkeys and Australia with its marsupials such as the kangaroo. Human settlement began 40,000 years ago, and perhaps earlier, when people came from the north on watercraft such as bamboo rafts from islands of Southeast Asia. With little contact from beyond, the Australian Aboriginal people developed their culture, religion and arts along with 'stone age' technology until changes were brought by Western contact and British colonization in 1788. Although much of the inland area of Australia is arid desert, it is estimated that the Aboriginal population before contact was at least 300,000 people, perhaps twice that figure.

In the two centuries since that colonization, Australia has acquired by continual immigration a population now approaching 17 million. These are mainly people of European extraction with Christianity of various forms as their religion. While originally the immigrants were from the British Isles, there is now a rich ethnic and cultural mix, as shown by recent studies written for the Bicentenary (Jupp 1988; Gillman 1988). In religion there is a trend towards pluralism and multi-culturalism (Habel 1992). However in this study we are concerned with the distinctive indigenous religion and arts of the Aboriginal people. These now number 163,000, or just 1 per cent of the total population. They are scattered over all parts of Australia, from urbanized to rural and remote desert areas; their traditional culture is represented more clearly in the Northern Territories and Western Desert (see map, figure 2). There remains great diversity of cultural traditions, as indicated by the 250 languages spoken by Aboriginal peoples at the time of contact. The diversity of traditional arts can justifiably be studied according to several major regions of the vast continent – from Arnhem Land in the north, to the Central and Western Deserts, the Kimberley area in the north-west and Queensland in the

2.   Map of Australia.

north-east (Caruana 1993). At the same time in the last two centuries there has been constant modification of the traditions through education and Christian missions (Swain and Rose 1988). The effects of an accelerated pace of social change in recent decades will be discussed later in this chapter.

Art, religion and life

Aboriginal bark-paintings can be perceived as a mirror, reflecting a group's essential cultural character, telling us about the people's values, religious concepts and thoughts, their social and cultural life. (Helen Groger-Wurm, in Ucko 1977: 150)

These are the ways of art. A people which dances and sings, carves and paints, is akin to ourselves, and the more we know of the Aborigines' art, the more akin to us they prove to be. (A.P. Elkin, in McCarthy 1958: 7)

The wholeness of primal religion which is able to unite the diversity of arts in a total performance, has been emphasized in the opening chapter. It is a characteristic beautifully displayed in Aboriginal religion, as the two quotations just cited bring out. But it was not at first appreciated by Westerners in the 19th century who regarded the Australian aborigines as having no religion at all, or only debased forms of magic, superstition and revellings. Even sympathetic researchers and scholars at the turn of the 20th century saw them still as examples of the childhood of the human race at the beginning of the evolution of religion: Durkheim stressed the sociological importance of their 'elementary forms' of religion as in totemism, seen as a quintessentially simple form of religious life (Charlesworth et al. 1984: 1–3). This contrasts with views from more recent researchers such as Elkin who brought empathy to the understanding of their culture and art. An appreciation of the complexity rather than the simplicity of Aboriginal religion, despite the 'primitive' technology of their culture, is evidenced in the testimony of an American researcher among nomadic desert Aborigines in the 1960s:

> Gradually I experienced the central truth of Aboriginal religion: that it is not a thing by itself but an inseparable part of a whole that encompasses every aspect of daily life, every individual, and every time – past, present and future. It is nothing less than the theme of existence, and as such constitutes one of the most sophisticated and unique religious and philosophical systems known to man. (Gould, excerpted in Schechner 1976: 167)

This writer goes on to describe the impact on him of the final rite of initiation rituals performed beside two bonfires. Suddenly the three naked novices emerge from between the two fires, running in a line in perfect step with one another and with the rhythm of the singers. 'From a choreographic point of view this is a brilliantly engineered dramatic climax . . . .' Then another sound is heard, that of the bullroarer or sacred board which is whirled round to produce the voice of the totemic kangaroo. The spine-chilling sound terrifies the women and children, who flee the dance-ground to return to their bush camp. Then two men bring in a sacred emblem to be seen by the novices for the first time; for the duration of the ceremony this is the actual body of the Dreamtime kangaroo. The positioning of this is done by the two high-stepping dancing figures so quickly and expertly that it has the dramatic impact of 'a dream while still awake'. After this the singing stops and young men form a 'human table' in front of the fire for the ritual circumcision of the three initiates (Gould 1976: 172–3). (On the life-cycle and male initiation in the Western Desert see also Tonkinson 1978: ch. 4.)

This example illustrates vividly how all the arts are brought together, including some of the ritual objects which are to be described further in this chapter. Within this total performance the basic principles of the arts in

3.   Walbiri sacred site, Great Snake.

Aboriginal religion are seen at work. Following R.M. Berndt's discussion of 'the arts of life', we note, first, the religious basis of the arts which all had the pervasive sacredness of Aboriginal religion as their inspiration. Secondly, these arts are related to the necessities of life in the material world, the land and the environment in which one has to survive − therefore rituals are a form of work as well as expressing the play of the imagination. Thirdly, these arts are symbolic in pointing to something beyond the various objects and rituals, for instance the kangaroo is connected spiritually to the mythic being of the Dreamtime, binding past and present. Fourthly, the arts communicate to people in a social context. They symbolize nature but also society and are directed to social ends (Berndt and Phillips 1973: 31−7; Berndt et al. 1982: ch. 1).

Clearly we are dealing here with religion and arts in a very different understanding from that of the Western tradition. Religion is not based on theistic belief in one God above all creation. The arts are not simply for the aesthetic satisfaction − 'for art's sake' − but for life's sake. An example of this is seen in the illustration of a Walbiri (Warlpiri) sacred ceremonial site in Central Australia where people are in the presence of a large rock painting of the Great Snake, Yarapi (figure 3). Known under various names in Aboriginal mythology such as the Rainbow Snake and Julunggul, the serpent is a primeval creative figure of ambivalent sex, the source of fertility and therefore respected and propitiated. The rock painting is regularly restored

and its vitality imparted as members ritually run their fingers along the Great Snake image to renew their ties of identity with it. On the rock around the image are other graphic signs used by the Walbiri to indicate features of the land, nature and mythology; for instance the horseshoe-shaped markings may refer to the camps of mythical wild dogs. The image relates to the living powers from the 'Dreaming' and to this central concept we now turn.

The Dreaming, the land and the ancestors

The Aboriginal religious cosmos is summed up in the term 'The Dreaming' (Isaacs 1980). This is the modern English rendering for a number of related words in different Aboriginal languages – *alcheringa* among the Aranda of Central Australia, *djugurba* in the Western Desert, *wongar* in the far north in East Arnhem Land. The Aranda term referred to the primordial beginnings of the world when the ancestor spirits shaped it and laid down its essential features and law. It had links with ideas of immortality and eternal vision, hence with 'dreaming'. Although the term 'Eternal Dream-time' has been used, the word 'time' suggests too much the past era of the ancestors. As W.E.H. Stanner writes in his vivid essay on this, 'One cannot "fix" The Dreaming *in* time: it was, and is, everywhen' (Stanner 1958: 514). Within this overarching sense four connected meanings can be delineated (Charlesworth et al. 1984: 9–10). First, as a narrative mythical account of the foundation of the world, it tells of the uncreated and eternal ancestor heroes. Secondly, the Dreaming is embodied in the land as a result of the ancestors waking and bursting through the earth; they left their mark on the sites as they went around shaping the rocks, waterholes, flora and fauna and important customs. Thus they bestowed a sacred character on life to this day through the spiritual power of the Dreaming. Thirdly, the Dreaming can mean the 'Law' in the sense of the Aboriginal way of life which is based on the moral and ritual regulations given. Fourthly, it can refer to an individual's vocation based on ties to a clan, totem and sites which are affirmed by saying, 'This is my Dreaming'. (We shall see examples of this in artworks.)

All these aspects add up to a very concrete and 'this-worldly' religion. The Dreaming is not an exercise of the imagination in sleep or fantasy but a spiritual outlook incarnated in traditional rites and in things and places in the world. Tradition is dominant in everything since one must look to the ancestors' pattern which is the eternal Dreaming. (As G.K. Chesterton said, tradition means giving your ancestors a vote.)

Above all it is the *land* which is the locus and central focus of everyday experience of the Dreaming. What may appear as a barren or featureless landscape to an outsider becomes for the Aboriginal a rich pattern of myths and traditions associated with the rocks and waterholes from the Dreaming,

4. Ayers Rock, Central Australiia. (Photo, A.C. Moore.)

with ancestral ties giving ownership and identity to the people. In artworks there is a continuum from the Dreaming through the artists to totemic designs and to the topographical features of the landscape. 'The single most common subject matter of Aboriginal art is the landscape-based myth' (Sutton 1988: 16). This is because the land has such strong emotional bonds for the Aboriginal who sees the landmarks as sacred, as the present-day incarnations of the ancestors who are in them still to influence the present. Purpose and knowledge go with this sense of belonging to the land. In the 1971 film *Walkabout* it is the young Aboriginal who is able to rescue two white children abandoned in the desert and to help them survive by his knowledge of the natural resources as well as the tracks which will lead them home eventually. 'Walkabout' for the Aboriginal is not a happy-go-lucky ramble but a knowing and re-visiting of the sites of one's ancestral land. In addition to the sentimental attachment to one's birthplace and homeland there is a belief in the ancestral imprinting of both the landscapes, with their networks of places and routes, and of the people who belong to the land. The ancestors walked here and sat down there; they still live on in the land.

The close link with the land can be seen in Ayers Rock, an enormous monolith of sandstone in the arid heart of Australia, south-west from Alice Springs (figure 4). Its striking beauty and colour-changes seen from the surrounding plain make it a popular attraction for tourists who may climb up the steep single access track to get the view from the flattened top. But for

the Pitjandjara people it is called Uluru, signifying a sacred repository of knowledge of things eternal. It has remained unchanged for them since the Dreamtime beginnings when it rose miraculously out of a large flat sandhill. In this period of creative emergence, *tjukurapa,* the topography of the rock was shaped by ten different mythical beings. There was a battle between the peaceful carpet-snakes and their attackers, the poisonous snakes. Among the other totemic beings were the sand-lizard, the hare wallaby, the spirit dingo and the willy-wagtail. These all left their mark and became features of the great rock and of the surrounding environment with its seasons and pattern of cultural life (Isaacs 1980: 34–44). The land and its features are thus personified as the ancestral heroes; and in turn the rock is living evidence of the reality of the Dreamtime myth. For instance, 'the grey patch on the southern cliff of Uluru is not an extensive patch of lichen, but the metamorphosed smoke from the burning camp of the greedy sleepy-lizard' (Mountford 1965: 198).

Ayers Rock is also the site of some forms of art. There are indentations on rocks in patterns caused by human engraving of a simple sort, as one could find in palaeolithic art elsewhere; but these are attributed by the Aboriginals to the totemic beings of the *tjukurapa* times (Mountford 1965: ch. 8). There are also sacred objects such as boards engraved with secret-sacred designs. Finally there are cave paintings in 12 major sites around the base of Ayers Rock, now given names such as caves of 'resting', 'fertility', 'hunter' and 'initiation'. But here they are not secret and being comparatively secular can feature a variety of subjects and be visited by non-initiates; they continue to feature living art of human and animal life, though not initially clear to the understanding of the outsider.

Another expression of the Dreamtime myths comes in the group of figures of sacred beings, carved in wood and painted, from the far north of Australia in north-east Arnhem Land (see figure 5). The largest figure, on the left of the illustration, is Banaitja, one of the ancestors who is seen as the source of totemic designs and sacred ritual which he taught the people. The other two are the mythical Wawalag sisters, likewise stylized and coloured with red ochre, black, yellow and white, in the distinctive style of incised carvings from this region. The famous myth tells of the elder sister (shown here in the centre with drooping breasts) who had borne a child and the younger sister (smaller, wearing a skirt) who in their Dreamtime wanderings from home named the natural species they found on the way. When they polluted a waterhole, the great snake Julunggul arose in anger to swallow the sisters and child, then to regurgitate them, which happened several times. This myth is open to various interpretations (L. Hiatt, in Charlesworth et al. 1984: ch. 1). At the level of the natural seasons, the snake could stand for the wet season swallowing up the dry. Or the snake could be chaos leading to cosmic renewal in the act of regurgitation. The ritual application of this seems to be in

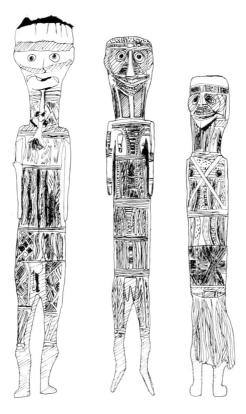

5. Ancestral beings, wood-carvings. Arnhem Land.

the initiation rites where youths are taken from their mothers, swallowed ritually by the Great Snake (represented by a large drone-pipe) and reborn as men. The many-sided applications of such myths are evidence of the continuing relevance of the Dreamtime events. Because they tell of the re-ordering of the world by the ancestors, these figures provide permanent patterns, archetypes, for humans to follow and re-live in the cosmos now.

One further example comes from north-western Australia, in the Kimberley district. In this area the torrential monsoon rain was believed to come from the Wandjina spirits in the clouds. In the times when they roamed the land they united under their leader Wodjin to do battle at Tunbai; by flooding the people out they were able to defeat them. After further wanderings they finally 'died' into the paintings which are still featured on many walls of caves throughout the area (figure 6). These Wandjina figures typically have eyes and nose but no mouth. One of the explanations given by aboriginals was: 'They can't have mouths! If they did it would never stop raining and all nature would die!' (Kupka 1965: 76). Because these paintings embody the Wandjina spirits they have been feared and revered for their

6.   Wandjina figures painted in caves. Kimberley.

powers over life and death. Touching the paintings was normally forbidden and the Wandjina would have to be addressed when visitors were brought into the caves and announced. However the paintings could be ritually renewed by re-painting from time to time; although they were attributed to the work and incarnation of the Wandjina spirits, such re-touching would renew their powers and make them available still for life and fertility.

The importance of the Wandjina for fertility relates not only to rain for growth but for conception of life. In traditional belief conception and birth

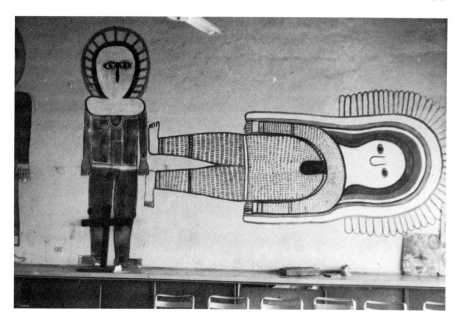

7. Wandjina mural in church. Mowanjum. (Photo, E. Kolig.)

were caused not by human fertilization but by the pre-existent soul being implanted in the mother by the life-spirits from the clouds. The little child spirits belonged to the Wandjinas and lived in water, especially fresh water pools from which came fish or turtles; a man eating these would thereafter dream about the child spirit and convey it to the mother-to-be. Such beliefs can be synthesized with modern knowledge of biological conception, by saying that the child spirit still comes from the Wandjina (I.M. Crawford 1968: 33–4). Otherwise, much of the ritual related to the Wandjina has fallen into disuse and the paintings have become dilapidated.

But this decline has in turn elicited new responses. One is the incorporation of Wandjina figures into Christian churches, as shown by the photo of murals (figure 7), painted like frescoes of saints in mediaeval Europe, in the mission church interior at Mowanjum in the Kimberleys, taken in 1972 (E. Kolig, in Swain and Rose 1988: 388–9). This represents a transition from the earlier mission attitudes when Aboriginal people had to choose between their traditional beliefs and conversion to Christianity. In recent years the indigenization of mission churches has allowed for much more Aboriginal input into church life, including artwork, as an expression of Aboriginal identity. This leads to the second response, at the level of cultural identity. Through education and other modernizing influences, literal belief in the rain-making powers of the Wandjina has been vanishing and is no longer effective as a reason for ritual. However, even while drained of these traditional

8. Wandjina mural on art shop. Mowanjum. (Photo, E. Kolig.)

motivating beliefs, visits to the caves have been revived recently for the enhancement of Aboriginal identity. Young people are encouraged to renew the fading Wandjina images by over-painting them. This may not please the archaeologists but it is intended to restore consciousness of the ancestral past. At the same time the images have been used for tourist art. Whereas traditional Wandjina paintings were on rocks in caves, now they are transferred to the saleable medium of bark-painting. Since this medium has been brought in from Arnhem Land and is not traditional for the Kimberleys, it is open to new ways and is largely taken over by women painters now. They have not yet turned to bright modern acrylic paints but this could develop as the supply of bark suitable for painting becomes exhausted from available trees. The striking public use of the Wandjina theme is shown in a 1990 photo (figure 8) of the mural on the outside wall of the art sales house in Mowanjum. It has been painted by a member of the Aboriginal community. Accompanied by two birds of mythological significance the Wandjina is a living symbol of the people's cultural identity.

A symbolic universe

The Dreaming is the overarching cosmic order within which Aboriginal people, both as individuals and as communities, are related to the environment as a living landscape. In this the ancestral past is a reality continuous with the present. It is a meaningful universe, filled with symbols. As in all human culture, symbols are the means of opening doors to the unseen. Objects of the natural world such as plants and animals or rocks and stars are not just isolated features of the visible world but parts of an inter-connected order, 'a humanized realm saturated with significations' (Stanner 1965: 227). An important concept supporting this Aboriginal world-view is what has been called 'totemism', reflecting the essential unity of all things in a bond between humans and the world of nature. A totem is a thing which confers this unity among diverse people who have the totem as part of themselves and can even call it their 'Dreaming', having, for example, honey or a sacred place as their totem. However, the fact that Australia is 'a continent with a lot of totems' does not meant that the religion of the Aboriginal should be described as a glorified totemism; they are seen in true perspective as parts of the ultimate order of the Dreaming (Stanner 1965: 225–9).

Stanner goes on to point to the vehicles which serve the symbolism and help to interpret the imagery of Aboriginal religion. He lists a range of 'raw materials', quoted below, which are relevant for our study:

(a) conventionalized movements that mark out in space geometric designs (lines, curves, circles, spirals, zigzags);
(b) postures, stances, gestures and facial expressions;
(c) silences, laughter, wailing, expletives, cries, invocations, instructions and commands;
(d) charts and songs;
(e) stories, tales and myths;
(f) mimes and dances;
(g) many uses and products of the plastic and graphic arts to make abstract and representational designs;
(h) a host of stylized acts – the whole repertory of theatrical forms . . . performed within ritualized processes or described in the associated myths. (Stanner 1965: 232–3)

Looking now at the visual art expressions we find the more representational or figurative images of the Dreaming in the Wandjinas and the Dreamtime beings pictured in Arnhem Land art; more examples of these occur in the next section. The more geometric form is seen especially in ceremonial and secret art in Central Australia and the Western Desert. However even here the designs are not just geometric but are representational in Aboriginal eyes. Desert art offers 'a hunter's eye view of the world' with its concern for the traces of people and animals and stereotyped shapes; they create an artistic system of about 14 basic graphic elements and the four colours: red, yellow, white and black (N. Peterson, in Cooper et al. 1981: 46–7). These colours are applied to a ground drawing in the illustration of a group painting (figure 9); the ground has to be prepared first by being

9.   Ground designs by group. Central Australia.

smoothed out, hardened, then dampened with water. The design is marked out first, then sprinkled with blood, with white and red feathered down being arranged on this (Berndt 1964: 369). Such ground paintings are mainly found in Central Australia among the Aranda, Walbiri and Warramunga people. The subject of the painting here is the mythical emu (the large Australian bird like an ostrich) with footprints represented by the arrow-like graphic sign. The concentric circles can mean a number of things from a campsite, rockholes, cloaca, to a breast or fire or a fruit relished by emus and humans. Peterson suggests three possible interpretations from such combinations of the two signs shown here: emu ancestors sitting down, or moving across the landscape on ancestral tracks, or carrying the fruit. Various interpretations may coexist and clearly many designs could be generated from the graphic signs with their variant meanings.

From this it might be concluded that understanding such art is little more than guesswork dependent on arbitrary arrangements of signs. An iconography depends on some system, as in a language, being a form of writing in images. Within the limits of the particular tribe, however, there is such a system which is understood by initiates and can eventually be explained through a series of examples; in this sense the art of Australian Aboriginals draws on various iconographies which belong to limited tribal groups in their own traditions. A fine example of how this works out is given in the study of

Walbiri (Warlpiri) iconography resulting from the fieldwork of Nancy Munn in 1956–58 based in Yuendumu, Northern Territory, north-west from Alice Springs. She was able to collect a variety of totemic designs painted for public camp ceremonies and also to see normally secret men's ceremonies (Munn 1973). The ceremonial regalia included headdresses of mulga branches, painted shields and poles and string crosses carried on the head or in the mouth. Designs were painted on these and also on the bodies of performers impersonating the ancestors. As in the case of ground designs previously mentioned, the four colours were used along with blood and bird or vegetable fluff stuck on to the body. The ground designs were obliterated in dancing. However information on these designs and their related iconography and myths was obtained by encouraging the men to draw 'visual texts' as diagrams on paper with pencil crayons.

In her aim of relating these varied forms of designs and providing a structural analysis of the graphic system in the social order, Nancy Munn found an important link in the sand-drawings of the Walbiri men and women. A basic repertoire of graphic signs was used in different contexts and combinations as they fingered the sand during conversation and story-telling. Women would recount everyday experiences and dreams; men dwelt on more masculine accounts and ancestral myths. Their pride in these sand-drawings as a way of talking was expressed in the saying, 'We Walbiri live on the ground' (Munn 1973: 58). The significance of this for the Walbiri community life and tradition is that children learn these signs and their meanings from the context of the stories and conversation of their parents. As with learning a verbal language from infancy, the process is absorbed without formal instruction; the signs are recognized and understood as having different meanings in different stories. Later on, the youths are given instruction for sacred ceremonies which apply the same basic signs to objects and body-painting. Again there is room for different meanings in the graphic signs as in the songs, understood within the overarching mystery of the ancestral Dreaming.

The designs are important in the wider life of temporal activities and bodily behaviour. This can be seen from a key example of the graphic signs in Munn's analysis, the 'circle-line notation' in which circles are linked to straight lines. As we have seen earlier, the circles, spirals and concentric circles can refer to campsites, fruit, fire and so on. The straight line refers to a path to a site, a means of going out and coming in, as with the ancestral sites and paths trodden in the Dreamtime. But these can also refer to sexual differences, symbolized by the circle for the female, the line for the male. The interplay of male and female and the basic life-experiences of birth, sexual intercourse and death can all be seen as forms of 'coming out and going in'. In these wide-ranging forms the circle-line model is a 'spatio-temporal icon' for the Walbiri cosmic order (Munn, in Forge 1973). In the more specific applications the patterns drawn in the sand are also repeated in the ceremonial designs and acted out by dancers in their movements. The body comes into intimate contact with the patterns, in dancing them as well as in body-painting. Visual codes are able to regulate experiences by drawing on the senses of sight and touch of the individual. The iconic symbolism is a bridge between the microcosm of the Walbiri people as individuals in society and the macrocosm of the world-order in which they share.

A concluding application of this is to be found in the designs used on 'secret sacred' objects such as the bullroarer and *tjurunga* (*churinga*). Both of these are sacred to cults for the initiated, kept in secret cult places and shown only to those authorized. They are believed to mediate the indestructible ancestral power of the Dreaming. The bullroarer is a flat oblong board with rounded ends, about one metre long, which has a hole for the thong with which it is whirled in the air to produce a rising and falling sound. It is valued for the energy it conveys, especially to young initiates, and is considered the incarnation of a primeval hero or ancestor (H. Petri 1960: 134). Bullroarers are found in Aboriginal tribes throughout Australia, as well as in Melanesia. *Tjurungas* are found in southern, central and western Australia; the name comes from the Aranda language and refers to a variety of objects as well as to their associated cults. Like the bullroarers they are flat decorated objects, but the wooden boards are sometimes much larger and they can also be made from smooth stone, flat and oval in shape, and can be much smaller and more portable. The *tjurunga* here illustrated (figure 10) is of stone and incised with symbolic motifs in geometrical style, with circles and curved wavy lines. These designs correspond to the graphic signs already mentioned as recurring in ceremonial designs and body-painting, as well as those on rock carvings and weapons.

Tjurungas are especially sacred and secret because they are totemic objects linking the owner personally with his Dreaming. They are seen as true incarnations of the bodies of ancestral heroes and may be shown to the initiated as representing parts of a hero's body. They convey reassurance to the owner as a personal cult totem, which conveys power through handling and rubbing. Taking a *tjurunga* on hunting expeditions will ensure success; lending it to another strengthens friendship. Therefore the incising of designs on the stone is a ritual act accompanied by sacred songs. It is not only a matter of the individual owner's identity but also of his group and the land over which it has rights. With all these associations the *tjurungas* are kept in a sacred storehouse and handled with reverence, as Elkin reports:

> I know of nothing more impressive than to see a group of Aborigines sitting in a secret ground contemplating their sacred symbols and chanting the song versions of the myth appertaining to them. (Elkin 1964: 208)

10. *Tjurunga*, sacred stone with designs. Central Australia.

Expressions in visual art forms

Of the varied forms of Aboriginal visual art the most ancient appears to be
rock art. Because engravings and especially paintings on rock are often found in
caves and rock-shelters one may easily assume that they are prehistoric
parallels to the palaeolithic cave paintings in Europe. But there are differences. Aboriginal cave paintings are not found in dark remote recesses since
these would be feared as the abode of spirits. Further, there is much evidence
of the art being overlaid at intervals of time and it is very difficult to date such
works. Because of the strong sense of continuity with tradition, rock paintings
known to have been done in recent years are hard to distinguish from those
thought to be ancient. For these reasons caution is necessary in judging the
rock art as prehistoric. What does appear likely is that it preceded other visual
art forms so that one may regard 'paintings on bark, bull-roarers, and
churingas as "portable" rock images' (Petri 1960: 136).

Already we have discussed the Wandjina figures found in impressive cave-
galleries in the Kimberley area. These feature anthropomorphic figures of
humans and spiritual beings. But a wide variety of subjects occur in rock art
elsewhere, as in the Northern Territory, and are listed as: mythological (other

than human) creatures; fauna; material culture (implements, weapons and ritual objects); linear; and indeterminate figures, identifiable only locally (McCarthy 1958; compare Berndt and Phillips 1973: 91–154).

In the case of *bark-painting* there is also a range of subject matter from the naturalistic to the geometric. Probably it originated in the painting of the bark walls of shelters for dwelling. The bark, like other materials such as pigments, has to be obtained and prepared by the artist, as is typical in a primal society. The bark is peeled from the stringybark (eucalyptus) tree soon after the rainy season, then dried out and flattened. The red and yellow colours are obtained from natural ochre stones, the white from clay and the black from charcoal. With these pigments the surface of the bark is covered by designs based on crosshatching, diamond and other shapes which have symbolic meanings. In Arnhem Land in the north this form of painting has been brought to a sophisticated level and now has a ready sale with tourists. For secular purposes artists are free to depict a wide variety of scenes from everyday life as well as hunting scenes, animals and the Land of the Dead. Other subjects connected with ancestral traditions and Dreamtime beings come into the secret-sacred category, for which each clan has its own patterns. Bark paintings of these are painted in secret to the chanting of songs and kept in storehouses on the ceremonial ground until shown to initiates.

In the face of economic and social changes imminent in Arnhem Land in the 1960s the need was felt to preserve the heritage in a collection of bark paintings for a collection at the Australian Institute of Aboriginal Studies at Canberra. Helen Groger-Wurm arranged for a team of artists at Yirrkala to paint traditional themes and to tell the 'true inside' meaning, on the understanding that their accounts would be correctly recorded; this is an example of friendship and mutual trust leading to benefits for all concerned (Groger-Wurm 1973; also Berndt and Phillips 1973: 201–24).

The illustration here (figure 11) is based on a Western Arnhem Land bark-painting of a Spirit Being called Nagidjiji hunting a kangaroo. It is of interest first because it shows the so-called 'X-ray' style of displaying not only the outwardly visible features of the kangaroo but also its internal organs (heart, liver and bone-structure, including the spinal column). This style is found in rock art also of the Arnhem Land area. It combines realism in depicting totemic species and ancestors with a sense of mystery that makes them extraordinary Dreamtime figures. The Aboriginal artist knows that the internal structure of a creature is essential to figures seen from the exterior: 'Therefore he draws the internal organs in a stylized way to indicate that a particular animal or creature is more than its outward manifestation' (Berndt and Phillips 1973: 157). Also of interest is the use to which such bark paintings could be put in tribal life. Imitative hunting magic is suggested by this example; other depictions of distorted and grotesque figures were used for

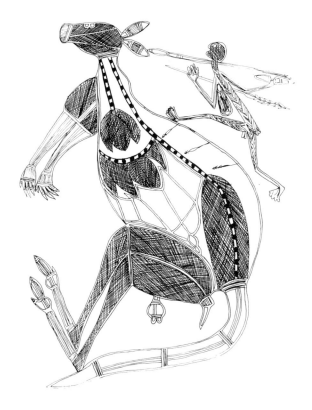

11.   Kangaroo in 'X-ray' style, bark-painting. Arnhem Land.

erotic love magic or for revenge by society. A figure of stick-like elongated form, featured frequently in Arnhem Land bark-painting as well as in rock-art and sculpture, is the Mimi spirit being; Mimi are trickster spirits which live in caves and eat yams and even human flesh.

Body-painting is an art form linked to bark-painting because designs from the latter are replicated on men's chests, arms and thighs, for important rites of passage such as circumcision and finally death. As Howard Morphy points out, in Eastern Arnhem Land the designs on the body or coffin of the dead person help to transfer the soul back to the ancestral world. 'Art is linked in with the concept of the cycling of spiritual power down the generations from the ancestral past to the present' (Morphy, in Eliade 1987: vol. 7, 14). Art here is able to bring the spiritual into close contact with the body, as we have noted earlier in regard to Walbiri body-decoration and dancing as well as to the handling of *tjurungas*.

Initiation rites are important occasions for 'painting' the body, from smearings of blood to much more elaborate painting of sacred designs with ochre and feather down, and added decorations such as headdress. However, not all such decoration is confined to men; women use ochres for their own religious rituals with less complex designs. Nor is it confined to sacred ceremony: 'There is painting for secular or camp dancing and entertainment, for love magic, or simply for personal adornment' (Berndt, R.M. and C.H. 1964: 366). Vivid examples of this from south-east Australia are recorded in the lithographs of Blandowski, a geologist and naturalist who made collecting expeditions in the hinterlands of Victoria and South Australia in the 1850s. While women supply the rhythm with clapping-sticks, the ranks of men dancing in the festivals display bold and elaborate striped and dotted patterns on their bodies − 'this incredible transformation of men into living designs' (Cooper et al. 1981: 35−7). The often harsh conditions of life did not prevent the imaginative use of colour and celebration in times of abundance.

Body-painting and facial designs apparently satisfied the needs which masks answered in places such as Melanesia. Outside influence from Melanesia would account for the masks found at Cape York at the northern tip of Queensland where the Torres Strait islands are a link to New Guinea. In these islands masks were made of tortoise-shell to represent ancestors and totems such as fish. The wooden mask featured in the frontispiece of this book has the typically piercing expression with its long nose and beady eyes. It is made of wood and decorated with human hair. Probably it was not worn over the face but either carried or worn on the head of a person completely concealed in an enveloping costume (Linton and Wingert 1946: 124). The name of the wearer had to be kept secret. This mask was used at the harvest dance during ceremonies associated with the return of ancestor spirits to the islands, no doubt to promote fertile crops.

The category of *ritual emblems* includes not only sacred art objects to be treasured but also more temporary constructions. The 'thread-cross' (figure 12), called a *waninga* by the Aranda, is used to mark a ceremonial centre for a particular activity and then dismantled. It is constructed from an upright pole or a spear crossed by horizontal sticks and decorated with strings of human hair, wool, ochres and tufts of feathers. Such thread-crosses are regarded as sacred because they symbolize totemic ancestors who once emerged from the shapes of a storm-cloud or a honey-ant nest. They may represent inspired dreams and experiences of medicine men and mediums. Smaller versions of thread-crosses are sometimes carried on the backs of dancing performers, worn in the hair or carried between the teeth. Like body-painting this is a temporary art form which brings the Dreaming into close contact with the body and its ritual action.

Sculpture in the sense of substantial objects carved in the round is not a widespread Aboriginal art form. Its richest development is in the north in Arnhem Land. The sacred objects under the covering term *rangga* include stick emblems with designs and decorations. These parallel the flat *tjurungas* of

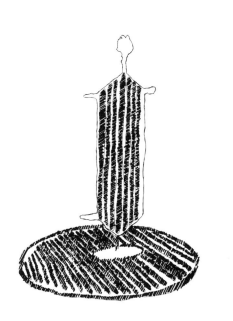

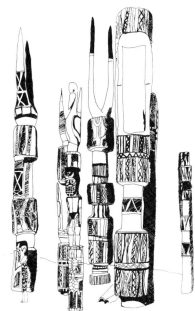

12. 'Thread-cross' emblem for
    sacred place. Aranda

13. Pukumani mortuary
    posts. Arnhem Land.

Central Australia: they likewise relate to ancestral lore and are not normally displayed. Carved and painted wooden images depict great Dreamtime figures, such as the Wawalag sisters illustrated in a previous section. In the secret-sacred rituals of the *maraiin* cult in western Arnhem Land wooden figures of birds, animals and fish were kept in storage until used in rituals based on social groups where members would posture with them to the accompaniment of songs. From spirit beings such as the elongated Mimi to natural creatures and decorated posts, a variety of themes appears in Arnhem Land sculpture (Berndt and Phillips 1973: 157–200).

One further impressive form of sculpture from this area is the *mortuary post* which is one object among others associated with elaborate rituals of death and burial. To represent the land and myths associated with the dead person, ground structures are prepared. A long hollow log is made as a container for the bones from the corpse which are solemnly placed in the log with songs to the spirits and the country, the soul having already gone to the land of the dead. The large mortuary posts, around 2 metres in height, are carved and painted with ancestral designs of myth and land; the name *pukumani* implies *tapu*, or set apart, for the rituals and posts. Of those illustrated here (figure 13), the pronged posts and abstract forms may be stylizations of the human figure. A large number of posts of various designs may be carved for an important

14.   Mortuary posts over graves, Barthurst Island. (Photo, E. Kolig.)

person. Unless they are preserved in a museum, these striking sculptures do not last long. The photograph taken in the Bathurst and Melville Islands in the early 1970s (figure 14) shows mortuary posts over graves at a burial ground. Within a few years the wood is likely to be destroyed by bush fires or by termites. It is the Dreaming, not the material object, which is to endure.

Expressions in music and dance

Most of the examples we have discussed with illustrations here have been expressions of the Dreaming in visual and spatial form. But the fact that these are featured in the context of ritual events such as initiations is a reminder of the temporal 'happening' side of the arts. Religion is defined in terms of

15. Corroboree dancer, after G.F. Angas 1845.

cosmos, as ultimate space and one's land, and also of transformations in time towards the ultimate, through the experiences of one's life. Music and dance are powerful expressions of the latter.

Australian Aboriginal music and dance are frequently performed together, even though the forms vary from region to region. At the general popular level the word *corroboree* has become familiar in Australian English usage to signify this close link of music and dance (S. Wild, in Jupp 1988: 175). The corroboree includes singing and percussion sounds with dancing and dancers' calls and shouts. Some have a sacred purpose but the everyday camp music is more public and secular. This was observable by early European arrivals in the late 18th century. Although they were ignorant of the religious basis of Australian Aborigines they were fascinated by the strange and vital performances at corroborees. Apart from brief descriptions, there was little attempt to study, record and understand the complex skills and traditions involved in these until the early 20th century, when W.B. Spencer made cylinder recordings of songs from Central Australia, to be followed by mid-century with extended analyses, tape recordings and films of Arnhem Land music, ritual and dancing (Elkin 1964: ch. 11). In recent decades ethnomusicologists have made thorough studies of songs of tribal peoples of South and Central Australia (Ellis 1985; Moyle 1986; T.G.H. Strehlow 1971b and others). Likewise, dances of the more public sort have been filmed and notated for study (E. Allen, in Berndt and Phillips 1973: 275–90).

The appeal of Aboriginal dance through its more immediate colour and pageantry was captured in the paintings by George F. Angas, a British visitor to South Australia in 1845. The illustration here (figure 15), after one of his published 'Portraits of the Aboriginal inhabitants in their various dances', is a useful starting-point. This male dancer, like others he depicted, has vivid white stripes painted on his body and face and bunches of leaves decorate the knees. The dancer carries a ritual object in the form of a decorated pole with leaves at the top; others could carry boomerangs, spears or shields, while some wore feathers and elaborate headdresses. There were different regional styles of decoration as of dancing. Aboriginal dances featured skills such as the 'leg quiver' rippling from muscles in the thighs, and leaping and high knee stamping with one foot; dancing on all fours was one of the clever imitations of animals. When performances were held on a dance ground at night they could have a powerful dramatic effect in building up to a climax, as noted in the description earlier in this chapter from the Western Desert imitation.

This leads to the more ceremonial and secret significance of dancing. Sacred rituals may involve dance steps which are different from those used in camp entertainment. The dancer represents a spirit ancestor and becomes ritually united with the ancestor whose activities and journeys are danced out. He is summoning spiritual power into himself, and after a dance people press the dancers to absorb some of this power. At the more general level, dancing is a pervasive experience of Aboriginal life, learned or absorbed by infants who clap to the rhythms and copy their elders from the edge of the dance ground. As they grow they will learn a variety of traditional dances, with new ones being 'dreamed' by dance-owners and imported by exchanges with other communities. In recent decades Aboriginal dance-groups have presented dances for tourists; more professionally styled concerts have gone on tour successfully, combining traditional myths and sequences with colourful modern sets and spectacular effects. (For instance, at the 1988 Brisbane Exposition, the Australian pavilion used laser technology to make the Rainbow Serpent flash through the stage sky as part of a Dreamtime story.)

Music is an essential part of this since it activates the dance with rhythm. For traditional rituals, song texts provide the charter; the singing of them is believed to activate not only humans but the sacred powers of the Dreamtime ancestors. Songs therefore accompany each stage of the important initiation ceremonies, and for mortuary rituals songs serve to direct the spirit to its home in the world of the dead and to offset any dangers from the dead. Songs also help to breathe life and power into cave-paintings to keep them good. A person respected for knowledge and authority is one who 'knows many songs'.

The key figure is the expert song-leader, the 'Songman'. The illustration (figure 16) shows him beating time with his pair of sticks. He is an

16. Songman. Arnhem Land.

experienced singer with a good voice for leading, but more importantly he is the inheritor of a line of tradition on which he has been taught. 'The Songman is the owner of his heritage of songs and of those which he composes, and no one can sing them without his consent and without "paying" him' (Elkin 1964: 295; also Moyle 1986: 139–40). This ownership is recognized by the community which believes that songs and dances came from the ancestors and tell of the ancestors who are related to their land. While this expresses a conservative attitude of mind it does not prevent some changes occurring to the repertoire through a certain flexibility of ownership by the community. Especially with modern transport and the migration of people from their locality to find work or to be re-settled in a new area, there is a diffusion of songs to new areas and the opportunity for transfer and exchange with other communities. It is possible to learn and buy new songs. Also the songman himself may have new songs revealed to him in dreams; these are also said to come from the Dreaming, mediated by spirit familiars, and may be adopted from the songman.

The hundreds of song texts consist of a fixed string of words to be repeated several times in performance and with some freedom insofar as the leader can begin and end at various points. The short text may describe a place or an event related to the Dreaming; it is only a part of the story, which is known to the hearers in its fuller form. A series of songs which recount one long myth is called a 'songline'. Men and women perform songs exclusive to their sex. Singing is usually done by two or three persons, but local styles may

17.   Didjeridu player. Arnhem Land.

differ by singing in unison or in polyphony. The people who join in dancing
do not usually sing the words but they will answer the leader's calling of
names of spirits or clans, using various 'dance-calls' such as squeaks, shouts,
humming, wailing and ululations. They also add to the sound through the
rustling of bunches of leaves tied to the legs and through rhythmic hand-
clapping and slapping of the thighs and buttocks. These forms of body
percussion add to the rhythm from the songman's sticks or paired boomerangs which he uses for accompaniment. They help to compensate for the lack
of drums. Whereas Melanesia features an abundance of masks and drums,
Aboriginal tradition has had neither.

The singers are often accompanied by a player of the *didjeridu*. This is a
well-known musical wind instrument, a dronepipe made of hollow wood
such as stringy bark timber which has been naturally hollowed out by
termites. Usually about 1.5 metres in length, it is given a mouthpiece made
of wax or hardened gum. As seen here (figure 17), it is played by blowing
into it like a trumpet. Aboriginal performers have developed highly skilled

techniques of circular breathing, lip control and tonguing to produce not only a deep fundamental note but also harmonics and percussion effects. These go beyond the use made of similar trumpet and megaphone-like instruments in other parts of the world (Trevor A. Jones, in Berndt and Phillips 1973: 269–74). The didjeridu originated in Arnhem Land and its use spread to the Kimberley area. In rituals it has been used as a symbol of the Rainbow Serpent and associated with rites of initiation and fertility. In recent decades it has spread to all parts of Australia and been popularized for entertainment by whites as well as Aboriginals.

The adaptation of Aboriginal songs and dances to changing conditions has already been mentioned in the case of inter-group exchanges. In the case of modern urban popular culture, contact has led to Aboriginal groups playing syntheses of 'pop' music, 'country and western', rock music and Christian hymns and Gospel (S. Wild, in Jupp 1988: 179–81). A recent example of the fusion of cultures is seen in 'Yothu Yindi', a ten-piece band which combines improvised jazz with indigenous Aboriginal language, as in their very successful album *Tribal Voice* (1992). The members are drawn mainly from the Yolngu people, Arnhem Land, the lead singer being the principal of Yirrkala community school.

In view of the importance of music and dance both for Aboriginal religion and for modern popular culture, it is important to relate such examples to the wider scene of changes in religion and culture. Music has been a key form of expressing Aboriginal experience and view of the world; it can be a form of therapy; now it can be a way of crossing cultural barriers. An ethnomusicologist (Catherine Ellis 1985) finds in music education a way of developing Aboriginal music as 'education for living'.

Modern changes: tradition and innovation

While our focus has been mainly on traditional Aboriginal religion and the arts, the impact of modern change has also emerged in the examples discussed. Even prior to European contact, change and adaptation took place; the layers of successive paintings in rock art are an indication of this, to mention only one example in the area of art. It is now evident that Aboriginal society with all its conservatism is not static and unchanging. Its symbolic universe based on the Dreaming is believed to be eternal; yet its symbolism is flexible and open-ended enough to be interpreted afresh and to incorporate social change. From his study of ritual innovation in Arnhem Land, Robert Bos concludes: 'Even though The Dreaming is regarded as having been laid down once and for all by the supernatural beings, this in no way precludes an ability to come to grips with new experienced realities' (Bos, in Swain and Rose 1988: 435). This view seems to find support in recent studies which reassess the response of Australian Aboriginal peoples to religious, social and cultural changes affecting the arts.

In religion, first of all, Christian missions have had a strong influence over the past century-and-a-half. The results have not necessarily been uniformly 'successful' in terms of the original goals of Christianizing and civilizing. Evaluation of the missionary impact is open to different judgements, as is evident from the range of revealing essays edited by Swain and Rose (1988). One important reason for this lies in the diversity of forms of Christianity seeking to missionize a very different religious culture. 'Australian Aboriginal religion is a non-theistic religion based on the sacred and sacramental character of the land, and it requires a considerable effort of mind and imagination for a European to come to grips with it' (Charlesworth et al. 1984: 7). The Western and Christian emphasis on events in time is in contrast to the Aboriginal emphasis on space and land; as noted already, the arts relate to ancestral places, and songs follow the tracks of ancestors through the land. In the setting of the Walbiri people seeking to indigenize Christianity to their location, Tony Swain highlights the contrast by calling their religious outlook 'geosophical – that is, a view acknowledging that all wisdom and truth is fixed in the earth' (Swain and Rose 1988: 459). Despite the contrast of the two cosmologies, Aboriginals have found ways of juxtaposing them as 'two laws' which are complementary and provide living-room for Aboriginal survival; in this, suggests Swain, their response to the mission presence is coherent, reasoned and intelligible.

Some fine examples of Aboriginal Christian art have emerged from this coexistence. In the Uniting Church in Maningrida, Arnhem Land, a series of bark-paintings by George Garawan illustrates the life of Christ, using familiar Aboriginal symbols, style and composition. Large stylized footprints point to the figure of Jesus walking on the sand to call disciples from their fishing-boat (Takenaka and O'Grady 1991: 92–3). For the Daly River Catholic mission in the Northern Territory, Miriam-Rose Ungunmerr was invited in 1974 to paint a series of Stations of the Cross; she did this, in Aboriginal style and acrylic paints, drawing on her work as a teacher and adviser in Aboriginal art (Takenaka and O'Grady 1991: 138–9). More recently and more radically indigenized is the carved wood sculpture by George Mung in Turkey Creek, a Catholic mission in the Kimberley area. This figure of 'The Pregnant Mary' depicts the infant Christ as a black dancing figure on the white background of his mother's chest encircled by her arms (Crumlin 1991: plate 15). It is reminiscent of the Russian icon of the 'Virgin of the Sign', but its power is convincingly the result of an Aboriginal expression of Christianity.

A different type of solution was attempted in the syncretism of the 'Elcho Island Adjustment movement' which flourished for a few years in Arnhem Land from the late 1950s. From the meeting of primal Aboriginal religion and

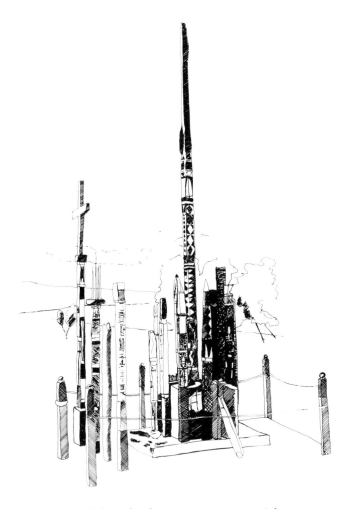

18.   Elcho Island movement, memorial 1958.

the universal religion of Christianity (in this case the accepting Methodist mission) came this new movement's effort to strengthen Aboriginal control of their affairs, improve their prospects and unite local groups. One means of achieving these goals was the assembling in 1958 of secret-sacred *rangga* for public display in a 'memorial', illustrated here (figure 18). These are traditional posts and poles with painted emblems and a figure of the ancestral Laindjung – Banaidja. The addition of the Cross gives a partial place to Christianity. However, the memorial fell into disrepair when, like many such movements, it did not achieve its goals. Since 1979 the Elcho Islanders have mostly followed an enthusiastic Christian revival called the 'Black Crusade' which has also spread to other parts of Australia (Bos, in Swain and Rose, 1988: 426–9).

While the message is that of conservative evangelical Christianity, the meetings and symbolism owe much to the local Yolngu culture. Although this is only one locality it does illustrate the tensions, hopes and changes seen in religious movements more widely. Changes in modern transport and communication make possible the mobility and innovations seen in religion and society.

Social factors are changing the form of Aboriginal culture and religion. The effects of modernization have been studied by Erich Kolig, not in order to portray them as a dying race or the helpless victims of Western culture but rather to see their response as they increasingly draw on their religious heritage to transform it (Kolig 1981). Modern communications, for instance, enable Aboriginal groups to cross the barriers of tribal and linguistic divisions and move towards a pan-Australian Aboriginal unity. This means less exclusiveness. Some traditional attitudes can support the increased sharing of religious rituals and artworks, for religion is a 'commodity' which a person or group owns and may wish to sell (Kolig 1981: ch. 8). This leads to 'cultic imports' which lead on to a wider ethnic community open to eclecticism. The type of leader who can negotiate most effectively in this modern world is one who is bi-cultural but also has a strong identity in Aboriginal roots. The strictness of traditional codes of the elders and severe punishments give way to a more broad leadership. Religious rituals are less exclusive to the tribe and become associated with a more playful and gracious ceremonial spirit (designated by the term 'eutrapelia' from the Austrian religious thinker, Hugo Rahner). Even if traditional divisions of sex-roles remain strong, there are pragmatic moves to emphasize shared religiosity. There is increasing egalitarianism within the Aboriginal community of religious heritage, and there is greater openness and individual responsibility. But as Kolig observes, these changes come with a price: a change of consciousness. Aboriginal religion survives by losing its traditional austerity and gaining tolerance and fluidity; it is now the vehicle of an emergent pan-Aboriginal identity (Kolig 1981: ch. 11).

These transformations have parallels in recent Aboriginal re-workings of traditional spirituality for the modern age. Despite the emphasis on land and place and the disinterest in time, there is a new temporized myth along the lines of an Aboriginal 'Eden' and a colonial 'Fall'. Despite the loss of much tradition, spokespersons appeal to a sense of identity through having something in the 'blood' and through oneness with 'Mother Earth'. These new adjustments are described by Tony Swain as 're-inventing the Eternal' (in Habel 1992: 122–36). In terms of the tensions of the past two centuries of change they need to be understood as efforts to come to terms with Christianity and modern changes while maintaining as much as possible of Aboriginal religion, integrity and autonomy. We have outlined these issues as the background on which modern Aboriginal artists can be best understood.

In face of these changes, Aboriginal culture and its arts seemed to many to be doomed. It was given some recognition in Australian society as the distinctive 'primitive past' which could be sold to tourists in such forms as painted boomerangs; the result of this was a deterioration of the integral understanding and practice of the arts by Aboriginal people. Fortunately a renewed understanding has developed in the last 50 years. Today, of the 30,000 Aboriginal people in the Northern Territory, about one-fifth produce art and craft for sale (West 1988: 11). Encouragement for Aboriginal art has come about through the concerned work of anthropologists, missionaries and educationists. Among non-Aboriginal artists a pioneer was Margaret Preston who in 1925 enthusiastically turned to Aboriginal art to find a distinctive Australian symbolism; in 1950 she returned to this to depict Biblical subjects such as Adam and Eve in Aboriginal form in an Australian Eden (Crumlin 1988: 40–45). Some other Australian and European artists also showed similar interest and appreciation. More recently a German artist Nikolaus Lang spent two years 1986–88 in Adelaide and South Australia working on tableaux based on the Australian landscape and natural materials such as skins, fibres and ochres from Aboriginal life (Lang 1988).

Modern Aboriginal artists

The renewal of Aboriginal art in the 20th century can be traced through four stages. During the first half of the century mission schools encouraged bark-painting in Arnhem Land and the development of Aboriginal talent in more European art forms at some central Australian missions. For instance, at Hermannsburg in the 1930s the Aranda painter Albert Namatjira began to capture the landscape in watercolours, leading to a whole school of Aboriginal painters in the following decades (Hardy et al. 1992). Although the technique of painting was European and the watercolours were popular for sale among Westerners, the subject-matter was the land in the familiar light and colour – the contours full of meaning for Aboriginal religious tradition.

The second stage came with a breakthrough catalysed in 1971 by the schoolteacher Geoffrey Bardon at the desolate and unpromising settlement combining several tribal groups at Papunya, about 250 km west of Alice Springs. As an art teacher he encouraged older men to help in painting murals on the school walls. This led to them continuing painting, using their traditional designs and colours. Then they began using European colours such as acrylics. These richly coloured paintings could be large works, sometimes painted by collective effort. They soon found a ready market with private collectors and institutions. Two new features are noteworthy here. Whereas traditional art was done for local ceremonies and was often ephemeral (as with the mortuary posts in the north) these were artworks designed to last and to be sold for collections. Secondly, acrylic painting tends to alienate the art from religious practice by putting traditional designs on canvas for sale to outsiders. As we have seen, even traditionally religion and art could be exchanged as commodities within understood restrictions. But the new style and context bring problems, as Christopher Anderson points out: 'Aboriginal painters are now confronted with the alien notion of a form of personal expression that overrides ancestral heritage and obligations' (in Sutton 1988: 140). Danger also lies in becoming dependent on a commercial market which could dry up and allow the art to evaporate.

The third stage in the 1980s has seen the emergence of successful 'acrylic artists' among Aboriginals whose works fetch high prices on the international market; they are exhibited in other countries such as the USA, with the impressive 'Dreamings' exhibition (Sutton 1988). This raises the question of their interpretation. An Aboriginal painter told Christopher Anderson (in Crumlin 1991: 114), 'You know, white fellow, he just put the picture on the wall and he looks at it. He doesn't understand it. It's just a pretty picture for him.' The outsider accepts it as a dazzling new abstract full of coloured dots and lines. But these dots and lines have significance of a different sort for the Walbiri artist. The dots are not fill-ins but signs of the spirit ancestors. Likewise the cross-hatching on bark-paintings from Arnhem Land is not just idle pattern but the expression of the totemic spirit in the land. In pointing this out, Judith Ryan calls these works 'mythscapes' since they create abstract maps of the mythological journeys of the ancestral beings of the Dreaming (Ryan 1989). The paintings still have a religious base in the invisible, eternal sense of the land which they make visible. The land is a sacred icon.

A powerful example of such work is given here in the large acrylic painting commissioned by Bardon in 1980 (figure 19). The artist was Tim Leurah Tjapaltjarri, assisted by his brother Clifford Possum who shared his Dreamings related to their homeland; this was the Anmatjera country near Napperby Station, linked to Yuendumu, north of Papunya. As Bardon explains in his personal account, this huge painting, seven metres wide, is 'a vast inspirational spirit journey' and 'a visualization of his life' (in Ryan 1989: 46–7). It is a stylized map of his ancestors' and his own tribal lands which he takes from the white owners of the cattle-station to appropriate as his own Dreaming. The major Dreamings of the artist's own life are shown as inset 'windows' in the painting (for instance, the Yam Spirit Dreaming, labelled in the accompanying diagram – figure 20). The title *Napperby Death Spirit Dreaming* refers to the spirit being who is shown at the right as a human skeleton. While he journeys along the central line he is eternally present in the landscape. The artist is a hunter, as implied by the spears and boomerangs. 'The background dotting reflects visual qualities of the landscape: grass, sand, earth, leaves, smoke, imprinted with tracks and footprints' (Ryan 1989: 47).

The mosaic-like patterns of dots in these acrylic paintings derive from the dots of white down fluff used on objects and bodies in ritual designs of the Walbiri (Sutton 1988: 107–13).

The fourth stage has developed out of these successes of the 1980s. If the acrylic painters from Papunya and the Western Desert used innovation in the service of their traditions, newer artists now consciously confront the tension of tradition and modernity. They are largely urban artists, in some cases with art-school training and higher education. They draw on various styles of European art, from sophisticated realism and surrealism to 'pop art' and folk art, as in the work of Lin Onus, Trevor Nickolls and Robert Campbell (J. Isaacs 1989). There is a strong element of political protest against racism and for Aboriginal rights in modern society. At the same time there is a conscious sharing in modern Western society and urban problems; this is brought out by the striking exhibition 'Balance 1990' (Eather and Hall 1990) which included both Aboriginal and white artists sharing their influences and challenges, through a wide variety of art themes, in order to break down barriers. This does not mean a loss of identity with tradition for these modern artists. Sally Morgan in Perth, Western Australia, is a writer as well as a painter of dazzling acrylics in her distinctive style (Isaacs 1989: 84–9). Fiona Foley of Sydney stresses that being 'urban' does not lessen her link with tradition from her coastal Queensland upbringing and her political activism for Aboriginals; her paintings translate the symbols of ritual art into modern abstract compositions (Isaacs 1989: 40–47 ; Crumlin 1991: 102).

This leads to a consideration of the place of woman artists in the modern phase. We have already noted this as an issue facing primal religious cultures in other parts of the Pacific area. In Aboriginal tradition women had no leadership role in art; they could assist senior male members of the family in preparing paintings and were able to work on secondary 'craft' activities such as rug-weaving, batik and silk-screen at modern mission centres. These were not recognized areas of high artistic worth for Aboriginals and the greatest personal success for Aboriginal women artists came when they worked within a European framework, as J.V.S. Megaw notes (in Jupp 1988: 171). Banduk Marika is the daughter of a bark-painter at Yirrkala; but she went away for 14 years to work as an actress and printmaker in Darwin and Sydney. Her strong linocut designs draw on traditional themes of religion and the land (Isaacs 1989: 20–23). Aboriginal women are now demanding and receiving recognition of their traditional and ritual rights within Aboriginal society.

Among modern Walbiri people at Yuendumu, women had been permitted to apply acrylic designs to practical objects and some ritual objects which could be sold to tourists for profit. Then in 1984 a group of senior women who had ritual power for participation in traditional ceremonies pooled their knowledge to produce flat acrylic paintings, which they did successfully for

19. Painting by Tim Leurah Tjapaltjarri, c. 1939–84 assisted by Clifford Possum Tjapaltjarri, b. 1943. Anmatjera, Papunya, Northern Territory, *Napperby Death Spirit Dreaming*, 1980. Acrylic on canvas, 213×701cm. Felton Bequest 1988, National Gallery of Victoria. C. Aboriginal Artists Agency Limited. Licence granted.

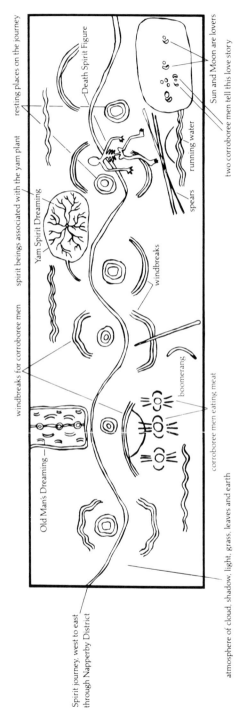

Spirit journey, west to east through Napperby District

Old Man's Dreaming

windbreaks for corroboree men

spirit beings associated with the yam plant

resting places on the journey

Death Spirit Figure

Sun and Moon are lovers

two corroboree men tell this love story

running water

spears

Yam Spirit Dreaming

windbreaks

boomerang

corroboree men eating meat

atmosphere of cloud, shadow, light, grass, leaves and earth

20. Diagram of *Napperby Death Spirit Dreaming*, reproduced from *Mythscapes: Aboriginal Art of the Desert*, by Judith Ryan. C. National Gallery of Victoria.

21.   Senior women demonstrating body-painting. Lajamanu, Northern
Territory. (Photo, by Harsh Prabhu.)

sale. They used the Walbiri store of symbols carefully so as not to violate laws of secrecy. They enjoyed a new freedom to experiment, made possible by the new 'foreign' medium of acrylic; thus they could mix different Dreamings based on sand-stories, parts of stories of sites and various ritual designs (F. Dussart, in West 1988: 34–8). Their example spread far north to the Walbiri settlement at Lajamanu (Hooker Creek) where men and women began to paint their Dreamings in the more permanent medium of acrylic. The patterns which Nancy Munn had observed in sand and ochre designs 20 years earlier were now adapted from finger-work to brush-work; the resulting series of men's and women's paintings were purchased by the National Gallery of Victoria. Men's paintings differ in mythological content and follow the men's rituals in emphasizing ancestors' routes of journeys and straight lines. Women's paintings follow rituals of fertility and designs emphasize camp and home, using more curved lines and clusters of units (Ryan 1990: 14). The two types are complementary, being both based on their Dreaming. The cheerful vigour of their tradition is conveyed in the photo of senior women demonstrating body painting for 'women's business' at Lajamanu community school (figure 21).

These new developments seem to be leading to a strengthening of traditional lore and ritual as part of the Aboriginal life. A similar result is indicated by Howard Morphy from his study of the Yolngu in eastern

Arnhem Land. Producing bark paintings there for tourists has widened the audience of outsiders but has also heightened the concern of the insiders to maintain knowledge of the ancestral past. Traditionally art has been religious in its basis: 'it is a means of transmitting religious knowledge from generation to generation and it is a means of transferring spiritual power from one generation to the next' (Morphy, in West 1988: 32). With a mixture of gains and losses, the modern artists still represent these aims.

It is by no means easy to evaluate the survival of religion in all this. Has it been modernized in a new 'Aboriginal identity'? Clearly identity is important in religion. But it is not the whole of religion, as our discussion in the previous chapter indicated. Identity is experienced within a cosmos, an interrelated whole which is more than the visible world and society. What this 'more' is continues to be the mystery of religion, pictured through the imagination and experienced as magical transformation. A landscape may look barren and empty but it is transformed for the Aboriginals who can sing, dance, paint and see their Dreaming. The landscape becomes a living mythscape.

CHAPTER 3

MELANESIA

The Melanesian mind is entirely possessed by the belief in a supernatural power or influence, called almost universally *mana*. (Codrington 1891: 118)

Melanesia has been revealed as the home of about one-third of mankind's languages, and that means — considering how languages are so crucial in defining discrete cultures — just as many religions. (Trompf 1991: 10)

A hundred years separate the works from which these quotations are taken. At first sight they appear diametrically opposed. Codrington, the 19th-century missionary scholar in eastern Melanesia, found in the concept of *mana* a religious theme central to the 'Melanesian mind', indeed to the whole Pacific. His chapter on religion was to prove influential and to be much quoted by students of comparative religion seeking parallels in 'primitive religions' the world over. But since then the 20th century has produced an ever increasing number of studies of Melanesian societies, their cultures and religions, their arts and their languages. The emphasis has been on complexity and diversity. At the same time Western influence has been transforming the societies and religions. Peoples who were then being colonized, pacified and missionized are now likely to belong to independent states; the 'New Hebrides' have become 'Vanuatu'. The work of Trompf comes out of this new situation, building on the wealth of diverse material from students of anthropology, linguistics and religion. Under the title 'Melanesian Religion' he is able to include both the traditional scene (the Old Time) and the changing Melanesia of missions, cargo cults, and secularization (the New Time).

The two writers have nevertheless some important common ground in their approach: both are concerned to learn from the Melanesians. Codrington was remarkable in his patient collecting of data on Melanesian 'anthropology and folklore'. Over a period of 25 years, from his mission centre on Norfolk Island, he listened to informants from the various islands (which did not, however, include New Guinea). His preface shows a deep concern to overcome prejudices from his European and missionary stance: 'one of the first duties of a missionary is to try to understand the people among whom he works' (Codrington 1891: vii). He cautions against hasty judgements. Writing a century later as a researcher in the history and phenomenology of religions, Trompf is likewise concerned to overcome ignorance and misconceptions by providing a sympathetic and comprehensive introduction, based largely on his research in Papua New Guinea. These pre-contact peoples 'were not the ignoble savages outsiders have often made them out to be (although there is no need to re-ennoble them through a compensatory romanticism either)' (Trompf 1991: 12). We can at least seek to understand the main features of their cultural life and religion.

Characteristics of Melanesian culture and religion

'All generalizations are false — including this one!' A logical poser such as this seems ready-made for Melanesia because of its tremendous diversity. It must be questioned whether 'Melanesia' refers to a single culture area with distinguishing traits. As Ann Chowning points out, 'Melanesia is best regarded as a geographical region within which some culture traits occur with greater frequency than they do in some of the surrounding areas' (Chowning 1973: 2). Again, in relation to physical anthropology the name Melanesia, meaning literally 'black islands' refers to black skin colour in contrast to the brown Polynesians; but in fact Melanesians are not a single type but varied and differentiated over long periods. The attempted division between a Melanesian type and a presumed earlier Papuan type is therefore difficult to apply with consistency to present-day peoples or to correlate with language differences.

What then can be said of Melanesian religions in their diversity? Some recurring themes and 'family resemblances' can be pointed out at a general level. A relevant place to start is the concept of *mana*. As the opening quotation showed, Codrington viewed this as a 'power or influence' attaching itself to persons or things. But a recent article on 'Rethinking Mana' (Keesing 1984) indicates that the word has been misinterpreted. Originally in Oceanic languages *mana* was a stative verb or at most an abstract verbal noun indicating that things were potent and efficacious in working; thus things or acts could have a quality of 'mana-ness' and persons a quality of 'being-mana'. A magical stone may 'have mana'; but it would be erroneous to substantivize *mana* as if the stone contained some invisible power to be elaborated in a cosmology or theory of psychic dynamism. Keesing has also described a living expression of the normative Melanesian concept in his extended study of Kwaio religion in the central mountains of Malaita in the Solomon Islands. The Kwaio term *nanama* is used to convey an active sense of '*nanama*-izing'. This happens when a priest sacrifices in a shrine, or when powerful magic is applied. This does not add some mysterious or magical ingredient to the gardens or the pigs but rather protects them and ensures that they will grow well and realize their potency. When the dead, the ancestors, are pleased with the living they give them protection for good living. The emphasis is on acting and achieving results rather than on giving reasons and explanations. Indeed, Keesing suggests that '*nanama*-izing' is a kind of conferring of grace which relieves the Kwaio of the need for metaphysical speculation (Keesing 1982: 46–9).

Although this example is drawn from one small part of Melanesia it serves to open up a whole chain of characteristics of religions throughout the region. We cannot expect to find a uniform pattern of belief in one or many gods or varieties of spirit-powers (Trompf 1991: 12–16). Underlying the profusion of myths and rituals is a religious experience based on abundant life, growth and death. The term *mana* is a focus for this, understood in a dynamic sense as we have seen. Sometimes Melanesians are categorized as 'materialist' and 'pragmatist' because of the concern for practical results in health and wealth. But the practical living belongs in a universe which includes spirits and ancestors, humans and the natural world all in one living cosmos, an ordered universe which is interrelated and which has to be maintained through right relationships.

Ennio Mantovani sums this up as the 'biocosmic religious experience'; everything which is experienced as positive has its source in 'life', which includes the material, biological and spiritual. Hence in contrast to the transcendent otherness of theism, 'the symbolism of the biocosmic experience is horizontal, with a stress on the blood, the womb, the tomb, the phallus' (Mantovani 1984: 32). He has applied this fruitfully to the interpretation of the pig-festival of the Chimbu in the Highlands of PNG. One can see the pig-kill as expressing values of community exchange and also of abundant life through the long rows of pigs and heaps of food. It is a repetition, an efficacious symbol, of the primordial killing of a man's brother which produced pigs from his grave. Through the symbolism of graves, flutes and dancing the ancestors participate with humans in the festival and share in the life that flows from the killing. Sex and violent death are symbolized here but in the biocosmic setting which is not only biological but spiritual – a 'life' which is 'health, wealth, well-being, good relationships, good name, prestige, meaning etc.' (Mantovani 1984: 161–2).

Within this biocosmic setting there is room for great diversity among Melanesian cultures and religions. Their general characteristics are modified in local situations and by ongoing historical changes. Nevertheless these features recur in the examples to be discussed in this chapter and we now list them briefly. As in most societies, death is to the forefront of personal and social concern. It implies the transition to the world of ancestors whose presence affects the living. The spirit-world includes the dead and ancestors; but also there are spirits associated with and embodied in the features of the natural world such as the forest and the sea and special places. Because of the interrelatedness of the 'biocosmos' there is no problem about using magical techniques to secure advantages or protection in everyday life through gardening, hunting or love magic. It has been said that there is no distinction between religion and magic in Melanesia. In the negative sense of sorcery, it is often feared as the cause of sickness and death. In the wider and more positive sense of magic, Mary MacDonald calls magic 'the characteristic form of traditional religion in Melanesia'; it is 'an elaborate metaphor operating throughout Melanesian cultures to facilitate involvement in the life of community and cosmos', comparable in its symbolic power to literature, theatre and art (in Mantovani 1984: 207−8).

Melanesian religions are generally lacking in concern for cosmogony, in contrast to Polynesian myths of creation or emergence of the cosmos. A contrast is also often drawn between hierarchical and hereditary leadership in Polynesia and the Melanesian 'big man' who has to achieve his status in his lifetime. However, this does not exclude the emergence of various forms of religious leaders − specialists in magic for diseases or in priestly sacrifices, visionaries, diviners, sages and prophets (Trompf 1991: 24−5). Since in primal cultures religion is closely interwoven into all aspects of life, their activities relate to the practical necessities of economic success and social power. In traditional societies prior to pacification warfare was a major concern with perpetual 'payback' fuelling inter-tribal feuds and the admiration of the warrior. 'The heartbeat of Melanesian religions, I estimate, lies in that constant round of give-and-take − or of payback, both vengeful and conciliatory − from which has been generated great warriorhood, the excitement of ceremonial exchange . . . . (Trompf 1991: 19−20; Trompf 1994). In relation to manhood and warfare, initiation is a crucially important rite of passage. An element of secrecy is involved in the imparting of secrets to the young by older men in the spirit houses which contain skulls and ancestral treasures. These have been typical sacred places for such purposes and elaborate masks and decorated boards may be kept there. Above all, festivals and ceremonies enacted for great occasions such as harvests or death provide the life-situation for Melanesian arts.

Arts in Melanesian religions

A whole range of arts is to be found in Melanesia − from music and song to dance and drama, from story and oratory to sculpture and design. They are not represented equally in all the areas. As with religions, so with the arts; they are diverse in form and content. How then to make sense out of this diversity? In the visual arts European scholars have sought to classify the major art styles and their connections through peoples and their migrations through areas of

Oceania. For instance, Felix Speiser (1966, 1941) included in his six styles the 'Curvilinear' plane surface style diffused from the early 'Papuans', the 'Beak' style with the nose elongated like a beak in the Sepik area, the '*Korwar*' style from far western New Guinea with the cube-shaped head form, and the distinctive complex *Malagan* style from New Ireland. While these categories proved useful in defining types and furthering discussion, they are not able to be applied with exactness. Moreover, they imply a static view of styles of tribal art whereas it is likely that changes and borrowings have continued in distant as well as in recent centuries. Attempts to show interconnections across the Pacific area result in some interesting comparisons. For instance, C.A. Schmitz (1971: 43–7) compares Melanesian forms with large staring eyes as a basic style of a 'Melanid Neolithic tradition', while a 'Bronze age' human figure is parallel in New Guinea, Polynesia and Micronesia. Such examples tantalize the viewer to speculation, but the limited number of examples and the interpretation of the evidence leave the nature of the linkages uncertain.

Bearing in mind these criticisms, a more cautious and tentative historical framework is outlined by Douglas Newton (in Gathercole et al. 1979: 46). In New Guinea the pre-agricultural period saw the 'use of ochre paints, mainly red, probably for body decoration', along with simple shell ornaments. In the early agricultural period (after 4000 BCE possibly) the stone bowl-pestle complex could have spread from the Highlands to the Sepik and Gulf areas and eastwards to the Solomons. Austronesian phases from 3000 and then 1500 BCE saw the development of outrigger canoes with carved horizontal prows and then vertical canoe prows. Designs on lapita ceramics led to two-dimensional art, while stone funerary monuments appear in island Melanesia. The historic period of art styles throughout Melanesia maintained continuity from the 15th century CE to the late 19th century.

A further problematic area is that of interpretation. Our concern in this study is especially with the religious significance of the art, and in Melanesia, as in other parts of the Pacific area with primal and pre-literate cultures, traditional works of art were often collected by people without knowledge of the language and religion from which they could be understood. Hence the many works to be found in museums with little more than a label saying 'totemic mask', 'sea spirit' or 'ancestor figure'. Ideally the inquirer should be able to consult the artist and the community where the object was used. Even if this were possible, questions about the meaning of art designs and representations might not be understood in ways that could satisfy an outsider; the answer may be little more than 'the ancestors said it should be like this and so we have always done it in this form'. Again the inquirer should not jump to conclusions by expecting a work to have certain fixed associations. An ancestral board that looks powerful and terrifying is not necessarily to be seen as 'high art', 'exotic' and 'religious'. Douglas Newton warns against this: 'we forget that these appurtenances of his daily life cannot be exotic to a Papuan; that through daily habit a great deal of the terror surrounding many of the most ferocious appearing objects must eventually wear off; that his conception of religion may be very different from ours' (Newton 1961: 33). On the other hand, there may be very real terror associated with memories of violent initiation rituals when objects were first shown to youth, leaving an enduring emotional impact.

This raises the question of secrecy, which prevents a local expert from divulging the sacred meaning of an object which should be known only by insiders. Yet sometimes 'outside' enquirers may be given the information because they do not belong to the restricted groups of women and children within the society itself. Further, a secret is never simply a secret but may have various levels. A sacred bullroarer may be shown in some versions to the uninitiated. As Newton points out perceptively (p. 35) there is an emotional dynamism and tension between the desire to have a secret, concealed from inferiors, and the desire to display a secret, thereby asserting one's superiority. In other cases works may be inaccessible after ritual use, not by being hidden but through being destroyed, having fulfilled their function.

In the face of these problems and the resulting uncertainties about the interpretation of Melanesian artworks by local informants, some scholars have emphasized the non-verbal nature of the visual arts, music and dance and sought other avenues for the meaning of their symbolic and ritual patterns. Psychoanalysis, sociology, structuralism and semiotics have been drawn on by Western scholars. The results can be searching and subtle, showing the complexity and diversity of meaning. However, as will appear in studies to be cited below, there is still the need for researchers to listen to the people themselves in their language, based on close contact and inter-action with the informants. It is through such first-hand work by explorers, missionaries and administrators that information has been gathered to present convincing pictures of the life, beliefs and art of the many cultures in Melanesia.

What then can be said in general about Melanesian arts in their diversity? First, religious themes and ceremonies account for the meaning and function of much of what has been available. Writing as an anthropologist, Raymond Firth emphasized the richness of the 'ritual life' of the people in the cultural background of their art: 'Funeral ceremonies, initiation ceremonies, fertility ceremonies are common, and are represented by a material equipment of masks, costumes, insignia and implements, the greater part of which is subjected to some degree of aesthetic elaboration' (Firth 1936: 24). This does not exclude elements of decoration and recreation in the arts, as with musical instruments, dance wands, clothing, designs on weapons and canoes and emblems on betel-nut apparatus. Even here religious themes may be echoed. In Melanesia the themes are usually related to ancestors and to various spirits and supernatural beings which combine human with animal form, including fish, birds and reptiles.

The arts are not related to either religion or aesthetic values in any abstract sense; they are not for 'art's sake' but for 'life's sake'. We can say, secondly, that effective power is the goal, in terms of our preceding discussion of *mana* and magic. Magic is interwoven with religion in the power attributed to sacred ancestor boards kept in the men's houses. When masks are prepared for a ceremony, the paints and material used may be seen as magically potent. In constructing a canoe and decorating it with carving, Trobriand Islanders used magical spells to ensure the canoe's success at sea. In addition to these practical expressions of magic we can add the more metaphorical sense of magic as a powerful means of swaying the imagination through the arts and transforming its direction to unseen worlds of wonder.

These features will become apparent in the examples which follow. But it cannot be expected that an example from one cultural group will be duplicated elsewhere. One aspect of the diversity of Melanesia lies in the emphasis or specialization given to some form of the arts. Some excel at singing, doing little carving, while neighbouring people may have developed elaborate sculpture. In the Highlands of PNG oratory is a great feature, while the visual arts are not developed except in body decoration. In the Sepik area, on the other hand, amazing cathedral-like *tambaran* houses are the focus of ancestral art objects and decoration flourishes also in everyday objects. In selecting examples we shall seek to cover a representative range of art forms which can be related to the religious life and ritual of local groups. The major areas of Melanesia will be covered, commencing with the far west of New Guinea (Irian Jaya), moving south-east to the Papuan Gulf up to the Highlands and down to the Sepik, then on to New Britain, New Ireland, the Solomons, Vanuatu and New Caledonia (see map of Melanesia, figure 22). Fiji is on the edge; originally Melanesian in population and language, its exposure to Polynesian culture makes it more appropriate for inclusion under Polynesia. While not all areas can be included, it is hoped that some justice can be done to the exciting diversity of Melanesia by bringing out a series of representative, inter-connected themes in religion and art.

North-West New Guinea: *Korwar* figures

The far west of New Guinea is adjacent to the Indonesian archipelago and some artworks show the influence of Indonesia from earlier times. It is now part of Irian Jaya, the western half of New Guinea under Indonesian rule. Previously it was part of the Dutch East Indies and had long been contacted

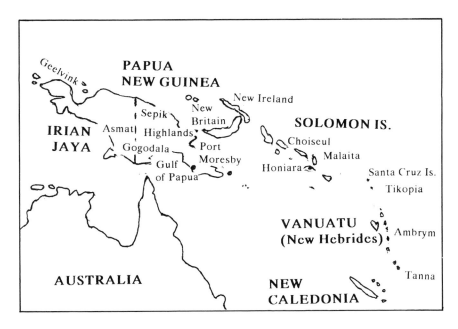

22. Map of Melanesia.

by Spanish, Portuguese and Dutch explorers. The latter provide the name of Geelvink Bay, the source of *Korwar* figures. Because this area was among the first to be contacted, the rituals and art associated with Melanesian tradition have declined; the distinctive figures have not been made in the 20th century and (as in many other places) information about their making and use has been lost or become difficult to verify.

The word '*Korwar*' denoted the spirit of the dead and came to be extended to the skull and wooden ancestor figures which could contain the skull of an ancestor of a family or clan. Those made entirely of wood could well be later imitations of prototypes which contained a skull (Baaren 1968: 85). The wooden *Korwar* (figure 23) is distinctive as a sculptured squatting figure supporting an outsize head. The face is based on a rectangular shape with a large mouth which shows a row of teeth. Sometimes there is the addition of feathers or an additional figure or an open-work panel in front of the body with tendril-like designs.

The carving of a *Korwar* is said to have been done in the person's lifetime so that at the moment of death the spirit could enter it (Linton and Wingert 1946: 134). Since the *Korwar* represented an honoured ancestor it was kept in the house by its family. It was a mediator between the living and the dead and could be consulted in order to find out, for instance, the cause of a death. For this purpose a shaman or *mon* was used to call up the spirits; but if the *Korwar* gave a misleading answer of false prophecy the owner might break it and

23.   *Korwar* skull-container. Geelvink Bay,
Irian Jaya, Western New Guinea.

throw it away, or sell it. Beyond this, van Baaren insists that it was part of an ancestor cult of offerings and worship. The term 'ancestor worship' can be used to cover a number of expressions of appeal to ancestral symbols as grave memorials or for protection. In Geelvink Bay the initiation ritual at the young men's house represented the ancestor's important place by the central pole linking heaven and earth as an *axis mundi* (Baaren 1968: 17−18).

This is a good example of a scholarly reconstruction of the meaning of an artwork in its religious context. The skull draws attention to the basic themes of death and the ancestors in Melanesian religions generally and indeed in most religious cultures of the world. Proverbially death is the 'one certain event in life' to which all the stages of a person's life eventually lead. Death is an ever-present threat in an environment of high infant mortality, sickness, warfare and the perils of rivers and forests. As Trompf points out, death in Melanesian culture was not objectified in speculative thought: 'Death was, far more commonly, an event in one's environment which induced *action*, usually a set pattern of actions, and virtually automatic responses' (Trompf 1991: 35, chap. 2). Wailing, elaborate funerary rites and even imitation as a form of ritual 'death' all witness to the importance of death for both the individual and society in the religious world-view. However, in this biocosmic world-view death does not have the last word for it is subsumed in the life-giving energies of the universe.

The power of the ancestors expresses one such ongoing form of life. The skull is a manifestation of its vital force in the *Korwar*. This has led some students of masks to speculate on the origin of sacred masks in the sacredness of decorated skulls; but this is not warranted from the evidence (Pernet 1992: 81–4). The important message conveyed by the *Korwar* is veneration of the ancestor who is the source of power and wisdom. Having crossed the divide of death the ancestors become the bridge between the living and the dead and provide a sense of unity for the family and clan. There is a certain ambivalence in approaching the ancestors, involving both trust and fear. As we have noted concerning the Kwaio religion in the Solomons, when the ancestors are pleased they offer protection and fertility. But if something is done wrongly they may bring retribution in danger and disease. So the skull is treated both with affection and with awe. That such attitudes are ancient and perhaps universal is suggested by palaeolithic burials with signs of careful tending of the dead. Skulls have also been found beneath floors at Jericho in the Near East, dated at around 7000 BCE. These are not evidence of 'ancestor worship' but indicate concern for the dead with reverence. To return to Melanesia of the present century, a beautiful example is given by Albert Maori Kiki in his autobiography describing his earlier life in the Papuan Gulf area. He was given a secret name, Maruka, after the great ancestor of the tribe whose presence was invoked in times of danger. Only his mother could call him by this name and she too was remembered:

> My mother died in 1958, the year I got married. From time to time my wife and I prepare a special meal and we set aside plates for my mother and for her father (whom she loved most) and we call their names and leave the food there while we eat our own share. This food will later be put away, it can never be eaten. We do this so we can think better of our dead. (Kiki 1968: 19, 5–7)

Asmat: artists and ancestor-poles

Moving to the south-west of New Guinea, in West Irian, we come to a very different situation from the previous example. With the Asmat people there was little outside contact and they remained fierce head-hunters and cannibals until the 1950s. Their 30,000 people were spread over a large area of jungle and rivers. Theirs was still a stone-age culture using stone and bone axeheads and knives. Their art was rich and impressive, and the introduction of steel tools was to make some of their work even more monumental. Its themes came from the culture, drawing on images linked to head-hunting and the relation of humans to the tree and the pig. All this was recorded in splendid description and detail by the 1961 expedition which brought back a range of artefacts and artworks from the Asmat (Rockefeller and Gerbrands 1967). Associated with this, a Dutch ethnologist made an intensive study of eight Asmat artists to present a first-hand account of their life, work and attitudes as individual artists, not just as conventionally anonymous 'primitive' craftsmen (Gerbrands 1967).

The Asmat *wow-ipits* (woodcarving-man) is certainly a clever craftsman using accepted forms and designs, but he can also be an artist in the sense of drawing on a fuller range of aesthetic expression and using his individual freedom more imaginatively. The average man in the community knows how to cut down trees and handle wood, but for a specially decorated shield or a carved canoe prow he will turn to the special skills of the *wow-ipits*. The artist is paid in food during the weeks of his work, but prestige is his main reward. His skill in making hourglass-shaped drums and statuettes from wood for regular ceremonies relates him to the ancestral traditions. These are focused spatially on the *yeu*, the large ceremonial house where the dead are buried and boys are told stories of their ancestors; it is the symbolic centre of the Asmat cosmos. In turn it is based on the archetypal myth of Fumeripits (Rockefeller and Gerbrands 1967: 11–24).

In this foundation story the cultural hero, Fumeripits, was the first to build a *yeu* house by drawing an outline of it on the sand, where it suddenly appeared. To fill the empty house he carved men and women from trees, and then by drumming he brought them to life and to dancing. Further, he had to defend his six *yeu* houses against the monster crocodile which he cut into pieces to become different kinds of men (black, brown and white). The myth thus provides the charter for the central Asmat values. Fumeripits is the creator of humanity out of wood, and wood is of vital importance to creativity and fertility, especially in the sago tree. Man is a tree and the tree is man. Fumeripits is also the first woodcarver and the first drummer, roles which are renewed by being re-entered at *yeu* house ceremonies. By cutting up the crocodile he justifies killing in order to create life, hence also head-hunting and cannibalism for fertility. The artist himself finds his charter in Fumeripits as he re-enacts the primordial myth by woodcarving and drumming. At the same time, he is a practical person who does the job he is commissioned to do. He does not expect that by drumming and singing he will repeat the miracles of Fumeripits who brought the wooden images to life and carved trees into people. He is 'a man of this world' (Gerbrands 1967: 161).

These Asmat values come together in the ancestor figures carved on canoe prows and especially in the great *mbis* poles (figure 24a). These monumental pieces, from 6 to 8 metres in height, are carved from mangrove with flat roots, one root being retained to make a wing-like projection with open-work carving like a decorated canoe prow. The lower part of the pole is often hollowed out like a dugout canoe, so that the whole work represents a 'soul-ship' (Renselaar 1956). The two figures depicted as humans in figure 24b are ancestors who live on after being killed by enemy head-hunters; they are reminders to the living to avenge them. Carved designs often include spiral

24. (a) Asmat *mbis* pole. South-west New Guinea.

24.   (b) Asmat, two figures on *mbis* pole. Otago Museum (photo).

forms and squatting figures of the praying mantis – 'a powerful symbol in this cannibalistic and head-hunting society of a creature in the natural world sharing similar proclivities' (Newton, in Gathercole et al. 1979: 59).

Before pacification of the Asmat, *mbis* poles were made for ceremonies re-enacting the Fumeripits myth of the creation of mankind. The motives were fertility and the renewal of life but also head-hunting, to avenge the dead. Accompanied by singing from head-hunters, the outlined figures would be cut from the mangrove trunk. The more skilled carving would be completed in a shed by the man's clubhouse. The eyes and mouth would be the last to be done, because of their importance in making the image vital, just before the ritual in front of the clubhouse. A mock attack was staged by men dressed for war, in order to chase away spirits of the dead. The ritual was concluded by men and women joining in a dance. After several days the sacred *mbis* was taken to the sago forest where its soft wood soon decayed; but this was because its supernatural power helped the sago trees to prosper. (Recently, Catholic Maryknoll Fathers have drawn on the sacred associations of sago flour in the baptism of Asmat converts to Christianity.) The ancestor pole thus achieved its purpose through this ceremonial occasion. (In more recent times it can be made for tourist purposes.)

From this Asmat example we can understand the traditional interrelation of Melanesian religion with fertility in food production and with head-hunting raids in warfare. This may be surprising or shocking to 'Western' attitudes, accustomed to dividing religion from economics and military activities. Here, among the Asmat, warfare was traditionally part of the realities of everyday life for which a warrior had to prepare himself. In the struggle for power and leadership the prerequisite was skill as a warrior; the trauma of initiation was heightened for a youth by having a freshly cut human head thrust before him. Shields used in Asmat head-hunting raids were decorated with symbols associated with head-hunting, such as fruit, the flying fox, the cockatoo and the hornbill; also a shield would be named after an ancestor and signify relatives.

This apparent obsession with warfare was not mainly for conquest or for exterminating enemy tribes, although these could become goals of revenge for wrongs done. There was the ongoing struggle for power but this was framed in a system of balances to ensure reciprocity in all the relations of life, including wealth and prosperity, as well as the righting of wrongs by violent 'payback'. Warfare as a means of solving problems has not completely ceased, despite a century of efforts at pacification by missionaries and governments. It may take new forms of inter-tribal hostility – gang violence in a modernizing Melanesia – or it may be replaced by non-violent forms of asserting power through feastings and oratory; but an underlying belief-system continues to account for the appropriate forms of 'payback', the reasons for death and sickness and for rewards and punishments. This is the 'logic of retribution' (Trompf 1991: ch. 3) which pervades Melanesian religion.

Gogodala: tradition revived

In the last decades a revival of traditional religious art has emerged in an area where it had almost disappeared. This is in the Western province of PNG, where the Gogodala, numbering about 10,000 people, live along the flood-plain of the Aramia river, north of the Fly river delta. Formerly they lived in communal longhouses and practised religious cults centred on their ancestral totems; totemic organization of society was expressed in totemic clan designs called *tao* – mostly abstract forms based on concentric circles – which were used on ceremonial objects and painted on the bodies of ritual performers (Newton 1961: 34–7). Fertility and initiation were at the heart of the great Aida cycle of ceremonies and the male cult named after the ancestor of the Gogodala who had brought them their ritual knowledge and social custom; 'Aida' was also the name of the sacred dance rattle kept in the longhouse (Crawford 1981). Some ethnographic records were made before the old order was changed by the arrival of Christian missionaries in the mid-1930s. Zealous native convert missionaries persuaded people to give up their heathen ways, and to burn the drums and ritual objects of the Aida cult; the longhouses and elaborate initiations were abandoned in favour of family houses and Christian upbringing. The old songs and dances were banned.

However the process of destruction was reversed with the work of Tony Crawford since 1972 in recovering and documenting Gogodala artefacts from museums throughout the world. He was able to explain to the Gogodala people the importance of their vanishing culture and persuade them to practise their arts once more. As a result, Gogodala women and men won success and acclaim as dancers at cultural festivals while their bold and colourful visual art was also commercially successful. A longhouse was rebuilt as a cultural centre, despite initial opposition from the mission. It was no longer an either/or between the Old and New Time; the Gogodala themselves were choosing how much of their heritage they would continue along with the Christianity they had adopted.

The artist, while an ordinary person in society, is respected as a skilled carver and painter. Traditional artefacts include masks, plaques, ancestral figures and various items such as weapons, paddles and musical instruments, finely decorated. An item of key importance was the canoe, the main form of transport for the Gogodala. The canoe that was jointly owned by members of a clan visibly expressed their solidarity. Hence they would ask a stranger 'What is your canoe?' (Newton 1961: 34). Even the individual man's canoe 'was not just a vehicle but an image of his primary or ascending totem to

25. (a) Gogodala model of canoe as goanna. PNG.

which he paid deep homage. It was a single dugout, up to 16 metres in length, intricately carved, incised and richly painted all over in red, yellow, black and white. The prow was elaborately carved to represent a primary totem "devouring" a clan father' (Crawford 1981: 50). The owner's totemic *tao* design was painted on the sides and feather decorations were clustered at both ends of the canoe. The great clan-owned canoes were similar in style but much more majestic, their prows being decorated by master-carvers. Being up to 30 metres in length and capable of carrying 60 paddlers they could be used as war canoes to reach an enemy longhouse; more peacefully, they were used for racing in competitions between village clans to celebrate the settling of a dispute. Nowadays races are held to celebrate special anniversaries such as Independence Day, Christmas or New Year's Day or the official opening of a new school or church (Crawford 1981: 284). The rich photographic record in Crawford's large work provides a splendid opportunity to see the vitality of these communal celebrations in contemporary form and to compare them with photos from half-a-century earlier. Even the 'death' of an old and outworn racing canoe, called *duda: gawa*, becomes an occasion for elaborate ritual and feasting so that the vital spirit of the sacred canoe is released properly without causing harm; this release happens finally when clansmen line up with axes to chop up the canoe and share it as firewood (Crawford 1981: 262).

A third type of canoe, the *gi gawa,* is a smaller ceremonial canoe not to be placed in water but displayed on a platform for initiation ceremonies (see figure 25a). Similar in style to the racing clan canoe, it is from 2 to 7 metres long. It is a sacred object representing a totemic ancestor such as a crocodile, snake, lizard or fish, often with parts of a human figure between its teeth. In all these canoes there is a link with the ancestral spirit world, not just through the totemic designs but through the spiritual force, or *ugu*, of the canoe which was 'instrumental in controlling most happenings' (Crawford 1981: 50). The *ugu* could also be embodied in the form of a *kuku* effigy, a limbless hardwood figure with the clan insignia; it was expected to dispel evil spirits and sickness and to protect gardens and promote fertility. The revival of the art and ritual is linked to the traditional Melanesian 'biocosmos', still a living reality for the

Gogodala as they participate in Christianity and the modernizing changes of the 20th century.

Gulf of Papua: masks and boards

Moving eastwards along the southern central coast of PNG we find in the Gulf area impressive masks and sacred boards associated with elaborate ceremonies for spirits and ancestors. The pervasive *mana*-like element of vital strength is called *imunu,* the power that gives things their individuality, such as a strangely twisted stick or a ritual object. 'The word itself is perhaps onomatopoeic, referring both to thunder and the noise made by whirling bullroarers' (Newton 1961: 8). The latter is a basic form of board, flat and elliptical, which is whirled on the end of a cord to produce a thundering noise, attributed to the voice of spirits of sky and thunder. Although not frequently used, the bullroarer is important because of its sacredness; it probably originated prior to other forms of sacred boards (Williams 1940: 165) which were carved or painted to embody the spirits. In the great masks the ancestral dead who had retired to the bush, as guardians there, returned again.

At the eastern part of the vast Gulf of Papua are the Elema people of Orokolo Bay. While differing from the western area, in not having the tradition of head-hunting for instance, they provide examples of the dominant religious and artistic forms of the Gulf. The *eravo* was the huge, ceremonial clubhouse for men, rising to 15 metres in height at the front. It contained the *hohao,* carved wooden tablets which were sacred if given the name of a bush spirit who indwelt the board and could wander around its home.

The Elema honoured the spirits in two especially notable and spectacular cycles of ceremonies – for the bush spirits (*Kovave*) and for the sea spirits (*Hevehe*). These were enacted in the late 1930s and recorded in detail (Williams 1940) and here (using the historic present tense) we shall discuss the *Hevehe* as featuring the cult of masks. Preparations for this may take from 10 to 20 years, continuing sporadically with the building of the *eravo* and then construction of the giant masks in the secrecy of this house. The work is slow and painstaking, undertaken by men representing the various clans. Ownership of the *Hevehe* mask is vested in a family, of which the eldest is the controller, and in addition there are several persons closely concerned with it (Williams 1940: 237–8). First, the man who makes the mask is its 'father', the *hevehe-oa.* His wife is its 'mother', contributing the sago-leaf draperies as well as cooking duties. Then the person for whom it is made, the male initiate, will be the first to wear the mask personally. The initiate in turn will give pigs to another person, the *aukau,* who has special ceremonial duties during the cycle of festivities. This illustrates the network of social relations and obligations supporting the masks in the setting of dancing and feasting.

25.   (b) *Hevehe* mask. Elema people, Papuan Gulf.

The form of the *Hevehe* mask (figure 25b) is based on a loop of cane, making a surfboard shape between 3 and 6 metres in height, affixed to a much longer pole, a sago midrib which reaches down between the wearer's thighs to balance the mask. The result is 'an outlandish figure, like nothing on earth . . . . But its ungainliness is largely redeemed by the surprising grace and agility of the wearer' (Williams 1940: 243). An inside picture of the making and iconographic meaning of the *Hevehe* mask has been given by a PNG national (Kiki 1968). Each mask has to be an exact copy of the one destroyed after the previous festival, and a consensus among the older people is necessary to ensure that this is so. The more experienced men 'with a skilful hand' actually make the masks: it is not an art taught via formal apprenticeship, but is instead a clan tradition. On the flat bark cloth covering of the cane frame they paint significant clan designs. The lower half represents the face of the clan ancestor while the upper half is decorated with various geometric patterns which, however similar to those on another clan's mask, can convey quite different meanings. A long line down the centre symbolizes a magic rope. The spatial ordering of the world is indicated by such patterns as zigzags round the edge for clouds on the horizon; a painted area at the top standing for land which the clan hopes to find and settle in the future; and a series of rectangles below this for the land held at present. The *Hevehe* mask typically shows the face of the clan ancestor with eyes consisting of concentric circles; they are surrounded by a star-like pattern which can mean a variety of things according to the clan that uses it: 'For example: the tail of the *maria* fish; a *lakatoi* sail; a firefly, which stands for lovemaking, and is the symbol of a particular ancestor; "jellyfish feet", which is a metaphor for the twinkling of the star, the symbol for Malara, the protector of the Kauri clan' (Kiki 1968: 47). Clearly, one cannot expect to find a single unified system of iconographic meanings in the masks. As with many other examples of the arts in primal religions, apparent simplicity covers a rich and complex variety of potential meanings; one can learn these only from the local people and artists who draw on their traditions and mythology in their art. This does not, however, preclude observers from building on this knowledge subsequently by making comparisons with other masks and artworks; this may illuminate the local example with further understanding from the study of religion, art and anthropology.

We return to the live setting in which the *Hevehe* mask is exhibited. It is in the happening of the festival cycle that the mask has its ultimate justification and meaning in the eyes of the people. The practical purpose of the cycle is to gain protection and fertility from the spirits and the great masks representing them are intended to attract their attention, to honour and to entertain them. This is consequently a suitable time for initiation ceremonies to introduce young men into the full male cult; they would be the first to be exposed to the newly made masks and thereby share in the power of the spirits, so near at this time. Before the fully public disclosure of the masks there are preliminary 'descents' where the novices learn to wear the giant masks. During these weeks there are preparations for feastings and occasions for songs, dancing and speeches of exhortations. The power of sound is important in all this. At one stage the booming sound of the bullroarer is intended to frighten away the women and uninitiated as its awful voice calls on the masks as its 'younger brothers' to come forth (Williams 1940: 301–2).

The climax of the *Hevehe* is the public emergence of the masks in *mairava*, the occasion of 'Revelation or Disclosure' (Williams 1940: ch. xxii, 346). During the night, after hours of drumming, singing and dancing, the swift approach of an invisible sea-monster, *ma-hevehe*, is signified by blood-curdling voices coming in from the beach, as it brings drums into the men's house. From inside suddenly a thunder of drums bursts forth and continues for two hours. This is what the *Hevehe* have been waiting for during all these years in the *eravo*. Women now join in a jubilant dance and excitedly call them to come out: 'I want to see you and to touch you. Come out!' As the light of fires gives way to dawn the door of the *eravo* flies open and the supreme moment has arrived. The majestic *Hevehe* stream out (122 in number at this Orokolo ceremony) and wend their way through the crowd, dancing to the beach. Women and children joyously receive each one and join in groups, dancing as they accompany the *Hevehe* on its path to the seashore and back. As the morning advances the masks are taken over by different wearers and dancing continues.

This happy celebration goes on for a month. By then the masks have been the means of generating power for good; but this power could be dangerous if the masks are left in their highly charged state. Therefore at the end of the lunar month there is a final procession of the *Hevehe*. After being thanked for their stay they are ceremonially 'killed' by an arrow being shot at the face of a representative *Hevehe*. Without reverence, all of the masks are carried out to be heaped up and burned as so much rubbish. The ashes are later thrown into the sea and the *Hevehe* spirits thereby go back to join the great spirit of all *Hevehe*. The *eravo* is now empty and eventually falls into decay. The masks have fulfilled their purpose in the cycle of preparation and festivities over the preceding years and climactic month.

By concentrating on one type of mask – the *Hevehe* – we can see that its religious power lies in its vital relation to a whole range of expression of religion through ritual and the arts – music, dance, speech and story-telling as well as visual art. It is not an object kept forever in sacred isolation from life. Its sacredness comes to its consummation in the ceremonial happening. At the same time we recognize that there are many types of masks with diverse functions throughout Melanesia. Among the Elema people there are, for instance, the smaller *eharo* masks which feature a variety of creatures such as birds on a conical head mask; they may be of totemic or mythological significance but are no longer seen as sacred and are of interest in dance, comedy and entertainment. Other forms of art associated with religion and legend such as *Hohao* boards embodying the spirits of clan heroes have suffered destruction in the Papuan Gulf area and even in more recent revival have an 'uneasy survival': 'The carvers nowadays see their own work as a degenerate art form' (Beier and Kiki 1970: 36).

Gope is the name given to elliptically shaped carved boards, about a metre in height, which are often labelled loosely in collections as 'memorial tablets' or 'ceremonial slabs' (see figure 26). Their bold design is carved in low relief with painting in red, white and black to indicate they are the home of a powerful protective spirit with magical powers. Their sacred status earned them a special place in the men's ceremonial houses, often crowding the interior. Their function was first of all protective, and in some forms they

26.   *Gope* board. Papuan Gulf.

were hung from house gables to twist in the wind and ward off sickness and evil spirits. More aggressively a *gope* could be consulted as an oracle before a raid on a village and as the sender of its spirit in advance to undermine the enemy.

Because of the vividness and power of the mask it is tempting to speculate that religious art finds its origins in prehistoric rituals associated with animal and human disguises in skins or masks. But the universality of masks can be questioned, along with other sweeping claims concerning them (Pernet 1992: part one). We shall confront the absence of masks in the following section. Further, in view of the diverse forms and functions of masks, one must look at the mask in its context and ritual use and not insist that its qualities be generalized to all. Some masks are for buffoonery, others for social control by creating fear. If we ask about the more specifically religious use of masks in relating people to a sacred cosmos and spirits we find many examples of these. The preparation of masks may be surrounded by sacred and secret prescriptions. The appearance of the completed mask in action may evoke awe and wonder at the mystery of the supernatural powers. Further, for the wearer who sees through the eyes of the mask it may be an occasion of transformed identity, of experiencing for the time the joy and power of the figure represented. This does not mean that the person is in a state of trance or literally changed in personal identity; but in acting out the part with great expectation one sees the world 'as if' transformed by the spiritual occasion. In these ways the mask can convey awareness of a sacred cosmos (Moore 1977: 54–7).

Central Highlands: personal art

In contrast to the elaborate masks, paintings and wood-carvings to be seen in the areas of PNG so far discussed, we find areas where these are given little prominence. In the fertile and populous Central Highlands of PNG few masks are used except for such comical forms as the Asaro mud-men masks of the Eastern Highlands. There is a lack of the initiation societies and cult secrets with which masks are associated elsewhere. Masks are not generally used here for acting out myths in dance-forms. Yet there is no lack of ceremonial life nor of vivid expression in the ritual arts. What forms then are used? A useful short summary (by Newton in Gathercole et al. 1979: 62–3) will show the alternatives:

> Personal decoration, especially in the form of headdresses of iridescent beetle-shells, flowers, massive shells, boar tusks, paint and above all the splendid plumage of many species of birds-of-paradise, was carried to a pitch of great magnificence. With all this, their painting and carving were elementary by comparison with other areas of the island. Much of it was based on simple geometric forms, mainly circles and diamonds, engraved, painted, and woven or pyrographed on two-dimensional surfaces. The most elaborate of these are on the painted shields and the *genua* boards displayed at festivals. Anthropomorphs and zoomorphs are relatively rare, though some wooden figures of both types have been collected in the last couple of decades; these perhaps owe their existence to outside influence. More traditional, apparently, are figures plaited out of cane in the Western and Southern Highlands.

If we go on to ask why the Highlands should provide this contrast, there is no simple explanation. In general it can be said that different cultures – of which there are many existing side by side in Melanesia – develop traditional emphases in some of the arts and not others. When only so much human energy and material for the arts may be available, the resources are channelled into specific forms of music and dancing, or oratory and theatre and selected visual art expressions. More specifically, this question has been discussed for the central Mt. Hagen ceremonies and some insightful considerations are given in the course of the Strathems' study of 'self-decoration' which we shall now take as a focus (Strathem 1971).

The personal art of the Highlanders is indeed remarkable as a spectacle. For exchange festivals and for public parades at an annual show, performers invest much time and resources in preparing their body decorations using paints, shells, plumes and furs. They will be admired for their rich and valuable

27.   Personal art. Mt. Hagen, Central Highlands, PNG.

adornment but also criticized by people of rival clans. The first impression of an outsider spectator is vividly conveyed by David Attenborough (cited by O'Hanlon 1989: 14–16):

> The sing-sing ground was packed with hundreds of wildly charging dancers. They formed themselves in platoons, five in a rank, ten ranks deep, and, pounding their drums and yelling hoarsely, they stamped fiercely across the ground. Their dance, though simple, absorbed them totally . . . they seemed almost in a state of trance . . . . It was one of the most spectacular sights I have ever seen.

Such displays have obviously warlike features which are intended to impress and frighten enemies by a show of superior power. Below the surface there are memories of clan hostilities and killings in the past. The men decorate themselves with dark and aggressive tonings (figure 27).

However, the power displayed should be seen in the more pervasive and positive context of fertility, health and productivity. One aspect of this is the use of decoration to attract the opposite sex at such gatherings. Another is the important place of dance and decoration at the exchanges of wealth such as the *moka* exchange, the aim of which is to enhance the prestige of a 'big man' by his giving away pigs and other wealth which he has accumulated. Dance plays an important part in gathering people together and bringing the crowd to a pitch of excitement with the colour and movement just before the pigs are given away. In studying this among the Melpa people of the Hagen area, Strathern draws on symbols of the bird of paradise (now a national symbol used throughout PNG) as suggested by a 'big man' in conversation. The bird goes through a natural cycle of acquiring plumage, dancing, moulting and then regrowing: 'The birds display before mating. The people dance before giving away their wealth. Wealth grows "on the skin of the people" and is then disbursed' (Strathern, in Spencer 1985: 129). People dance and wear plumes when giving away wealth goods, as building up and disbursing wealth expresses maturity in the life-cycle of a person in the *moka* exchange system.

More specifically, religious cults also promote prosperity. One which is concerned with fertility and male purification honours the Female Spirit who appears to men in dreams as a beautifully adorned young bride who yet remains a virgin. It is the men who practise the spirit-dance and decorate themselves fully in secret, then dance out of the enclosure to stream round the ceremonial ground, their white plumes waving. The crowd shouts, 'The Spirit is coming!' (Strathern 1971: 56). Another cult for clan strength and fertility is intended to enhance relations between the sexes, allowing women to take part in the climactic dance. Beforehand the performers place their feather head-dresses inside the tall pole-house so that they will be made bright by the spirits of clan ancestors there. Both of these religious cults have features of the great exchange festival displays and are followed by the distribution of meat. The decorations for these cults assert group prosperity and well-being, displaying 'a person in an enhanced or ideal state' (Strathern 1971: 59).

If we ask about the meaning of this personal art and body-decoration it is evident from the foregoing that prosperity, health and fertility are predominant concerns. Strathern also suggests, in addition to the basic message, a whole battery of messages transmitted through different combinations of items. This has been explored further by Michael O'Hanlon's ethnographic study of the Wahgi people who are neighbours of the Mt. Hagen Highlanders and use both 'festive' and male 'martial' adornments. A common emphasis among anthropologists has been that art traditions form systems of communication which are not translatable into conscious and verbalized statements, so that direct questioning of informants in the society will not help. However, this study shows that the Wahgi do talk about adornment art in terms of their own concerns; they assess the art as giving answers to questions about male strength and solidarity, unsettled scores and rumours about betrayals. While direct verbal professions about these may be suspect, the quality of the decorated appearance reflects the inner moral state: 'a man whose skin glows has not transgressed' (O'Hanlon 1989: 138, 17–21). A dull, sallow and lustreless skin is untrustworthy, but a bright, glowing glossy skin (like glossy, glistening and fertile pig-fat), is at the opposite side in evaluating the person's decoration. These attempts at 'reading the skin' do not provide final answers, yet the decoration provides a non-verbal form which is related to the social life and experience of the viewers; it provides a platform and stimulus which elicits talk about the art and moral judgments for ordering and authenticating their life. Here we can see a process which is going on in all response to the arts. In this specific study of the Wahgi we see an example of 'ethno-aesthetics' and of how the people apply their indigenous values in practice in the culture. When so many theories have been imposed on 'primitive art' by scholars from outside, it is important to explore every means patiently to understand what is experienced from inside.

We return finally to the earlier question about the importance of personal art in the Highlands. On the one hand we can observe in this culture a degree of sophistication in its traditional arts and astuteness in adapting to modern changes in technology, education, politics and religion which suddenly arrived in the 1930s. On the other hand the Highlands' emphasis on dancing and personal art can be seen as primeval and elemental, in so far as dancing is the simplest of the arts in needing no apparatus while bodily decoration is possible even for the poorest or most transient of peoples. Archaeological data suggest that the Highlands was the earliest area in PNG to be settled, probably before 25,000 BCE and various carvings of pestles and mortars are associated with human, bird and animal forms (Newton, in Mead 1979: 33–6). Prehistoric stones are still valued and used to this day as cult objects with spiritual significance. Traditionally stones of peculiar shape have been seen as magical and used for protection or to gain success in hunting and fertile production. Such stones may be inherited and kept safely in men's houses; they may be decorated with designs and with colours associated with fertility. Tentatively we suggest that the Highlands have preserved very ancient art forms and in the case of self-decoration developed it to a high level. Further, consideration of the cult rituals of Hageners shows that they are designed to achieve fertility, not reveal the spirits in tangible form through visual representational arts. The spirit world is not conceived physically but more abstractly as 'their unseen presence and influence over health and moral behaviour' (Strathern 1971: 176). When they do use decorations to associate themselves with powerful beings such as birds, they do so metonymically by taking parts of the birds, such as feathers, and attaching them to decorations; they do not represent the bird by making carvings or masks or by re-enacting myths about birds.

These close studies by Strathern and O'Hanlon serve to illuminate the subtle and often complex and elusive meanings which Highlanders may find in their personal art. Underlying them, the pervasive purpose remains the increase of health, fertility and prosperity within a Melanesian 'biocosmic' view of life.

Sepik: *Haus Tambaran*

The Sepik region is renowned for the abundance, variety and imaginative power of its art. Hence it often predominates in collections of PNG art and in books featuring visual arts of Melanesia. It has been the subject of large scholarly studies (Kelm 1966–68) and of many detailed reports and analyses by anthropologists (Lutkehaus et al. 1990). From the mountains and foothills to the low-lying plain of the winding Sepik river in northern PNG, the region includes diverse languages, cultures and art styles. While there are similarities in buildings and art objects, the symbolism of these may differ: for instance, the yam harvest among the Abelam and Arapesh stands for male fertility and aggression, whereas for the Kwoma the yam in the garden is 'basically feminine'. In societies such as the Kwoma, the artist is an influential man of knowledge who expresses his views in words and songs, carvings, paintings and pottery. His success is related to his other achievements as yam cultivator, politician, man of practical and mythological knowledge and, formerly, war manager (C. Kaufmann in Mead 1979: 330–31). Art styles may be recognizable as coming from distinct villages. On the other hand they have also been mixed through mutual plundering in war and trading in peace.

Both the natural environment and ancestral traditions provide the symbolic content of the religiously infused art. Stories of ancient times recounted how once water was everywhere, before creation. Then the crocodile appeared and split in two, his upper jaw becoming the sky and his lower jaw the earth. (This is reminiscent of myths of origin found in other parts of the Pacific and also other parts of the world; here it is used to explain the later division of people by earth and sky moieties.) When the first pair of brothers appeared, this led on to clan associations whose founders followed the tracks of crocodiles clearing the way (J. Wassman, in Lutkehaus et al. 1990: 24).

Other forms of the story attribute to the primeval crocodile the origin of the earth from his excreta and then the birth of man who was originally dependent on the crocodile to carry him. Then man rebelled by killing the sleeping crocodile with a large stone. In remorse for his deed he burst into a flood of tears which made his nose grow longer and longer as the months passed. The tears formed a stream which became the Sepik river. From the traumatic event came both the independence of humanity and the dominating feature of the Sepik natural environment. Also grounded or 'explained' here is

28.   *'Wanleg'* hooked figure.
Arambak people, Sepik, PNG.

the elongated nose which is a striking feature of Sepik carvings of the human figure, with a trunk-like nose in a curve connected to the chin and lower body. It may relate to the beak of a bird, expressing the close relation of the human to the animal and bird world.

Sepik art is curvilinear, in contrast to the angular figures of Korwar art. The human figure predominates, especially the head, but often stylized with such intense emotional power and fantastic transformations that modern European artists and critics have sometimes seen the art as 'expressionist', 'surrealist' and even 'abstract'. One example of abstraction is the incorporation of hooks which are often elaborately carved for practical purposes in hanging up belongings and skulls. In the case of the *yipwon* figures of the Arambak people of the Upper Karawari, groups of opposed hooks are carved as the body of a slender human figure in flat profile with only one leg visible (figure 28) (Forge 1973: 69–70). The significance of this distinctive style for the local culture is unknown, but legends recount how the figures were carved from wood pieces left over from the making of a drum from a tree growing from the grave of a female ancestor. These were given magical powers of speech and movement. Their having only one leg (*Wanleg* in Pidgin or Tok Pisin) did not prevent them from bounding along to help warriors and hunters pursuing their prey. Though now reduced to a lifeless state they are still valuable, and smaller *wanleg* are carried as protective amulets (Dennett 1975: 116).

Among figures from the world of nature, such as the cassowary bird or the serpent, the crocodile recurs in realistic and stylized forms. A canoe prow may be carved as a crocodile head, with a row of teeth cut out of the wood and eyes inserted for realistic effect. This relates both to myths of origin, which have already been mentioned as showing its archetypal importance, and to rituals associated with initiations, the crocodile being a totem animal. For these occasions the cry of the 'spirit-crocodile' is heard when water drums are thrust into water to produce a gurgling sound. In some parts of the Sepik initiations involve painful scarification of the chest and down the back, buttocks and legs so that the scars will resemble crocodile skin.

From these examples of specific themes we turn now to the *Haus Tambaran* (figure 29), the large ceremonial house found throughout the Sepik region, the focus of the male ancestral cult (as seen in the comparable *eravo* clubhouses of the Gulf of Papua). At Maprik in the Abelam Territory the impressive structure rears up towards 20 metres in height and serves as a focus like a cathedral in a village square. Huge faces of ancestors look out from the painted front gable which leans forward, providing shade and protection from the weather. Access to the interior is gained solely through the tunnel-like opening; it is a store-room for ancestor images and secret objects for male initiates only (figure 30). It is a meeting-house and centre for initiations into the ancestral cult which includes the cult of yams, the staple food. In his study based on the neighbouring Arapesh culture, Donald Tuzin shows that the term *Tambaran*, or *Tambaram*, has a wide range of meanings — the cult as a religious institution, but also the spirits, individual and collective, who are venerated within the cult, and then the ritual initiation grades and sacred paraphernalia (Tuzin 1980: xiii, 24–7). A sequence of five grades takes males from childhood to old age; women are excluded from the cult secrets yet they prepare the feasts and are essential in their roles as outsiders and spectators. The figures in the house and the mysterious sounds heard from the house are believed to be those of powerful supernatural beings such as the supreme ideal, but also fiercely personified, figure of the giant spirit Nggwal.

Meanwhile, the exterior facade of the house publicly displays a row of large flat painted faces, *ngwalndu,* whose great white circles of eyes stare out on the ceremonial ground. How are these understood by the people? Andrew Forge pursues this question in his studies of Abelam art as a means of cultural communication (Forge 1973: 168–92; Forge in Jopling 1971: 290–314).

29.   *Haus Tambaran*. Abelam, Sepik, PNG. Melanesian display, Otago
Museum (photo).

30.   Ancestor face from interior of house, Maprik, Sepik.

Painting is a sacred activity related to the *Tambaran* and to the yam cult. Paint itself is the essential magical substance of the yam and the means of transferring benefits to initiates and to the village; paint becomes highly charged by ceremony. However when it comes to identifying the content of these rich polychrome works the artists often refuse to state what they are painting until they are finished. The outside observer who seeks 'explanations' of the art and its meaning is told that 'the ancestors did it this way' or that it is powerful magic or that a name is given for an item. Even with the ritually essential motifs on the facade, they will deny that they portray the ancestors. Literally, the *ngwalndu* are not the ancestors. Yet the great white circles of their eyes suggest stars and fireflies which are identified as ancestors coming back to observe their descendants. Forge concludes that it is by a chain of puns, or by the ambiguity of poetry that the eyes are seen after all as the eyes of the ancestors. Sepik art is a means of communication but not one that can be verbalized. The meaning is not in representing something in the natural or spiritual world but rather in expressing a relationship that is not immediately accessible; this is at several levels of meaning, like a grammar which the users of a language know almost unconsciously. 'Abelam art acts directly on its beholders, properly socialized and initiated Abelam' (Forge 1973: 190). It conveys important meanings, about the nature of man and woman's creative power in relation to supernatural power for instance, which are cosmological and theological. Forge thus points to the system of meaning which underlies

31.   *Kundu* drum. Sepik, PNG.

the various combinations of colour and graphic art in the visual system. The art is more than a visual art style. The art visually evokes a whole chain of associations, deeply meaningful to both individual and society.

The same can be said for the interior of the *Haus Tambaran*. 'The Tambaran is more than the sum of ideas and artifacts associated with the men's cult; it is the very sign and symbol of Arapesh culture, the personified mystique of a way of life' (Tuzin 1980: 324). The visible expression of this is found in the ancestral figures, masks, skulls, shields and other treasures stored in the house, some of them very secret. But the visual is only one part of the complex of ritual dance, teaching and other activities in the men's house. Of particular importance are the arts of music and sound. The large slit-gong drum, *garamut,* is carved from a log of wood. Smaller hand-drums, *kundu,* are carried by individual dancers and may be carved with bird figures, human faces and ornate designs (see figure 31). Flutes and whistles are used in the *Tambaran* musical repertoire. Of special secrecy were the instruments used as the voices of the *nggwals* taking part in an initiation – the *bowas*, bamboo flutes and voice-distorters placed in the open end of *kundus* to transform the singers' voices into the eerie muffled resonance of the *Tambaran* voice (Webb 1987:

16). By performing this in the inner sanctum of the spirit house, the fearsome power of Nggwal is released to liberate the natural order and all the progeny waiting to be born: 'the voice of the Tambaram *speaks* creation, with a mysterious, intrinsic efficacy' (Tuzin 1980: 245). While the women outside continue to believe that it is Nggwal whose voice sounds forth and who feasts on the foot provided, the truth is revealed to initiates – that it is the men who eat the food and whose chorus of voices make the Voice. The effect of this revelation is not to destroy devotion to the *Tambaran* but to use its illusion and disguise to celebrate personal and collective identity. Tuzin interprets it as a transcending of a magically bound system to become an abstract religious ideal and a religious ethic (Tuzin 1980: 284–5). More recently, Tuzin suggests that the *Tambaran* cult, like the cargo cult, is an indigenous statement about 'cultural authenticity', attained momentarily in ritual action (in Lutkehaus et al. 1990: 368).

Whatever the future of *Tambaran* may be for religious and ethical practice in local cultures, the influence of its arts continues in the wider world of changing PNG. Christian missions have adapted the *Tambaran* motifs in the design of church facades and interiors including the Catholic Stations of the Cross, as in the Roman Catholic churches in the Sepik region at Ariseli (Tuzin 1980: 186) and at Ambunti (Trompf 1991: dust-cover picture). The Catholic cathedral at Port Moresby incorporates the facade design of ancestors into a striking modern tower. Sepik art has been developed by modern artists in decorations of public buildings, banks and the Museum and Art Gallery of PNG.

Another modern development is the Sepik 'story-board', a portable wooden picture carved in relief with scenes from local life. For the Kambot people along the Keram river (in the lower eastern part of the Sepik) story-boards were devoted to depictions of spirits and ancestors. They were originally painted on bark; but since these were too easily damaged in transit, dealers in the 1960s arranged for them to be done as carvings on durable wooden boards. With this there came a change in subject matter to scenes of everyday life. The spirit figures are seldom shown, apparently displaced by a process of secularization. While story-board art is popular for sale to tourists in PNG it also expresses the indigenous feeling for the interconnection of events and scenes; PNG pupils in drawing will naturally let one thing lead on to another. An example here from the Sepik (figure 32) shows more traditional figures from stories both above and below; men are vigorously poling a canoe on the Sepik river with crocodile and serpent nearby and stilt houses typical of the river area. In the second, quite recent, version (figure 33) the Sepik artist has repeated the three upper formal figures and rendered the men in the boat more stiffly, with additional symbols in a formal arrangement; the bird of paradise is included as the symbol of PNG

32. Story-board, traditional Sepik. (Photo, A.C. Moore.)

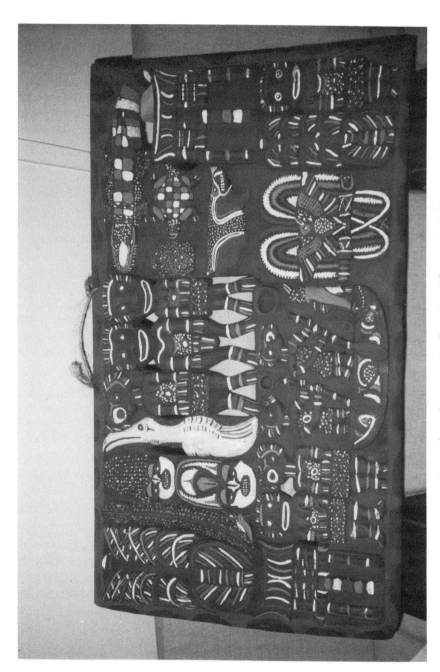

33.   Story-board, recent Sepik artist. (Photo, A.C. Moore.)

national unity. Traditional themes are thus developed, with some loss of the dynamic flow. But the art of the Sepik continues to exercise an important influence in the new nation.

New Britain: masks

Moving from the New Guinea mainland to the north-east we come to the large islands of New Britain and New Ireland. These were included in the 'Bismarck Archipelago' in the days of German colonial rule; they are now provinces of the PNG nation. They furnish further examples of Melanesian diversity and remarkable art forms.

Spectacular masks are the notable feature of New Britain visual art and there may well have been some interchange between the various tribal groups as well as with New Guinea across the water. However at the far west of the island the Kilenge people claim that one of their great masks, the *bukumo*, originated in the bush interior of their land (Dark in Mead 1979: 154). This is a 'Janus' mask with the face painted on both back and front, from which radiate spokes of canes almost 2 metres in length with feathers on the end. The effect is like a vast open fan which sways and vibrates as the wearer proceeds along the village path. This is for the special ritual use in initiations held at ten-year intervals, the mask frames being kept in the men's house in the interim. When the time comes for the boys to be recognized as men, with hair cut and ears pierced, there will be feasting and the appearance of the young men wearing *bukumo* at dusk; after participating all night at a sing-sing he will be told to go away at dawn (Dark 1974: 19–41). In addition, this redounds to the credit and prestige of the 'big man' who has paid the artist to exercise his skill in making the traditional ceremonial objects such as masks, decorated drums or a canoe.

As we have noted earlier, there is a variety of masks to fulfil a variety of requirements in different religious and cultural settings (see further Moore 1977: 53–6, 296; *EWA* ix: 520 ff.). At the other end of New Britain at the Gazelle peninsula interior, the Baining people had owl-masks with large staring eyes to represent bush spirits for the protection of children. They also constructed *hariecha* effigies on poles up to 12 metres in height attached to the back of the staggering celebrant; these were concerned with male and female fertility figures, friendly spirits for harvest and initiation. The Baining continue their extensive tradition of perishable art with dramatic ceremonies featuring female tasks and harvest (daytime) and male existence and struggle (night), symbolically covering the whole of life (George Corbin, in Mead 1979: 159–79). The *tubuan* dance-masks are linked to the female 'mother of masks'. Less friendly are the *Dukduk* masks of the neighbouring Tolai people.

34. *Hemlaut* mask, Sulka, New Britain, PNG.

Originating probably with the bush spirit cult, they have become the disguise of a male secret society to exercise social control. A tall woven conical cap covers the face and a bulky costume of palm leaves covers the body down to the ankles. As awesome apparitions from the spirit world they would in the past terrorize young men by beatings and extort food from households. Women still go indoors to hide from the *Dukduk* and may be forced to supply food on demand.

The secret society may supply the function of masks of the Sulka people (traditional enemies of the Baining), but these are quite different in form again (see figure 34). Their bizarre shapes are made of strips of pith sewn in place like basketry, being painted in bright colours. Thus it is the umbrella-like disc, decorated with stars and eye-like protuberances, which here crowns the mask's conical hat:

> Many of the masks consist entirely of geometric forms with no indication of the anatomy of a human head. In others, facial features appear in high relief . . . . The art of New Britain is most dramatically represented by the bizarre fabricated masks. (Linton and Wingert 1946: 151–2)

Recently research, by means of 'salvage art history' from photos of masks of the Sulka at the beginning of this century, has indicated five distinct types of these 'umbrella' masks (G.A. Corbin, in Hanson 1990: 67–72). The geometric patterns of these *hemlaut* masks contained representations of the praying mantis and its pincers or could be, as here, divided into four quadrants derived from a wild palm-leaf, with shell money and shell rings strung beneath. In all presentations the dancer would jump up and down, then throw back the mask on a diagonal plane to display the underside of the umbrella to the audience; this was called 'showing the writing', meaning the patterns to be 'read' iconographically.

New Ireland: *Malagan* rites and carvings

In north-western New Ireland a distinctive and intricate style of painted carvings developed under the name *malagan* (*malanggan*). The name may be derived from a cultic word meaning 'spirit . . . or belonging to the spirit world' in Tabar, the island which was one of the original areas of this tradition (Franz Karun, in Habel 1979: 45). The masks and carved figures were associated with ceremonies for initiation and especially for death rites and commemoration. During elaborate festivities which involved pig-feasts, dancing and speech-making, the *malagan* figures would be displayed in a bamboo hut, the size of a small room, for several months (figure 35). After this, most of the precious figures would be left to rot, to be destroyed or to be sold to outsiders. Their sacredness belonged to the ceremonies arranged by the clan which commissioned and owned them.

These carvings are rich and ever-varied in their combination of human figures with birds, pigs, fish and snakes to symbolize clan ancestors, totems and gods or supernatural beings. Recently dead relatives were depicted but also mythological ancestors. Symbols for the moon included a boar's head or tusks as well as snake, fish and clam-shell forms; rayed discs and the head of a bird could represent the sun. The valves of marine snails were often used for eyes. Families would draw on their own distinctive motif, the *kowarawar*, usually based on a circle with a central eye, to embody the magical powers of the *malagan* and its family (G.N. Wilkinson, in Greenhalgh and Megaw 1978: 229–33). These themes are combined in such dramatic carvings as a spirit canoe with its crew of ancestral figures or a giant tusked fish ridden by male and female gods with a man-god in front (depicted in Poignant 1967: 78–9). The complexity of the themes is matched by the intricacy and fantastic detail of the open-work carving, incorporating carved rods and careful painting in red, black and white. 'This manipulation of negative space creates a density of levels which is rendered even more mysterious by the shimmering layers of colour' (Newton, in Gathercole et al. 1979: 54).

What is the meaning of these *malagan* sculptures with their variety of figures? They are mostly connected with the complex of funerary ceremonies

35.   *Malagan* figures in shelter. New Ireland, PNG. Melanesian display, Otago Museum (photo).

of mourning and burial, taboo-removing, display of the *malagan* and feasting; then several years later there is a further series of ceremonies, this time for the commemoration of the dead person, perhaps along with others also. This is the obvious context of meaning. But an inquirer cannot expect to read off the sculptures as images of the dead or their spirits. A recent study by Michael Gunn on Tabar is revealing. When he asked people the meaning of the sculptures, they answered that it was 'that this particular person, as a leader of this lineage, owns this particular malagan' (Gunn 1992: 171). The leader who commissions the work certainly gains in prestige, as seen in the Melanesian exchange system with its socio-economic implications. Ownership means that he has the right to produce, use and transfer the ownership; also he must know the appropriate ownership chants to be called out on public occasions. But it is not just possessing a ritual object, but becoming involved in all the obligations of honouring the dead and maintaining the bonds with clan members. If someone marries into the clan and then fails in his duty to use a pig and work a *malagan,* he is told that he is a 'rubbish man'. Instead, 'when a person becomes a malagan owner he becomes a shareholder in the ritual world to which his clan or the clan of his affines belongs to. The more malagans a person comes to own, the more complex his ritual world becomes' (Gunn 1992: 174). In this setting the *malagan* sculpture is not an image which represents people or things; the image is of the relationship of the dead with the living, of the resulting bonds between people or clans and of the idea of the clan's totemic life-force which is its origin.

This understanding helps to explain why the *malagan* tradition continues despite the changes observed over the past hundred years. The adoption of Christian burial practice led to a decline in *malagan* art, which was largely replaced by concrete tombstones. Western education and patterns of work and money have upset traditional art production; now there is some modern secular production of the art. At the same time, however, there is a revival of *malagan* ceremonial, which could work to revitalize the art (P. Lewis, in Mead 1979: 378–89). Therefore, instead of expecting *malagan* sculpture to repeat the old forms, one may accept continuity in ownership which will change the art as the people change: 'Even malagans change over time, grow and change . . . . Malagan is dynamic, a living cultural tradition' (Gunn 1992: iv).

Solomon Islands

This group of islands, stretching from Bougainville in the west to the Santa Cruz in the east, includes diversity with unity in its span of some 1500 kilometres. It is basically Melanesian in culture (apart from a few Polynesian 'outlier' islands such as Rennell, Bellona and Tikopia) and over 60 vernacular languages are spoken in this chain of mountainous islands. Since British colonial rule gave way to independence in 1978, there have been seven provinces, with Honiara the capital in Guadalcanal, in the central group. Some differences emerge in the western and eastern groups.

The concept of *mana* has already been discussed in relation to the pervasive Melanesian sense of power as a living process. The traditional religions have no supreme deity but a variety of spirit powers. The place of the spirits as bringing *mana* to human life on earth has been well described by Esau Tuza, a researcher on Melanesian religions who is himself from the island of Choiseul in the Western Solomons. Because of the close relation of the living and the dead, the ancestors traditionally were remembered and their protection sought through the *sope* or skull-house, a simple yet awesome place for worship through offerings. Interspersed with sacred images and valuables, the skulls were arranged in straight rows; since skulls were too sacred to handle, it is unlikely that the over-modelling of human skulls as a form of portraiture would have been a practice of the old times. The rituals of worship and offerings in the *sope* were means of making *mana* operative (E. Tuza, in Habel 1979: 105).

With the coming of Christianity since the 19th century, information about rituals and festivals is often sketchy and available only through the 'missionized' memories of older people (K. Prendeville, in Habel 1979: 26). Records from missions in the Floridas, central Solomons, noted the belief in powers exercised by *tindalos* or 'ghosts of ancestors' in the vital areas of traditional life such as war, fishing, gardening and love; if angry they could wreck a canoe; some lived in the bodies of sharks; they were symbolized in emblems such as clubs and ornaments (Waite 1983: 12–16). But by 1900 the *tindalos* had been driven from public observances. To the south-east in San Cristobal (Makira) the term *akaro* or *adaro* was used for the ancestral spirits of the dead as well as for the living soul; other non-ancestral spirits dwelt in the forest, the sea and the forces of nature. Spirit images were carved and painted on canoes, fishing-floats, bowls and other artefacts. Studies in recent decades show that ancestral and sea-spirits still feature in the myths and visual arts of the south-eastern Solomons. Depicted in the wood-carving from this region is an example of the sea-sprite who is non-human but combines features of the fish and human (figure 36). It is ambivalent in its power to shoot victims in the neck with flying fish, yet also to inspire songs and dances through dreams. Clearly the dependence of people on the resources of the sea led to the valuing of fish such as the bonito, sea-birds such as the frigate bird and the shark. The houses for the sacred bonito fishing canoes became ceremonial centres. House-posts had carved figures at the top depicting 'the deities who controlled the bonito shoals and the predators — birds and sharks — which followed the fish' (Newton, in Gathercole et al. 1979: 51–2). These are featured also on wooden

36.   *Adaro* or sea-sprite, wood-
carving. San Cristobal, Solomon Is.

bowls, some of tremendous size, used for domestic and tourist sale purposes now, as well as in traditional religious use.

While communication between different cultural areas led to some common themes and styles of art in the Solomons, regional differences are apparent here. For instance, the theme of a dangerous creature holding a human head features a crocodile in the Western Solomons and a shark in the south-east. Yet these creatures are not seen primarily as enemies. From the central Solomons a traditionalist from Malaita insists that sharks are human and not to be eaten: 'We never fish for sharks. He is a person with us. We are related. The other ones we do not eat are rays and crocodiles because they are related to us too' (from a conversation in Brake et al. 1979: 19). Sharks may embody dead ancestors. They may also be of help in fishing for bonito. Sharks and humans share a common ancestry; hence shark spirits live in harmony with them and may even come in human form to mix with people. This serves to explain the wooden carving of the shark god Menalo in ceremonial dress, from the eastern Santa Cruz group (figure 37). He wears the local hair-style projecting backward from the head, as seen also in the finely carved *duka* figures of the Santa Cruz ancestors.

If we ask why gods and spirits should be embodied in animal forms such as the shark the answer is not hard to find in Melanesia and in the wider history of religions. Animals have been admired and envied for their superior and mysterious powers which represent fertility and cosmic life. Their otherness and superhuman powers evoke a response of awe which goes with religious veneration, as can be seen in the therio-morphic gods of ancient Egypt (Moore 1977: 68–71). In Melanesian art there are abundant examples of the blending of the animal and the human. In her careful study of style and symbolism of art in the Solomons (in Mead 1979: 238–64), Deborah Waite focuses on anthropomorphic images which lead on to hybrids such as human bodies with shark, fish or bird heads, also the 'sea spirits' already discussed above.

Turning now to the human figure, we note the importance of the human head throughout the art of the Solomons, including Bougainville with its squatting figures of a protective spirit with large bulging forehead. Of special interest here is the carved figurehead called *nguzunguzu* (figure 38), originating in New Georgia in the western province and featured on the prow of the canoe in the central Solomons also. Small but powerful in its impact, it is a guardian spirit attached above water level to the prow of the canoe. The *mon* canoes of the Western Solomons were magnificent works of art with their long upward-curving prows elaborately decorated in shell-inlay. They were supremely important as a means of transport, of fishing and of waging war. The attached prow figure was in some places named Kesoko who seems to have been renowned in myth as a head-hunter, a fisherman and a spirit of the dead (Waite, in Hanson 1990: 44–66). The face is made of blackened wood and its shape is prognathous in the horizontal extension forward with jutting jaws like an animal and large nose and nostrils. The head has no body, but only small arms and clasped hands. This may well be explained by its function on head-hunting expeditions, for which the head is a striking symbol. Its eyes are wide open so that it could keep a watch for enemy spirits in the sea, the water-fiends who might upset the canoe with winds and waves to devour the crew. The image on the prow was to guide the expedition safely to achieve success and return home with trophies.

The taking of heads was customary for special occasions such as launching a new canoe or completing a new canoe house; head-hunting expeditions were motivated by revenge ('payback', as we have noted in New Guinea) and perhaps by the search for *mana* to empower and protect. But head-hunting was suppressed by the colonial government in 1890. Since then the *nguzunguzu* carving has become a distinctive artwork of the Solomons, shorn

37.   Shark-god Menalo, wood-carving 1.5m. high.
Santa Cruz, S.E. Solomon Is. Otago Museum (photo).

38.   Canoe-prow with *nguzunguzu* figure, wood-carving. New Georgia, W. Solomon Is. Otago Museum (photo).

of its former associations and sold to tourists for souvenirs. On sale at a church-organized craft outlet for skilled carving work, modern examples can be found.

Anthropomorphic figures are also a feature of ancestor posts cut from a tree-trunk to be incorporated into houses of special concern. Their placing is most meaningful, so that the ancestor of the house is shown to be the central support. At the National Museum of the Solomons in the capital, Honiara, a series of houses has been reconstructed to display typical styles from the provinces. Here the 'custom house' from Makira in the south-east displays its ancestor in the front centre with an animal-headed hybrid dance-figure above him (figure 39). With houses of a more everyday type, ownership and significance are sanctified by legends and rituals of burial and sacrifice. In the case of modern public buildings, for educational and other purposes, posts have been incorporated to show traditional myths embodied in ancestral figures.

Other forms of art – visual, musical and arts of story and dance – were involved in the rituals of traditional religions. Although the Solomons did not generally make use of masks compared with their abundance in New Guinea, spirit figures were represented by wooden masks in manhood initiation ceremonies in New Georgia. 'Similarly, in the Makira area, initiation – the *mara'ufu* ceremony – also stimulated artistic production, notably of elaborately formed canoes, and of a decorated tower for the young men to climb, and of carved figures representing sea-spirits' (Romano Kokonge, in Laracy 1989: 61). For other occasions of life such as death, harvest, fishing and building, music and dance gathered the community together. A conch-shell sounded out the arrival of an important person. Occasions of death or war were relayed by patterns of drumming, for which the instruments were the group of smaller drums, *gogo*, and the large *maramura* drum giving the booming background. In addition to singing, instrumental music was played on bamboo flutes, bamboo panpipes and percussive instruments; in modern times these have been incorporated in various forms of popular music. Processions and dancing are further means of participating in a community celebration and remembrance of traditional myth and ritual (*Kastom*). In addition to this educative function, dances are intended to honour the spirits and give thanks for blessings and success.

Inevitably, many examples of these art forms have not survived the changes of the past hundred years and information is lacking to explain the meaning and use of various objects and rituals. Fortunately in the visual arts the beauty and craftsmanship of works are now more accessible to us through museum collections and the superb colour photographs in Deborah Waite's catalogue (1983) which are juxtaposed with old photos of the Solomons from the early colonial period to illuminate the traditional context.

39. 'Custom' house from Makira province, S.E. Solomon Is. National
Museum, Honiara. (Photo, A.C. Moore.)

Now that the context of traditional ('pagan') religions has been supplanted by Christianity as the predominant religion, what is the place of art in religion? This varies according to the form of Christianity (see Moore 1977: 264–77). The Roman Catholic and Anglican churches seek to draw on Solomon Islands culture and arts and 'baptize' them in the service of Christian worship. This is evident in their fine modern cathedrals in Honiara where Solomons inlaid wood-carving is used for the liturgical furnishings, as well as the crucifix and figures in the church tradition. At the moment of consecration in the Eucharist, attention is drawn through the sounding of a slit-gong, not of a bell as in Western Christendom. In churches of the Protestant traditions such as the South Sea Evangelical Mission and the Methodist (now United), the emphasis is on singing and the word, with little place for the visual arts. These four churches account for some 80 per cent of the Solomons population. A further 10 per cent belong to the Seventh-day Adventist church which has a strong emphasis on health education and a training centre at Betikama, near Honiara, for art carving; at the same time it rejects the traditional Solomon Islands culture of mythology, music and dance. This highlights a tension between the old and new orders to be dealt with in the education system, in which the church missions have all played an important part.

Indigenous attempts to bridge the gap have been made by some Melanesian independent churches (Trompf 1991: ch. 9; Loeliger and Trompf 1985; Cochrane 1970). An example of particular interest is the Christian Fellowship Church in New Georgia in the Western Solomons. Silas Eto, the founder, was a Methodist pastor-teacher who broke away from the Methodist mission in 1960 (Tippett 1967: 219–64). Much of the Methodist worship tradition is retained and re-worked, with singing as the great climax. To symbols such as the cross and the portrait of the Methodist founder John Wesley, Eto added his own special robes of office. However the emphasis was not on art but on the experience and practice of the Spirit. His own experience had been of the wind moving a string or vine in the bush, signifying the presence of the spirit. Strings were subsequently used as an aid to worship in his church's villages, to symbolize the spirit's activity and movement and the need to internalize its power above all (E. Tuza, in Habel 1979: 101–2).

A final example of art in the modern context is of an unusual imaginative artist from Bellona Island whose talent was encouraged by his Seventh-day Adventist church and school. This was Kuai Maueha (1933–81), a physically disabled man who overcame ridicule to express his feelings in powerfully distorted sculptures including Biblical themes. His work has been given recognition as interest in creative art has grown in the Pacific area (A. Wendt 1983; B. Kernot 1984).

Vanuatu (New Hebrides)

In the eastern reaches of Melanesia lie the islands grouped under the national government of Vanuatu. It achieved independence in 1980, having previously been governed by a joint French-British condominium as the New Hebrides. There is considerable diversity among the cultures and religious practices of the long chain of islands. They share in the common Melanesian linking of humans, ancestral spirits and the natural order in a living cosmos, also the achievement of prestige by effort in the accumulation of wealth, not by heredity. A widespread institution for this achievement was the series of rigidly graded societies through which a man had to progress throughout life until the ultimate transformation at death, to become an ancestor. The ceremonies for marking these stages combined the religious and the worldly, as in the killing of valuable tusked pigs.

Statues to mark these ceremonies in visual form were carved from tree-fern trunks and hard teak wood, then painted in earth pigments of bright colours over a clay covering. In the tropical climate such materials soon deteriorated or lost their colour; impermanence meant that new objects were made for further ceremonies. For rites held on the dance ground before the men's house, large figures were set up to honour the ancestors. These had enormous heads with saucer-like eyes and could be several metres in height. For mortuary ceremonies smaller figures were made to represent the deceased and their children. 'In spite of the gaudy colour and ramshackle construction, there is a remarkable spirituality about this strange, violent style; it is human, ephemeral and aspiring' (Newton, in Gathercole et al. 1979: 50). The grade-society markers shown here (figure 40) would be made secretly in the bush by the owner of the pattern. When the ceremony took place — in this case for the sixth grade on the island of Malekula - the candidate could be required to dance on a wooden platform above the marker.

Even more striking versions of the marker figures are the great *tam tam* or slit gongs which stand up to 3 metres in height on the grade-marker ground. These drums achieve a spectacular effect with economy of means: as Jean Guiart points out from his wide knowledge of Melanesian art in this area, the drums are monumental, especially in north Ambrym, a major art achievement in the sculpture of the head in which 'these faces give an impression of serenity and composure' (Guiart 1963: 229–31). Traditionally the *tam tam* with their slit 'mouths' were regarded as a human voice for 'speaking' messages of good or bad news (a fast or a slow beat) and for summoning people at the chief's command to a dance, ritual or other assembly. A modern adaptation to Christian worship is seen in the Pacific Regional Seminary of the Roman Catholic church centred in Suva. When the new chapel was built in the 1980s, a carver from Ambrym was commissioned to make three drums which now

40.   Grade-society markers, tree fern, from Malekula, Vanuatu. *Tam tam*,
slit-gong, from Ambrym. Display in Otago Museum (photo).

41.   Snake on cross symbol. Jon Frum cult shrine, Tanna, Vanuatu.

stand under a roof shelter near the chapel. The slit-gongs serve instead of a bell as a 'call to worship' (N. Lange 1992: 83–4).

Turning to the southern end of Vanuatu, the island of Tanna offers a quite different example of religious practice, in the Jon Frum 'cargo cult'. It began around 1940 with the expectation of a new order with plenty of cargo wealth as well as a revival of traditional customs discouraged by Western schools and missions (E. Rice 1974; Muller 1974). Cargo and a new order did indeed arrive with American troops in the Pacific war in 1942 and the expectation was fostered here with cult symbols of the Red Cross and the aeroplane bringing goods and troops. The excitement and eschatological expectations have subsequently settled into the practical forms of political and religious institutions; in the phrase of the sociologist Max Weber, 'the charisma has been routinized'. In the village of Ipekel near the sacred volcano Mt. Yasur, all-night dances are held on Fridays and a house dedicated to Jon Frum has a black Jesus on a red cross. The cult has become more of an independent church combining elements of 'Kastom', (Custom and primal religion), with Christian symbols and modern Western culture. Along with the red cross, symbolizing the blood of Christ and Western learning, goes the black cross of traditional culture and the magic which sustains life. The snake on the cross (figure 41) is a symbol of mystery and power in life, a perennial Melanesian theme; it may also be an echo of the Christian mission teachings from the

Bible (John 3: 14): 'This Son of Man must be lifted up as the serpent was lifted up by Moses in the wilderness'. The interweaving of the old and new in the cargo cult raises important issues about salvation for religions in the wider field and deserves further study and interpretation (Trompf 1991: ch. 8).

New Caledonia: house and ancestors

Finally, in the south-west of Melanesia lies the large island of New Caledonia. A century-and-a-half of French colonial rule has seen the evaporation of the traditional culture and, as elsewhere, the loss of knowledge of the meaning of surviving art forms. Powerful masks were made in the north-east; some with feather cloaks represented water-spirits and may have been used in secret societies. Sculpture was the principal visual art and here we look at its place in the house, particularly the 'great house' which served as the centre for men's ceremonies. This *moaro* was circular in shape, an exception in Melanesia apart from the 'round house' typical in the Eastern Highlands of PNG. The conical roof was thatched and the structure and carvings were of durable wood, a fitting sign of the abiding presence of the ancestors.

The impressive doorway is marked by heavy wood-carvings, especially the door-jambs on either side of the entrance (figure 42). These are taken from tree-trunks, convex on the front and almost human in size. They are guardian ancestor figures who may be male or female; dwellers in a house address the ancestor for help and protection and make sacrifices before it. The door-jamb (*tale*) is covered with geometric patterns in the main body. The face at the top typically has 'sharp pointed oval eyes set under low beetling brows, a large-nostriled, hooked nose suggesting a bird beak, and a wide tight-lipped mouth . . . an alert, aggressive, somewhat bellicose expression' (Linton and Wingert 1946: 78). Inside the house smaller posts set in a ring are carved with bearded faces of different features, contributed by different clans subject to the chieftain (Guiart 1963: 252–63). There was also a decorated ceiling plank to mark a platform where men slept in search of divinatory dreams. Figures from these carvings would also be repeated for relief-carvings on coffins. On the outside of the house, surmounting the high conical roof is a spire carved in wood, over 2 metres high; it has a face set in between stylized and geometric forms and this probably symbolizes the ancestor (see figure 43). The spire can also be regarded as a family crest.

While the specific form and carving of this New Caledonian house is unique in the Pacific it does express powerfully the attitudes and beliefs which are found widely in other cultures and religions. The house, both domestic and ceremonial, is a centre of meaning and vitality for those who dwell in it and remember their family and ancestors. The doorway is significant because one crosses this threshold between the outside world which is 'profane' (in the

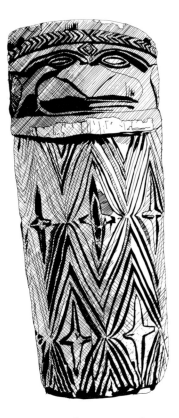

42. Door-jamb, ancestor figure.
New Caledonia.

etymological sense of 'before the threshold') and the world of the sacred
centre inside (Eliade 1959: ch. 1, 4).

Melanesia: changing traditions

The preceding sections have covered a range of art forms in different parts of
Melanesia. These are mainly 'traditional' expressions of the sort displayed in
museums or described in books on religion, anthropology and the arts. But it
is evident that the traditions have never been static and have, in fact, proved
able to incorporate changes and borrowings over the years. Since the 19th
century, and especially since World War II in the 1940s, the pace of change
has speeded up and affected the arts. We need to examine, by way of
conclusion three areas of change – the impact of social change on the arts,
the emergence of modern 'non-traditional' artists and the changes in religion
affecting the use of art in churches.

People in Melanesia continue to enjoy the range of traditional art forms

43.   Wooden spire, with model of house. New Caledonia. Display in Otago
Museum (photo).

from carving, painting, body decoration, story-telling, singing and dancing.
Many of these were embedded in the social life and religious rituals which
were part of the whole way of life of tribes and villages. Now they have to
contend with, or exist alongside, a new range of interests and activities

brought by 'Western' contact and international trends in economic development. A vivid impression of this is gained from any colourful book on modern Papua New Guinea (such as Sinclair 1985) which includes the rich display of traditional life and costume along with modern farming, mining, political independence, education, travel and communications. Radio and TV have brought Western values, from the desire for motor transport to guitars, pop-music and T-shirts. The desire for these things creates a consumer society in which money and money-gaining activities are valued more than traditional culture. The problem emerges in the school systems in Melanesia where competition is fierce to gain admission to high schools and tertiary education. To succeed one must concentrate on examination subjects which are required, and here the arts become peripheral. On the other hand, the arts can become highlighted in public shows of traditional costumed groups performing for large audiences and often including guitars and modern developments of indigenous traditions.

How does this affect the understanding and appreciation of 'art'? As Marsha Berman points out, the Melanesian concept is summed up in the Pidgin English phrase *samting tru*, something true. This means that the art functions as part of life, on a canoe or in a dance-mask or in the multi-media context of a religious and community ceremony. When the art lacks that real context in the social setting it becomes *samting nating*, something nothing, 'without significance or consequence, merely a pretty thing' (Berman, in Simons and Stevenson 1990: 61). A joyful celebration for the opening of a new school, hospital or church or for an official visit to a community can include modern innovations and still be *samting tru*. But if it is solely for pleasure it is of no consequence. When applied to Western standards of art as a product of the creative individual, 'art for art's sake', the work is seen also as *samting nating*, for it is 'only a picture'. Likewise, the masks or once-sacred designs that are produced for art galleries and airport sales to tourists are no longer true art.

Here we come to the problem of modern non-traditional artists who have emerged in Melanesia in the last two decades. An early lead was taken by Papua New Guinea where the rich traditional arts began to be developed in new ways through the new University of PNG and the National Art School (now the Faculty of Creative Arts); this was aided by the national feeling which culminated in independence of PNG and a striking new National Museum and Art Gallery in 1977. In the early 1970s a number of artists living in Port Moresby gained attention with their modern experimental works such as metal sculptures by Benny More and Gikmai Kundun and paintings and drawings by Akis and Kauage. It is interesting that they had come from the PNG Highlands, on which the Samoan writer Albert Wendt noted: 'The new artists come mainly from cultures without strong traditional arts or from those whose artistic traditions have been undermined . . . . Most of them have had little formal education and know little of western art or art history' (Wendt 1983: 202). Their work had sales in Australia and Europe and was displayed in exhibition catalogues and pictorial books in Germany (Heermann 1979). A fine representative exhibition of contemporary PNG artists organized from Australia, went on tour 1990–92, (*Luk Luk Gen! Look Again!* Simons and Stevenson 1990). The problem with this success is that the recognition of the artists has come from the expatriate community in PNG and from foreigners. In terms of the ordinary Melanesian these works are not seen as real art, *samting tru*, but just as pictures, however interesting: 'They have not yet found an audience amongst their own people' (Berman, in Simons and Stevenson 1990: 61). It may be that at the present stage artistic innovations are more acceptable in the *singsing* type of celebration with music and colourful use of the various arts.

It may also be said here that the changing institutions of religion provide some avenues for innovation in the arts. The record of the various Christian churches which now predominate in Melanesia is, as we have seen, a mixed one. Ambivalence towards the indigenous traditions has ranged from destruction of 'pagan art' to a cautious acceptance and encouragement by some churches. In one sense this is understandable, since Melanesian art has traditionally between interwoven with religious beliefs and practices; therefore missionaries found it too dangerous from their viewpoint to expose their new converts to the continuing pagan associations of the arts. In some cases bonfires disposed of the masks and precious objects of the old order. On the other hand, some churches made efforts to incorporate and build on the best of the old traditions in the arts. This is seen in several striking examples of churches incorporating Melanesian art in the last decades. A German Lutheran missionary has discerned four stages in these developments of sculptures and paintings as 'an indigenous expression of the Christian Faith' (Hermann Reiner, in Wagner and Reiner 1986: 451–67).

The first stage is marked by a naive representation of biblical themes, preached and painted for illiterate people. In the late 1950s an evangelist Qakomo painted a series of six scenes of the life of Christ according to the Apostles' Creed, from birth to Last Judgment. The simple style is effective, like an enlarged comic-strip; the pictures are in a church at Kotua, near Mt. Hagen. The second stage brings imitation of European models. This is seen in the early work of Dawidi, a teacher and master builder who did most of the carvings for his home church of Ngasegalatu, Finschhafen on the east coast of PNG (figure 44). The Lutheran rose symbol is included among indigenous symbols above the pulpit; the pulpit itself is on a canoe-shaped structure, recalling Jesus teaching from a boat on the Sea of Galilee: 'If Jesus had been in New Guinea, he certainly would have used a canoe'. Ancestor posts from the old time are on the outside of the church, to indicate the origin of the people

44.   Lutheran church of Ngasegalatu. Finschhafen, PNG. Interior designed
by Dawidi 1954–57. (Photo.)

who enter the house of God. Dawidi carved apostle posts for the inside of the
church to depict 'the new life of the reborn Christian'. This work was done in
1954–57. In later church interior art, Dawidi developed his own style, less
influenced by European models. Thus the third phase is exemplified by the
altar which he carved for the Martin Luther Seminary at Lae; the altar is an
elevated table with the legs designed as traditional drums, symbolizing
messages of strain and battle but also of joy and peace celebration. Traditional
motifs come to fulfilment in the fourth stage which achieves a homogenous
indigenous style in architecture, sculpture and painting. For a memorial
church to the missionary Johann Flierl at Simbang, Dawidi presented the
planning committee with the idea of building a church in the style of the
men's house of the Melanesian forefathers. This was accepted, but with the
extended vision of the men's house being for the entire community – a place
for people to discuss matters of daily life or the past on sitting places in the
open, also a place of refuge or sanctuary. The outer posts again recall
traditional houses and themes of the crocodile, snake and shark. The ceiling
includes old canoe decorations but the church also features the story of
Christian missions in PNG, climaxing in a large crucifix, with candles on the
altar to show the light of the Gospel.

Similar experiments and achievements are found in Roman Catholic churches, as mentioned earlier. In an excellent survey of 'Christian Art from Melanesia', Theo Aerts begins by facing honestly the unfavourable factors which have to be faced in these efforts, from the lack of suitable materials for monumental art to historical factors such as the setbacks caused by destruction of churches in the Pacific war of 1941–45. From the standpoint of the churches, especially in the earlier mission situation, it would certainly have been unrealistic to expect that the arts of the previous 'pagan' generation could be taken over as if divorced from their old meanings. They were associated with visions revealed from the ancestral spirits, with myths, rituals and magical spells designed for very definite purposes, such as warfare; also they were pieces of 'spiritual property' not for an outsider to use. Because the traditional art forms are sacred, renowned artists from this background have been reluctant to use them in the service of church art. Work of inferior quality may be the result (Aerts 1984: 48). Despite these and other problems some impressive buildings and artworks have emerged from the concern to synthesize Christian values and Melanesian traditions.

This concern has been criticized from both sides. Defenders of the Melanesian traditions may feel that Christian churches are plundering their indigenous heritage and misinterpreting its own sacred imagery. A perennial Christian reaction from some has been against any 'syncretism' which corrupts the Christian faith by blending it with pagan images of the old order. The argument against both of these positions is the evidence of history that traditions of religion and art have changed with the advent of new conditions and new experiences. Indigenous cultures themselves have not been static. Already, in the early centuries of Christianity, the churches had begun to borrow art forms from the surrounding culture of the Roman Empire as well as from the Jewish heritage to express the new faith. The recent attempts of the 20th-century churches to 'contextualize' Christianity in local forms have their roots — for better of for worse — in much earlier times.

In the Melanesian scene the churches have become widely, if also ambivalently, accepted as a home for the religious life of communities. Because of these roots in life, churches which are able to draw on indigenous Melanesian arts may eventually provide a more enduring and deep-rooted setting for meaningful Melanesian religious art. If they are able to offer this, working along with artist and educational programmes, the result could be accepted as *samting tru* — more effectively than either the commercial context of tourist art or the professionalism of 'art for art's sake'.

CHAPTER 4

POLYNESIA

Ye ancestral guardians from the sun's rising to the
  sun's setting,
From heaven and earth's joining at the horizon;
Ye ancestral guardians backward leaning, forward bending,
On the right hand in the heavens.
                    (Ancient Hawaiian prayer, cited by Handy 1927: 2)

These words evoke a sense of the vastness of heaven and earth as a voyaging people look towards the horizon of the ocean. From the majesty of the heavens in space the ancestral guardians move also in time as they have in the past. Here are themes at the heart of Polynesian religion. They have a unity which contrasts with the diversity of Melanesian culture and religion. Such unity is all the more remarkable in view of the distances separating the island groups of Polynesia. When Captain Cook was exploring the Pacific Ocean in 1774 he thought it extraordinary that 'the same Nation' should have spread themselves over all the vast Ocean from New Zealand to Easter Island. It was a previously uninhabited region which Polynesian seafarers, a brown-skinned people, explored and settled over a period of three thousand years (c. 2000 BCE to 1000 CE). While widely spread, their island cultures retained a close ethnic homogeneity based on their unified origins (Bellwood 1978a: ch. 1).

The name 'Polynesia', derived from the Greek meaning 'many islands', began to be used by Europeans in the 18th century. More precise usage of the term is based on modern studies of language and archaeology. Polynesians belong to the widespread Austronesian language family. They came from Southeast Asia (eastern Indonesia or the Philippines) and migrated through Melanesia to the area of Fiji before 1500 BCE. Polynesian speakers moved first to the Tongan Islands by 1300 BCE, then to Samoa and later to the Marquesas Islands in eastern Polynesia. By 700 CE settlements had spread to the Society Islands (Tahiti) and the marginal extremities of Hawaii to the north and Easter Island to the far east. It was not until after this, from 700 to 1100 CE, that Polynesians settled in the Austral and Cook Islands and finally to the south in New Zealand, (Gathercole et al. 1979: 67–9). As the map shows (figure 45), the area can be seen as a Polynesian 'triangle' including these settlements over the expanse of the Pacific. This is generally helpful as a guide, but in the western Pacific there are some exceptions. The Fijian Islands

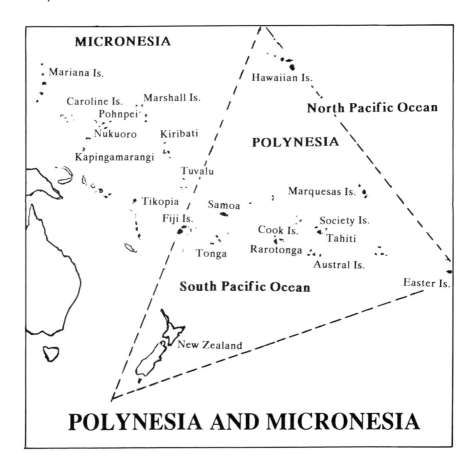

45.   Map of Polynesia.

are on the boundary of Melanesia, and further west are the Polynesian 'outlier' islands such as Bellona, Rennell and Tikopia. To the north-west in Micronesia there are the outliers Kapingamarangi and Nukuoro.

Religion and arts in Polynesia

Granted regional variations over the centuries of local development, there is an underlying common basis of Polynesian religions. First there is the evident linguistic link; for instance the war-god Tu of the New Zealand Maori is Ku of the Hawaiians; Tane is Kane. Secondly, Polynesian societies gave a high value to social ranking based on systems of tribal chiefs and hierarchies (Goldman 1970; Williamson 1937; George E. Marcus, in Howard and Borovsky 1989, ch. 6). This was reflected in the hierarchies of gods and ancestral beings, so much so that a scholarly researcher can say: 'Polynesian religion was an outgrowth of Polynesian social structure which focused on genealogical connections and the integration of the gods with nature and the human condition' (Kaeppler 1987: 435). Thirdly, there was an emphasis on genealogies by which one's inherited status could be linked to ancestors and thereby to the *atua*, the ancestral 'gods' or sacred powers of the various departments of life from the primeval emergence of things. But this was not tenaciously conservative or backward-looking. Indeed it has been claimed that in their looking forward to new things that would be better, the Polynesians were 'one of the least conservative of native peoples' (Linton and Wingert 1946: 14). It has also been claimed that Polynesians were less dominated by material concerns for prestigious wealth than the Melanesians and that this freed them for the development of elaborate genealogies and imaginative mythologies. This is a speculative judgement, but, fourthly, the Polynesians certainly showed interest in cosmogony and myths of the beginnings (Poignant 1967: 29–69; Andersen 1969). Myths recounted the emergence of the world from darkness and the primal parents. Rangi and Papa, or from an originating power Ta'aroa (Tangaroa). Throughout the length and breadth of Polynesia stories were recounted of Maui, the creative culture hero, demigod and trickster figure (Luomala 1949).

Fifthly, the concepts of *mana* and *tapu* were elaborated in diverse forms to show reverence for effective power in action and corresponding prohibitions or taboos to safeguard it. *Mana* is central to the Polynesian worldview and connects humans to the gods through the hierarchy of the cosmos. At the same time it is manifested in practice, especially in organic vitality, fertility and procreative power, through food and sex. Its power is ambivalent, both life-giving and death-dealing; Polynesian religions are therefore concerned with its ritual transformations (Bradd Shore, in Howard and Borovsky 1989, ch. 5). In addition to the respect for chiefly *mana* this led to specialization of roles to deal with the powers of life, as in the roles of men and women. Various 'experts' dealt with religion, the arts and practical crafts, after lengthy apprenticeship in their skills and traditions; the term *tohunga* in Maori signifies 'expert' (*kahuna* in Hawaiian, *tufunga* in Samoan). The priestly *tohunga* was equipped to deal with sacred power and avoid danger by carefully observing *tapu* regulations. In this he was a professional in ritual matters; some specialists could be the medium for the voice of a god. Sixthly, ritual in Polynesian religion was designed to exercise control over the influence of the gods in human affairs. Although the gods were understood to inhabit a realm distinct from the human and physical world, their activity in this world could be regularly invited and dismissed (F.A. Hanson 1987: 423–4). Finally, the locus of such rituals could be in various sacred places from the temporary *ad hoc* site to an open court or green, the *marae*, or a demarcated 'god house'. Examples of these occur in different regions of Polynesia. They are expressions of the sacred or holy in the world. The gods are awesome and majestic, yet they are also near and available to help because humans are connected to them by nature and ancestry. Polynesians participate in a dynamic sacred cosmos.

These points indicate an underlying unity along with diversity in matters of religion. The same can be said of the arts associated with Polynesian religions, to the extent that they are linked to the veneration of gods and ancestors remembered for their deeds of power. For this reason Gilbert Archey finds unity in sculpture as the basic form and important artistic achievement of Polynesia. His monograph *The Art Forms of Polynesia* (Archey 1965) concentrates on figure images abundantly illustrated from Central Polynesia to Hawaii, Easter Island and New Zealand. However in islands such as the Polynesian outlier Tikopia (Firth 1970) there were no figure sculptures at all but only a craft tradition applied to such objects as head-rests. To account for this Raymond Firth suggests (in Forge 1973: 26ff.) that such groups, long isolated, may develop their aesthetic traditions selectively and differentially. We have noted this already in the diverse regions of Melanesia where some excel in music and oratory rather than in the visual arts. In the case of Polynesia we can see that material expressions of religion are often classified by Europeans as 'crafts' rather than 'arts'. It is necessary to consider the arts of weaving and *tapa*-cloth, tattooing, story-telling and oratory, music and dancing, as well as carving of visual art objects.

To mention examples related to acts of religious ritual and celebration, the Polynesian use of chanting was motivated by the desire to influence nature and the gods by enhancing *mana* and empowering the gods positively, while driving away evil powers. Prayers, incantations and spells were uttered without a break for inhalation to avoid breaking the spell; the breath carried the words to their objective, the sing-song chanting conveying dynamic impulsion: 'Unbroken rhythmic accurate utterances were the essentials of effective ritual in these islands. The Polynesians recognized that the breath (*manawa*) was the medium upon which words were carried' (Handy 1927: 198). Likewise, dancing involved dynamic action to affect nature and to entertain the gods, even to arouse the gods to fertile activity by erotic dancing. Here the gods were linked to humans by desires common to both, as expressed in pleasing offerings at feasts and festivals (Handy 1927: 210–11).

The diversity in emphasis on various arts throughout Polynesia may be due to several factors mentioned by Archey (1966: 444, 465–6). Immense distances separated groups which could then explore local stylizations. This was helped by some tropical abundance which offered the potential for development in one or more forms. But at the same time there was a lack of some materials in Polynesia such as metal or pottery clay; arts were largely in the field of 'handicraft', such as woven textiles, plaiting, ceremonial regalia and personal adornment. The Polynesians were not lacking in artistic creativity which they manifested in oral literature, but they were hampered by lack of resources and lack of the stimulus of contacts with other cultures, due to the distances of the ocean. Therefore, concludes Archey, it is sculpture in wood and stone that stands out artistically.

A wider view of Polynesian arts in their cultural setting is represented by Adrienne Kaeppler's incisive programmatic survey (in Mead 1979: 180–91). She is dissatisfied with the 'outside observer's point of view' represented by Western scholars analyzing the formal aesthetic qualities and following theories of evolutionist or diffusionist development. Another approach, the ethnohistoric perspective, seeks to study changes within the arts of Polynesian peoples with the aid of historical documents and the more accurate dating of museum artifacts. This is potentially valuable to the extent that historical data are available. The most fruitful approach favoured by Kaeppler is based on the 'ethnoscientific' view of an underlying structure linking the arts, using ethnoaesthetics to understand Polynesians' own evaluations and criteria of art. This should be accompanied by a view of social and artistic change which avoids schematic classifications such as 'classic period', 'indigenous' and 'acculturated'. What categories then should be used? Kaeppler chooses four categories for a framework in the Polynesian arts – 'traditional art' from the time of European contact, 'evolved traditional art' incorporating some European methods and subjects; 'folk art' as the living art of the community; and 'airport art' for sale to outsiders.

Examples of these categories have already occurred in the previous chapters of this book and will be encountered further. Meanwhile, in this chapter on Polynesia we must make a selection of examples from each island group, keeping in mind the wider framework. As in the case of Melanesia, different artforms are emphasized in some regions more than in others. Even within the main tropical zone there was a slightly different context in each island or group, and much more so in the non-tropical larger islands of New Zealand, to be discussed in the following chapter. As Kaeppler observes, 'each Polynesian society conceptualized the relationships among social organization, religion, oral literature, music, dance and the visual arts in different ways' (in Gathercole et al. 1979: 94–5). Overall, 'the most important art in Polynesia was oral – poetry, oratory and speech-making' (1979: 78). In live performances the oral was combined with visual and olfactory arts and resulted in a distinctive local mix.

The study of Polynesian art must keep in mind both this wide range of art forms and the 'deep structure or underlying principles' of the aesthetics in the society concerned. Kaeppler exemplifies this in comparing the house forms in Tonga and Samoa where spatial arrangements reflect traditional social relations and hierarchies. Further, since societies are not static, these forms which used to express an 'aesthetic of inequality', in various dimensions such as clothing and access to sacred places, now show a shift to an 'aesthetic of equality' in contemporary Polynesian art (Adrienne L. Kaeppler, in Howard and Borovsky 1989, ch. 5).

Fiji Islands

The present-day Fiji consists of many islands of which the largest are Viti Levu, with the capital Suva, and Vanua Levu. Until independence in 1970 it was a British Crown Colony for almost a hundred years, during which time Christianity (largely Methodism) was adopted by the majority of indigenous Fijians and the population was greatly supplemented by indentured labour from India. For the preceding 35 centuries of settlement the name 'Viti' has been suggested as more appropriate for the ancient culture (Clunie 1986: preface). The original settlement prior to 1500 BCE brought people who were Melanesian in physical type and language and with cultural expressions such as pottery. The social organization and religious forms were Melanesian. Otherwise, the admixture of Polynesian settlers and their systems of rank and political organization, with hereditary chiefs, made the culture more Polynesian. Material culture, as in bark-cloth and canoes, followed Polynesian models and the art forms were influenced by Polynesian cultures in the following centuries. In these ways the Fiji Islands provide a link between Melanesia and Polynesia.

The respect given to chiefs as semi-divine through hereditary rank found a parallel in that given to priests of temples. These were dedicated to the worship of clan deities who were deified ancestors and heroes. The priests were costumed and officiated in care of the temple image and in sacrifices to the clan deity. They were sometimes the mouthpiece of the god whose 'voice' they could hear from a small god-house (*mbure*) modelled on the larger temples and with openings as the god's ears and mouth (Poignant 1967: 87).

Of the many ritual offerings and invocations offered in each temple dedicated to its clan god, we note one related to the 'anthropomorphic dish' illustrated here (figure 46). This is one of about a dozen such dishes to survive; they have usually been explained as shallow dishes for holding scented coconut oil to anoint the bodies of priests. The more likely explanation is that the dish is a *daveniyaqona* for holding the sacred *yaqona* drink (Clunie 1986: 80, 168–9). This is now the widely used social drink in Fiji, prepared from a narcotic root and served in large bowls with formal ritual; this form is due to the dominant Tongan and Samoan *kava* circle influences from the late 18th century. In the previous centuries of Viti, *yaqona* drinking was a religious ceremony of exclusive *burau* rites within the temple or spirit-house. At the beginning of the day prayers were offered and, as part of the offering to the god, *yaqona* was drunk by the priest, regarded as possessed by his ancestor

46. *Yaqona* dish in form of human image. Fiji Is.

spirit. The priest would kneel or lie down to drink it from a leaf-lined hollow in the floor or from a wooden or earthenware vessel which was not to be touched with the hands. It was an inspirational vessel, in this case carved from the sacred *vesi* wood in the form of a human image with strikingly flared arms.

These rituals were set in a social pattern with chiefs and priests at the top of the male hierarchy. Nowadays the organization of churches and social institutions is more democratic and all women are able to drink *kava*. Yet the old traditions continue in seating patterns in households, expressing hierarchical relations between kin when they eat and drink together. This may also help to explain the popularity of tapestry versions of Leonardo da Vinci's Last Supper, hung in many Wesleyan Methodist churches in Fiji; with the male disciples around the table, oriented as towards a chief, this resonates with Fijian tradition (Christina Taren, in Hiller 1991: 261–79).

Another sacred material was *masi*, bark-cloth beaten from the soaked inner bark of the paper mulberry bush. Skilled women workers hammered the bark into wide and gauzy strips of cloth, of which the finest were worn as turbans by priests and chiefs: 'It was a women's privilege to make *masi*, a man's prerogative to wear it' (Clunie 1986: 126). It had a variety of social and religious uses, such as the loincloth donned by youths at initiations and by men at re-naming ceremonies following killings. In the form of streamers it decorated weapons and persons in dance and warfare. It was an important medium of symbolic exchange which chiefs could wrap themselves in to donate to another clan or tribe for enhancing bonds with them. It was used for the curtain concealing the shrine within the spirit-house (Clunie 1986: 127). Because of these solemn associations *masi* cloth has been used to symbolize the divine presence in Christ on the cross in the modern chapel of the Catholic Pacific Regional Seminary in Suva.

In western Polynesia, such as Tonga, *tapa* (bark-cloth) was developed not only for clothing but for magico-religious purposes, with enormous sheets of tapa covered in ornamental designs for use in ceremonial contexts (S.J. Kooijman, in Forge 1973: 97–112). The Lau groups of small Fijian islands towards Tonga illustrate the Polynesian influence mixing with the more Melanesian traditions of *masi*. Where the latter are followed for local ceremonial contexts great care is taken in beating the bark-cloth and stencilling the patterns. However, for the tourist market far away in Suva there is little need for such skill and care, since tourists want a smaller size of 'Fijian *tapa*' to take home as a memento, without being aware of the finer nuances. The result is the mass production of commercial tapa of mediocre quality (Kooijman, in Mead 1979: 363–77).

The impact of tourism can be seen in other forms of art which might otherwise die out. Beautiful forms of traditional pottery are made for sale to tourists. Wood-carvings of old images and weapons also have an appeal as souvenirs, and hotels will decorate walls with the impressive Fijian war-clubs to add a note of 'authentic' Fijian identity. The identity of yesteryear is thus transformed into 'art' and becomes 'tomorrow's heritage', as Philip Dark observes. There is also a trend to combine indigenous forms and new ones with the growth of commercial interest in Fijian wood-carving in the 1960s. As a South Pacific centre the capital city Suva can promote a type of Pan-Pacific culture with wooden images which incorporate features from Hawaii or the Marquesas and serve as 'a satisfactory Pacific emblem' (Dark, in Hanson 1990: 261).

Tonga and Samoa

These two adjacent groups of islands in western Polynesia show similarities in their material culture such as house design, canoes and bark-cloth, yet it is difficult to form a detailed picture of religious beliefs and practices covering the 3000 years prior to European contact. There was veneration of Tangaroa as god of the sea, of key importance for seafaring and fishing people. But other major sacred figures featured elsewhere in Polynesia, such as Rongo, Tu and Tane, were not found in Tonga and Samoa. Little is known of any priests and temples in a developed institutional form, although religious ceremonies

47. Female 'goddess'
image, wood. Tonga.

were conducted in Samoa and Tonga from large burial mounds and special god-houses for invoking the gods (Bellwood 1978b: 71–5). There were few cult objects. It may be that the explanation lies in a more pragmatic activism directing energies elsewhere: 'Most of their energy seems to have been devoted to the manipulation of a highly formal socio-political system. Where the Tongans were disciplined warriors the Samoans were adroit politicians' (Linton and Wingert 1946: 24). Tongans were ruled by a warlike aristocracy of chiefs and eventually by a king based in the main southern island of Tongatapu; this continued from the late-19th century as a constitutional monarchy. Samoa developed a more flexible and open system of village councils (*fono*) in which men were awarded titles leading up to the hereditary chief and the talking chief. An important expression of this system was ceremonial *kava*-drinking, also the exchange of fine mats and other precious gifts.

Although only a few carved images have survived from pre-contact Tonga, mostly of human female figures, they have an impressive intensity. Small figures carved from whale-tooth ivory were apparently intended as pendants on a necklace or as suspension hook god symbols (Barrow 1972: 68–71). The larger wooden image illustrated here (figure 47) with its large head and stylized arms is a free-standing 'image of a goddess', 33cm in height, beautifully carved in hard shiny wood. It came from Lifuka in the Ha'apai group in the middle of the Tongan archipelago with its many islands. Whether it really was meant to depict a 'goddess' we have no way now of knowing. It could equally be an ancestor figure and in this case would embody ideal qualities. The senior female figure was very important in Tongan social structure and lineage. In terms of desirable female qualities this image, like the others, has the legs placed in the parallel position which is 'proper' in Tongan custom for women. Further, the generous shoulders, breasts and calves 'contribute to the statuesque quality of women' (Kaeppler, in Gathercole et al. 1979: 92, 174–7). Such a female ancestor served as a model and sacred archetype for women.

Of further interest is the rare piece of information attached to this image from the British missionaries engaged in converting the Tongans to Christianity in 1830. Encouraged by zealous converts and lay-preachers as well, people desecrated their old gods and destroyed them. The Wesleyan missionary John Thomas, like the famous John Williams, managed to collect four of these images to take to show back home. He mentioned that King Taufa'ahau (who later became King George Tupou I) hung several images in his house and laughed heartily at these now disgraced 'Idols'.

This rejection of 'graven images' appears to have discouraged Tongans from producing visual art in the subsequent century-and-a-half, and only recently has some wood-carving been revived for tourism. All the more effort was channelled into the arts of weaving and *tapa* work which became of very high quality. Traditional vocal music was developed to a complex level with four men's parts and two women's parts, a polyphony based on the melody or leading part, the drone and the decoration. Adrienne Kaeppler follows this through, using the approach of 'ethnoscientific structuralism' to show an underlying structure and interrelation of the arts. Although these dimensions of music and poetry may be fully understood only by a few, such as performers and artisans, the audience shares in the experience:

> But even without complete understanding of all the dimensions, the spectator is immersed in the artistic allusions of his society and can understand some correspondences immediately. At the end of a twenty to thirty minute performance the dancing ground is alive with song and movements of the performers and empathetic movements (especially of the head, *fakateki*), applause and shouts of '*malie faira*' (bravo) of the spectators. (Kaeppler, in Greenhalgh and Megaw 1978: 272)

Through the overlay of decorations and complex associations of the arts, both spectator and performer can attain some aesthetic experience in which various traditional religious themes are interwoven.

Polynesian religion reflects social rank and hierarchy, as is exemplified in the complex of funeral ceremonies. These were traditionally confined to royalty, chiefs and nobles and marked by burial mounds which could be used for other religious ceremonies subsequently. With the coming of Christianity, graves began to be used for all, commoners as well as nobility. The traditional concern with burial ceremonies was thereby extended; the distinctive Tongan type of grave became a shaped mound of glistening white sand which women decorate with a variety of colourful if ephemeral forms of folk art. A recent study of changing styles in graves in the area of the Tongan capital Nuku'alofa shows the mixture of traditional features and natural materials, such as shells, coral, flowers and leaves, with modern objects such as bottles, cans, quilts and billboards. The work is done carefully by women and regarded as sacred decoration (*tapu*), forbidden for others to take; it is highly valued by society. It is of special interest for the understanding of changing styles and values in Tongan art because it is made exclusively by Tongans for Tongans and is not a form of saleable tourist art. It also shows a de-emphasis of the role of chiefs and nobles in favour of commoners, the nuclear family and a rising middle class (J. Teilhet-Fisk, in Hanson 1990: 222–43). While most other parts of Polynesia have adopted the Christian headstone and Western-style tablets for graves, Tongan Christianity has remained distinctively Tongan and begun to introduce concrete graves only in the 1980s.

In other areas of art and craftwork, Tongans continue to make mats, *tapa* cloth and baskets for home and community use as well as for tourists. The art of wood-carving has been revived for tourist sales, drawing on models from elsewhere in the Pacific such as Hawaii and Tahiti.

Samoa

In the case of Samoa, there are even fewer examples of anthropomorphic carved images than those preserved from traditional Tonga. One was presented to Queen Victoria by the Samoan King Malietoa in 1841. It is not known whether Samoans had used such images in the veneration of gods or as the medium of spirits. That one was associated with the preserved bodies of two chiefs. While it has some Tongan and Fijian features it could be of Samoan making rather than a Tongan import as often stated. In general, the energy of Samoans has been directed into other arts such as oratory, singing, architecture, weaving and tattooing. While these arts may be viewed as expressions of social relations and values shared by Samoans, they also convey underlying religious symbolism which continues into the present (Duncan 1985).

The coming of Christianity from 1828 (first with Wesleyan Methodists from Tonga, then the London Missionary Society from the Congregational church, then Roman Catholics and later the Mormons or Latter Day Saints) brought religious changes and Europeanization. Yet these did not destroy the

Samoan traditions and sense of identity. The Samoan cultural life, *fa'asamoa*, bound the village social structure and family networks to traditional customs and ceremonies. In various ways the forms of Christianity came to terms with this and were, on the one hand, assimilated to Samoan culture while, on the other hand, reinterpreting the culture by baptizing it into Christianity. Religion and politics worked together in new alliances from the time of King Malietoa. At the end of the 19th century the eastern islands of Samoa became a trust territory of the USA, 'American Samoa'. The main islands, 'Western Samoa' came under the administration of Germany, then of New Zealand until becoming the independent state of Samoa in 1962. Through all this the church continued to be part of 'a most powerful and resilient social structure'. Some of the strength and vigour of the Samoan church in Polynesia is due to this: 'The Samoans are astute politicians and have been masters in handling the politics of church life' (Forman 1982: 23). But even more important is the strength which stems from continuity with the deep-rooted symbolism pervading *fa'asamoa* and which has proved able to adapt to Christianity and modern Western culture. This is evident not only in Samoa but also in the sizeable communities of Samoans who have migrated to Australia, New Zealand and America (Duncan 1990: 128). As examples of the continuity of traditional symbolism we refer to the following arts.

In the art of architecture the Samoan house (*fale*) stands out both in its conception and in its execution by traditional builders who worked without nails and used sinnet lashings (see figure 48). Roger Neich lists the three basic principles as round ends, open sides and a single room under each roof. These are evident in traditional dwelling houses and guest houses. Recent decades have seen changes in building materials (such as concrete instead of stones for the platform) and the use of European building methods, windows and rooms. Despite the resultant variety of houses representing degrees of Europeanization, the three principles persist strongly: 'these houses still maintain a distinctive Samoan appearance and are well adapted to serve the Samoan lifestyle' (Neich 1985: 19).

Traditional Samoa maintained *malae* or open spaces for ceremonies; there were also some god-houses probably built on rectangular or star-shaped mounds (Bellwood 1978b: 74) When Christian missionaries introduced the new idea of churches in the 19th century, these were built on European models which became an established style. However, it is noteworthy that modern Samoan communities in New Zealand cities such as Auckland and Wellington have drawn on the *fale* in some striking new church buildings. Likewise the Samoan Congregational Christian Church built in Suva, Fiji in 1988 has the rounded roof (though not in leaf thatch) and the traditional three pillars in the interior behind the altar and large cross. Here is a recovery of tradition with modern transformations.

48. Samoan house, *fale*. Otago Museum model (photo).

The plaiting arts and crafts include the making of fans and baskets as the work of women, along with plaited mats which are the strongest traditional craft in Western Samoa, with continual innovation. Mats are not only useful floor coverings but are exchange valuables and a source of pride for a family. Of the various types of mat, which are strictly ranked, the highest is the 'fine mat' (*'ie toga*) which is woven from pandanus leaves. This will be presented at special occasions such as funerals, weddings and the accepting of a title, accompanied by speeches. The sacred power of the fine mat is given a mythological founding in the story of three Samoans captured by a Tongan king who was going to burn them in a fiery pit. The Samoan lady among them, Futa, had woven a fine mat which she used to cover the three as they approached the king; the mat so impressed the king that he freed the Samoans. From this comes the name *'ie toga,* meaning Tongan mats, and the description of them as 'the shelter of life'. This has continuing social and religious relevance in restoring broken relationships; the exchange of fine mats could prevent a blood revenge in the past. In the *ifoga* ceremony forgiveness is confirmed when an injured party accepts the fine mat. In relation to Christianity, the fine mat covering the head can be seen as a symbol of the shelter offered in the forgiveness of sins (Duncan 1985: 7). Second only to fine mats as a valued ceremonial gift is *siapo*, the Samoan bark-cloth or *tapa*. Once worn as clothing, it is still used for bed covers, room dividers, table cloths and decoration. It is an important item for presentations and investitures. As a cultural art form, especially in the form of *siapo mamanu* where designs and colours are applied directly by freehand to create rich and complex patterns, it has enjoyed revival in recent years (Pritchard 1984). Samoan traditional designs have now also been applied to other art forms such as modern paintings by younger Samoan artists in Auckland and elsewhere in the Pacific.

As a final example of continuity, full body-tattooing from the waist to the knees (*tatau*) is a tradition still alive in Samoa while it has virtually faded away elsewhere in Polynesia. Although discouraged by the Protestant LMS missionaries it was approved of by the Catholic mission. It has in recent times had a revival as a form of initiation through standing up to the painful ordeal of tattooing and showing manly qualities. For some it is felt to be a spiritual experience of rebirth and completeness by being linked to one's Samoan spiritual heritage (Duncan 1985: 10).

Tahiti, Society Islands and Austral Islands

A millennium and a half after Western Polynesia had been settled, there was a great expansion eastwards in the period 300–1200 CE. At the heart of Polynesia the Society Islands appear to have been the point of launching further settlements to the Austral Islands, Cook Islands and then New Zealand in the latter part of this period. Meanwhile, the northern and eastern extremities had been settled in the Hawaiian Islands, the Marquesas and Easter Island.

The Society Islands, all volcanic in origin, include two connected groups – the Windward or eastern group, with the major island culture of Tahiti, and the Leeward or western group with the island of Raiatea as a powerful religious centre. In the traditional sense the term *Ma'ohi* covers the people and customs of the Society Islands (Oliver 1974: 7). Rigid class structures developed over the centuries, the chiefs having great power, with a subordinate class of lesser chiefs and landholders and the commoners below them. Such a society was large enough to afford many specialists and in the field of religious ritual the priests were probably hereditary from the upper class group, with some perhaps supported fulltime (Oliver 1974: 869). There were also shamans who in a state of possession or inspiration could serve as oracles, but drawn from all social classes; this survives into modern times in the *tahu'a*, a spirit-expert in healing and magic spells (Levy 1973: 159–77).

Priestly rituals were conducted at the public courtyard called the *marae* (figure 49). Being simple rectangular stone structures, many can still be seen in the Society Islands where they are 'the most enduring of the monuments to have survived from prehistoric times' (Bellwood 1978b: 81–4; Green and Kaye 1968). A few were built up into monumental stepped structures, but most are open or walled courts with floors of basalt or coral blocks. A raised

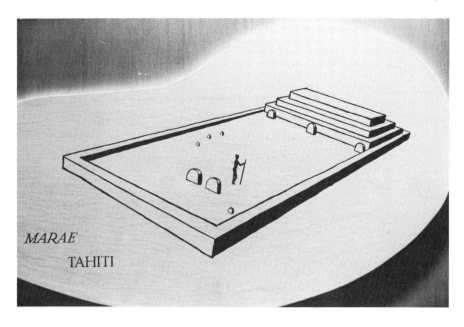

MARAE

TAHITI

49.   *Marae*, Tahiti. Diagram in Otago Museum (photo).

platform, the *ahu* at one end, was the sacred place of the boards or stone slabs representing the gods. Before them sacrifices of animals, and sometimes humans, were made. Prayers were addressed to the gods and ancestral spirits for ceremonies relating to chiefly burials, reception of visitors and declarations of war. A nearby storehouse was used for keeping drums, staff-gods and other representations through which the gods would come for the ritual when required.

Which gods were worshipped at these *marae*? There were diverse structures on the coast and inland, some being devoted to local spirits and to interests such as the success and protection of fishermen. Among the sacred powers of the Polynesian pantheon there were changes over the centuries. The great sea-god Tangaroa who was supreme in Samoa was regarded in Tahiti as the originator of all things in the myth of Ta'aroa; by emerging from his shell in the primeval darkness he gave rise to all the features of the earth which issued from the parts of his body and he called the gods into being (Henry 1928). However, by the time of European contact and reports in the 18th century, Ta'aroa had become an otiose, distant High God. The effective objects of ritual worship were instead the many-sided life-giver Tane, beloved of canoe-builders who invoked him, and then the war-god Oro, son of Ta'aroa, whose ascendancy was promoted by priests at a great *marae* in Raiatea. Oro was said to be a youthful and handsome chief who could also manifest himself in the form of a boar or the man-of-war bird, symbolizing the fierceness of the warrior. Images of Oro were decorated and taken round in a 'god-house' mounted on a double canoe. Oro was believed to enter and possess a human's body as a vehicle for instruction and also to inhabit images for such communications as well as for receiving worship and blessing social occasions by his presence (Oliver 1974: 900 ff.). A drawing made at the time of Captain Cook's visit in 1777 shows a human sacrifice to Oro about to begin near Attahuru *marae* in Tahiti, with skulls of former victims on the platform. (Cook described this representation of 'Oro' as a 'sacred repository' shaped like a sugar-loaf.) The cult of Oro came to an end with the conversion of Tahiti to Christianity in 1816.

The image of Oro illustrated here (figure 50) is one of several such symbolic images (*to'o*) surviving in this form, a 47 cm-long cylinder made of a wood core with a plaited covering of sennit or coconut fibre. It has the stylized features of eyes, nose and mouth, with navel and suggested arms; it would be originally embellished with red feathers. Why should a great god be represented so simply, almost abstractly? As the art-historian E.H. Gombrich noted, it is enough to convey a 'look of uncanny power'; the suggestion of eyes gives it the power to see, and that is lifelike enough (Gombrich 1955: 25–7). From the Tahitian viewpoint, the sennit braiding was highly valued as a distinctive artistic medium and could itself have sacred associations through respect for the intricate work involved. (Kaeppler, in Gathercole et al. 1979: 85–6). The shape of this *to'o* image has been discussed by Simon Kooijman by means of a comparison of several examples in the light of historical reports. The club-like shape could express the weapons empowered by a god of war. But Oro was also supported by the Areoi sect in Tahiti who were noted for their erotic dances and activities. As their patron, Oro would be the god of sexual desire and represented as a phallic symbol. Oro in this light had the functions of both a youthful god of fertility and a god of war (Kooijman 1964). Clearly there was no lack of artistic skill in representation if that had been sought, as indicated by the wooden anthropomorphic images (called *ti'i*) which were also used as vehicles of gods. It may be that there was little need for detailed iconographic god symbols in large-scale rituals on a *marae*. Barrow relates this to 'a general trend of the more esoteric and priestly religions of Polynesia to adopt abstract symbols in preference to the more naturalistic sculptured forms' (Barrow 1979: 41). Parallels to this can be found in the religious iconography of other cultures (Moore 1977: 29, 79–81). In the case of Tahiti it appears that the result of this trend was the takeover of the wooden images by sorcerers as magic dolls, as well as their use as boundary-markers (Barrow 1979: 41–7).

Remarkable wood-carved images were produced in the Austral Islands. Lying to the south of the Society Islands, their culture may have originally derived from there but developed further at a distance, as with other

50.   War-god Oro, wood and   51.   Goddess image, wood.
       sennit image, Tahiti.   Raivavae, Austral Is.

Polynesian groups. Distinctive design motifs and intricate carving are features of ceremonial drums, paddles and fly-whisks from Raivavae (Barrow 1979: 50–69). Massive stone images of deities also come from this island. A more modest image of a goddess is one which the missionary John Williams obtained around 1830 on the understanding that he would use it to show in England as an example of heathen idols (see figure 51). However it should now be seen as a fine example of pre-contact Polynesian sculpture achieved with stone-age tools. The image is 65cm high and is decorated with typical Australs motifs over the face, shoulders, arms, knees and back. Information is lacking about the name, iconography and worship associated with this goddess figure who wears a collar and a hat with a rim. There may well have been a rich variety of such images.

From the Austral island of Rurutu comes one of the most remarkable works of Polynesian wood sculpture, collected by LMS missionaries in 1821 and now in the British Museum, London (see figure 52). Standing 112 cm in height it has a round mask-like head with its features made up of tiny human figures in various positions; these also are placed symmetrically over the rest of the body. Because the figures seem to be 'sprouting' from the head and body of the male image the theme can be interpreted as the creation of gods and men. Therefore it has been in the past labelled by the Museum as 'Tangaroa Upao Vahu (Tangaroa-up-in-the-sky)', the Polynesian sea-god who had been

52.   God A'a, wooden image. Rurutu, Austral Is.

elevated to creator as Ta'aroa in the Society Islands. However, it is not known whether the great gods Ta'aroa and Oro were known at all to the remote people of Rurutu Island. John Williams of the LMS reported that this image was of their national god called A'a. Regarded as the ancestor by whom the island was peopled, A'a became deified after his death. The meaning of it is still that of generation and creative emergence, along the lines of Polynesian concern with genealogy and descent from ancestral deities. The back of the image is detachable, and originally the hollow body was filled with more small figures of gods and humans, perhaps so that they could be infused with the power of A'a. In its stance with thin arms and hands on the body with domed head and sharp jaw ridge, this appears to be related to the Tahitian wooden *ti'i* images (Barrow 1979: 58).

Cook Islands

Named after their Western 'discoverer', Captain Cook, these islands comprise two different groups – the northern Cooks which are scattered atolls and the southern Cooks which are mostly volcanic islands such as Rarotonga, Aitutaki and Mangaia. Their culture appears to derive from the Society Islands, the source of the Polynesian settlers who probably came in the 9th century CE. A similar hierarchical structure based on genealogy classified members of society as high chiefs (*ariki*), lesser chiefs (*rangatira*) and commoners. There were priestly experts (*ta'unga*) trained for their various specialist tasks. There was veneration of such leading Polynesian gods as Tangaroa, Tane, Tu and Rongo. Some islands such as Rarotonga had rectangular ceremonial courts similar to the *marae* in Tahiti; sacred structures also included small god-houses or 'houses for peace' (Barrow 1979: 72). Fine artistic work was done for religious rituals, reflecting the influence of the Society and Austral Islands but also of Samoa and Tonga from a later period.

The staff god illustrated here (figure 53) shows a typical Rarotongan religious symbol used in religious ceremonies when it would be carried upright on a ladder held horizontally by several bearers. It could be an image of Tangaroa, head of the pantheon, who would take up temporary residence in it during the ritual. The head is carved in a stylized way, distinctive of Rarotonga, with a high forehead and carved grooves and ridges making large eyes and broad open lips and tongue seen in profile. The ironwood carving continued downward with a series of small projecting 'bat-like' figures representing the successive generations of ancestors. Below this the main stem of the staff was left plain, to be wrapped in three layers of decorated bark-cloth (*tapa*) to protect the spirit of the image, then tied with sennit cordage. The lower end of the staff is represented as a phallus; indeed this whole staff can be understood in this way, as a symbol of the generative and creative power of the god, giving life and continuity to the ancestors and their descendants. These staff-gods were made in various sizes ranging from 1 to 6 metres in height and were venerated until their abandonment in face of the adoption of Christianity.

Other carved images from the Cook Islands include some of the same features and style. Fisherman attached to their canoes small (40cm) wooden images of gods. These were squat, compressed male figures with enlarged eyes on the massive head, a protruding belly and sometimes tattooed patterns on the lips and body. A more elegant form of this is a god image with small secondary figures on the chest and on the arms, reminiscent of the image of A'a from Rurutu. It was labelled by the LMS collector as 'Te Rongo and his three sons', in which case it would represent the father of agriculture and cultivated foods; again, it could be a figure of the creative Tangaroa (Poignant 1967: 36–7). Other striking images from other islands of the southern group are intricately carved maces and slab gods, and a stylized simple image from Mangaia using sacred materials of sennit and red feathers to represent the fertility god Tane (Barrow 1979: 83–90). These show something of the

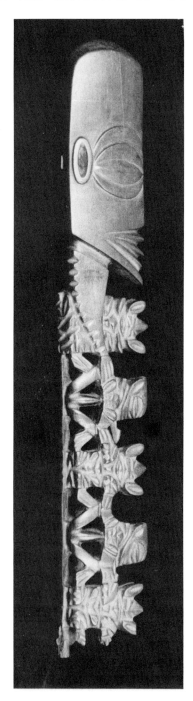

53.   Staff-god, wood. Rarotonga, Cook Is.
Otago Museum (photo).

quality and variety of the decorative ritual carvings. The coming of Christian missions in the 19th century led to the demise of such images and the introduction of new non-religious arts, such as the large fabric quilts (*tiraevae*) sewn by women, with bold and colourful designs based on flowers and natural forms (Rongokea 1992).

Turning to other art forms, we note also the Cook Islands' reputation for powerful singing, drumming and dancing. This synthesis is popular to this day, both for the people themselves who practise enthusiastically for competitions at festivals between village groups, and also as entertainment for visitors and tourists. In pre-contact times chanting and drumming predominated, accompanied by dancing. With the coming of LMS missionaries and native teachers, European hymns of the early 19th century were introduced from Tahitian missions in the style called *imene tuki* ('grunting hymn') with local adaptations. This became part of the culture, happily adapted to local needs. Describing a Protestant church service in the Southern Cooks in the 1950s, on the island of Aitutaki, Bernard Thorogood notes the powerful *fortissimo* sound and the emphasis on counterpoint and harmony, rather than unison, of the men's and women's parts; free verse, prose and chanting can also be used. Above all there is great joy and energy in the singing:

> The enthusiasm is shining on every face – and so is the sweat. For singing becomes a physical exertion, not a polite social duty. Bodies sway to the rhythm, the men grunt to beat the time and sometimes the women can sit still no longer and jump up to dance, revolving their hips and stretching out their arms. (Thorogood 1960: 14)

This writer also observes (1960: 12) that Cook Islanders have taken their special singing wherever they have gone and thereby influenced the church in Papua New Guinea. Another example of Cook Island singing is given in Kevin Salisbury's study of the Northern Cooks island of Pukapuka, 1000 km north-west of Rarotonga. The original cultural influence was from Samoa but more recently singing and drum-dance styles have come through the Southern Cooks from Tahiti. Singing and chanting accompany all the occasions of village life; all chants are owned by one or other of the villages, with exclusive rights for performance (Salisbury 1984: 44). They have local ways of singing the hymns and can interpolate new material expressing the Bible in indigenous form. Secular singing styles likewise are modified by new influences. This is evident in the Pukapukan community in Auckland where 1000 or more migrants now live as New Zealand citizens – more than the 800 living on the distant atoll. While modern forms of popular songs and dances are enjoyed, there is also concern and enthusiasm for retaining the traditions of pageants and music such as ancient chants, along with new compositions. This is just one example of Polynesian adaptation and continuity between old and new. It illustrates the increasing mobility and interchange between cultural groups in the Pacific; it also shows the use of modern mass-media communications such as radio and now videos to convey new items and also to record and preserve the traditional.

Easter Island (Rapanui)

This small island, completely isolated at the eastern extremity of Polynesia, is well known for the mystery surrounding its cultural origins and its impressive stone monuments. Potential information on questions about its prehistory was lost through the inter-tribal conflicts, the epidemics and the depredations by slave-traders from Peru and Chile in the mid-19th century which destroyed most of the people and the traditional culture. A colourful Hollywood feature film, 'Rapa Nui', was filmed on the island in 1993, using actors from several parts of Polynesia, to reconstruct the tribal and ecological disasters of the 18th century. However, vigorous studies by modern researchers in history and archaeology have pieced together some probable answers to these questions (Bahn and Flenley 1992; Fischer, S.R. 1993). It is clear that Easter Island was settled not from South America, almost 4000 km distant, but probably from the Marquesas Islands in Eastern Polynesia (Bellwood 1978a: 361–79) as early as the 5th century CE. Linguistic and archaeological evidence points to this.

Wood was in short supply as the population grew over a 1000-year period, making possible the large-scale effort of shaping and erecting the 600 immense stone statues on the island, a quarter of which lie unfinished in the quarries from an extinct volcano. After being shaped out of the fairly soft volcanic rock, the statues were lowered down to the base of the slope and erected on an *ahu* platform; only after this were the eyes carved (Bellwood 1978b: 118). This indicates a belief in the power of the image to be awakened once the eyes were put in, hence to be controlled by not activating them until the right time. The platform also suggests veneration of the gods at the *ahu* of the *marae* as in other parts of Polynesia such as Tahiti. It is possible that the massive but stereotyped statues represent chiefs who became venerated after their death when the statues were erected on the mortuary platforms of the clans.

Scarce though it was, wood was used for carving weapons such as clubs and images of humans and fish and lizard shapes. A 'bird-man' image, combining a human body with a bird head, was said to be the representative of its patron, the supreme god worshipped in Easter Island of old — the local god Makemake who functioned instead of Tane as creator of humankind (Poignant 1967: 40). The bird-man also appears in petroglyphs on rock outcrops. The standing images of humans, male and female, were carved of wood about 45cm in height and depict emaciated or aged figures to indicate their status as ancestors. The male 'ancestor spirit' (*Moai kavakava*) depicted here (figure 54) has a skeletonic spine at the back, raised ribs, staring eyes and the chin beard of the elders. It may be that the artists derived these physical characteristics from observing 'the bodies of the dead mummified or dessicated by the dry atmosphere of burial caves' (Barrow 1972: 139). This is how Easter Islanders thought that ghosts would look when they appeared. A further possibility of the stylized ribs is that they had a mnemonic significance for enumerating the ancestors, as suggested for other areas of the Pacific.

The use of these images was not for worship directly but they still held some religious significance. Since they represented ancestors who had died and become spirits, they could function as household gods and confer merit. At festivals they were taken out of their bark-cloth wrapping to be worn by male members of the household, suspended on their bodies: 'The more images a man could wear the greater chance he had of having his requests answered by the deity' (Linton and Wingert 1946: 42).

The old Polynesian religion and its associated arts are no longer realities of life for the people of Rapanui. The trauma of the 19th century broke their culture and reduced their numbers – from several thousand to a mere 111 people at one stage. Now a province of Chile, Easter Island has in the 20th century lost some of its isolation and been opened to tourism. For a considerable time previously the people had absorbed non-Polynesian influences from Europe and Latin America. Yet now there is also an expectation that they can produce traditional Polynesian carvings for tourists. The Roman Catholic church of the Holy Cross in Hangaroa in 1970 encouraged indigenous carving with the result that an impressive wooden statue of the Virgin and Child now stands beside the altar. A Cultural Centre was established to encourage the revival of traditional culture, but this confronts the dilemma, seen elsewhere in the Pacific, of conforming to a stereotype of indigenous art expected by tourists. In the fields of music and dance Rapanui is influenced by American popular disco music, Catholic hymns sung polyphonically and the Polynesian-Latin style popular groups called *conjuntos*. From research in 1982–83 Joan Seaver concludes (in Dark 1984: 68): 'Rapanui current lifestyle can no longer endow musical events with their original ritual symbolism. Obviously a new content and new meanings must result in fresh forms and presentations.'

Marquesas Islands

The name Marquesas was given by the Spanish explorer Mendana in 1595 and the islands have been part of French Polynesia since 1842. In the West they may be best known as the home of the painter Gauguin in his last years. The two groups of islands, although on the outer margin of Eastern Polynesia,

54.   Male ancestor image, wood. Easter
Island. Otago Museum (photo).

were first settled as early as the 2nd century BCE from Western Polynesia (Suggs 1960: ch.10). Life on these rugged islands was never easy, with the threat of recurring famines and droughts. Tribal divisions dominated the population which engaged in continuing warfare and cannibalism. These features did not prevent them from putting energy into remarkable constructions and refined works of art; their elaborate carving work has been compared as parallel to that of the later Maori carving in distant New Zealand. Their skill in stone construction led to fine stone platforms, *paepae*, for domestic houses. More impressive still were the *tohua*, assembly places for dancing and ceremonials in each village, some well over 100 metres long with high stone walls and platforms for seating spectators (Bellwood 1978a: 332–5). Along similar lines to the *ahu* in central Polynesia there were sacred groves with platforms for images, with a high-roofed house for storing sacred objects (Linton and Wingert 1946: 34). Temples were built as dwellings to house the gods coming to enter the images (Suggs 1965: 46).

The religion of the Marquesans was tribal and the worship focused not on major Polynesian deities but on the souls of deified chiefs whose powers depended on human sacrifices. As described by Linton, it was a pragmatic religion in which worship depended on the deified chief giving satisfactory answers to prayers. There was also a cult of the dead who were mummified and later given a final funeral at which much wealth, in the form of pigs, was displayed. One result of this may be seen in the *tiki* or votive images of wood or stone, some of them being 3 metres tall (see figure 55). While the body of the image follows a similar pattern to that of the Society and Austral Islands, the head is emphasized in a distinctively Marquesan way. The facial features are carved in low relief, as if in a pattern for decorative carving, with huge round eyes and arched brows, small flattened nose and horizontal mouth partly opened. 'This facial convention as a whole may derive from the sunken eyes and shrunken lips of a mummified head' (Linton and Wingert 1946: 37). Images with such features were made for many decorative and religious purposes. Very small *tiki* made of hard volcanic rock may have been used by sorcerers as receptacles for trapped souls. Others were used for healing and some were carried by priests to be invoked for success in enterprises (Barrow 1972: 96–7).

Marquesans applied these features and artistic skill to many objects of practical use (Linton 1923: 263–471). For instance, the long wooden clubs (*u'u*), as illustrated (figure 56), were heavy weapons but also used as an everyday walking stick and for leaning on while talking by slotting the upper end under the armpit. This is stylized as a human face with, once again, the Marquesan emphasis on the huge staring eyes. There are small secondary *tiki* heads in the centre of each of the circular eyes; another small head represents the nose, below which a pair of eyes like spectacles represent the mouth.

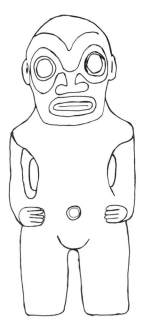

55. Grey stone *tiki*, votive
image. Marquesas Is.

Delicate surface carving is a feature of these clubs, and some of the patterns individual to each club may relate to the individual tattoo pattern of the owner of the club. This is an example, comparable to some Australian Aboriginal objects, where patterns of both tribal and individual significance are featured on things of everyday; utility, aesthetics and spiritual identity are woven together.

As a concluding example of such interwoven aspects of culture and life, the body decoration of tattooing deserves further comment. In varying degrees throughout Polynesia tattooing of some parts of the body was valued as a sacred art performed by experts under *tapu*. It was an art which, being applied to the body, did not survive the person's death. A painting from the 1830s of a Rarotongan chief depicts him with a high feather headdress and a wavy linear tattoo over his whole body and limbs but this is the only record we have of it there. Full body tattooing was known also in Easter Island. Women could be tattooed partially, but men were more lavishly decorated; it was a painful operation but worth enduring as a test of courage and in order to be seen as beautifully clothed in patterns which gave one a sense of pride and identity. The most complete body coverage was attained in the Marquesas, as shown in the classic study by Karl von den Steinen (1925–28, vol. I on Tattooing). This German doctor had been enchanted by Polynesia on a world tour in his younger days and returned in 1897 to spend half-a-year in first-

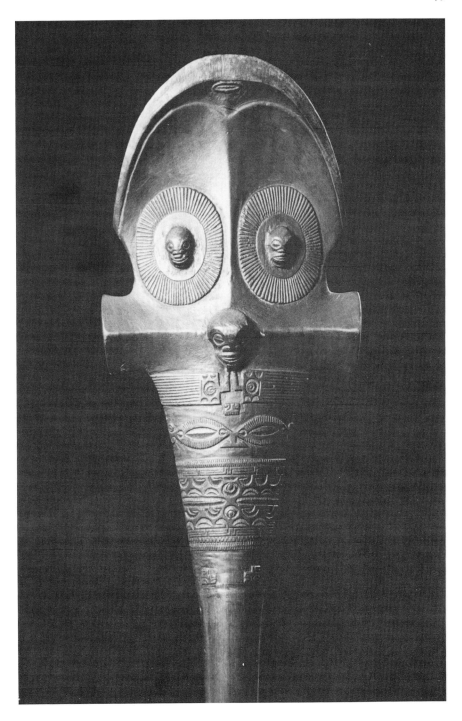

56.   Head of carved wooden club. Marquesas Is. Otago Museum (photo).

hand research on the Marquesas arts for the Berlin Museum. He subsequently combed the world's museums and other sources for information, photos and artifacts. The results of his life's work were published eventually in three splendid volumes, a classic of ethnology. Photos and drawings show the richness of the designs covering men from head to foot and women on the lips, arms and legs. The significance of these designs is first that they become personal art, permanently embedded in the human skin. But also the designs can be transferred to other media of bark-cloth and wood – for instance, the realistic wood sculpture of an arm with tattoo designs which could have served as a tattooist's model, or as a ritual object. As Kaeppler observes: 'There can be little doubt, however, that the stylized eyes, concentric circles, and the placement of various design combinations in space demonstrate the same principles which underlie the Marquesan aesthetic tradition' (in Gathercole et al. 1979: 88). Such studies are all the more valuable in the Marquesas, as in other parts of Eastern Polynesia, where the once-flourishing population and culture is now only a fragmentary remnant continuing some of the past traditions (Suggs 1965).

Hawaiian Islands

At the northern apex of the 'Polynesian triangle', the Hawaiian Islands were settled by the 6th century CE, probably from the Marquesas. They developed the Polynesian tribal system along similar lines to the Tahitian three classes, headed by the *ali'i*, the hereditary chiefly families. As the islands became more heavily populated and in later centuries completely isolated from other Polynesian groups, this became a rigidly defined feudal system of large kingdoms with kings controlling subordinate chiefs and orders of priests on temple lands. The Polynesian emphasis on genealogy and descent from the ancestral gods served this complex hierarchical society with symbols of rank and power. For instance, the elevated creation chant, the 'Kumulipo' (Beckwith 1972), was transmitted orally by a family of ruling chiefs to show its divine origin from the beginning of the world. Again, the visual art form of Hawaiian featherwork (figure 57), the most prestigious artistic medium requiring costly work and technical perfection, involved the work of all classes; but the rich red and yellow feathered cloaks and capes were worn only by high-born male chiefs. Priests also made feathered images which were used for invoking the presence of the highest gods. As Adrienne Kaeppler shows (in Gathercole et al. 1979: 82–3), this exemplifies the 'relationship between gods, priests, chiefs, and people, and an aesthetic tradition concerned with ongoing process and use in which works of art become chronicles of history objectified in visual form'.

Hawaiian religion followed the general Polynesian pattern of a hierarchy of

57.   Feather-cape, Hawaiian Is. Otago Museum (photo).

gods (*akua*) representing the major departments of life from the mythical beginnings of the cosmos (Buck 1964: 465 ff.). Thus Kanaloa (Tangaroa or Ta'aroa in Southern Polynesia) had the sea as his realm, so embracing for a seafaring and sea-surrounded island culture; but he was not accorded major worship in shrines. Kane (Tane) representing sexual fertility and growth, as well as forgiveness and revenge, was much more the object of prayer. Lono (Rongo) dealt with rain and healing. Ku (Tu) was the war-god in his highest form but was represented in many other forms of 'Ku gods'; Ku and the goddess Hina (Hine, Sina) were associated as the male and female reproductive principles (K. Luomala, in Eliade, *ER* 6, 217). Another form of Hina was the fierce and destructive Pele, the Hawaiian goddess of volcanic fires, called 'Hina-who-eats-the moon'. Many of the images which have survived appear to be representations of Ku with large head and fiercely grimacing mouth. These major gods were worshipped by all ranks of people but, as in other parts of Polynesia, there were many local gods, guardian gods (*aumakua*) and sacred powers connected to family and occupational groups. The reality of Hawaiian religion can hardly have been an orderly system.

Official worship came to be focused on sacred centres, at first in the form of the simple open-air platform. Then, as the hierarchical organization distinguished the aristocracy from commoners, there developed a more exclusive walled structure called the *heiau* (see figure 58) under the control of priests appointed by the king or chief, now ritually trained and socially prestigious. These uniquely Hawaiian temples provided for public religious rituals

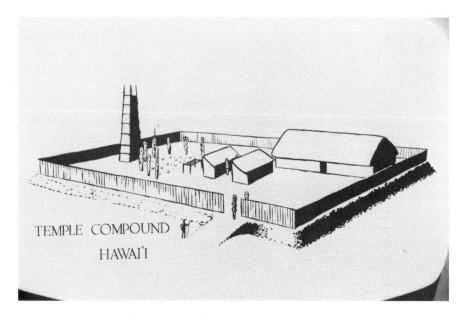

TEMPLE COMPOUND

HAWAI'I

58.   *Heiau*, temple-compound in Hawaii. Diagram in Otago Museum (photo).

conducted by the priests, elaborated sometimes for several days and involving offerings and, in some higher temples, human sacrifices. The two main types of temple were devoted either to Ku, involving priests of the highest order in rituals for war, or to Lono whose blessings were sought for crops and peaceful needs (Buck 1964: 513–27). The *heiau* was typically rectangular with high stone walls outside and courts and terraces within. A wall separated the area in which commoners could sit and make their ritual responses from the sacred enclosure to be entered only by priests and chiefs; there were rows of images, a platform or altar for sacrifice, offering-stands and small houses for sacred objects. An additional feature was the oracle tower, perhaps 15 metres high, which had three stages; only the king and high priest could climb to the highest floor to be possessed by the god and to deliver oracles on coming events.

What was the place of images of the gods in the *heiau* and elsewhere? On the outer walls the large fearsome figures on posts appear to have functioned as guardian images. Even inside 'the large wooden images seem to have been little more than stage properties' (Linton and Wingert 1946: 64). The most important image and focus of the divine power was usually much smaller, such as a roll of bark-cloth decorated with sacred feathers, as already exemplified in other parts of Polynesia. Also using feathers were portable images made of a basketwork frame up to 1 or 2 metres in height. They depicted some form of Ku with staring eyes and savage mouth lined with shark's teeth; this was designed to terrify the enemy and to heighten ferocity in battle; there is record of two human sacrifices being offered to such an image of Kukailimoku before the battle which ended this religious regime in 1819 (Barrow 1972: 152–3).

Most of the large images were destroyed in the reaction against the burdensome system and its replacement by Christianity. One of the images to have survived from the famous Honaunau Bay temple on the large island of Hawaii, where there also was a royal mausoleum, is the so-called Bloxam image (figure 59). It appears to be one of the forms of Ku with a fierce visage and crested head-piece but with the unusual feature of outstretched arms. It was one of the two wooden images (133 cm in height) standing beside the altar from which Andrew Bloxam was given permission to take out any 'curiosities' in 1825 (Buck 1964: 492–4). At the same time, however, the dismantling of the great gods of old and their temples did not at first dissolve the local and family cults. These continued to venerate ancestors and tribal guardians in the form of small 'god-sticks' pegged in the ground and goddess images for household ceremonies (Duff 1969: 69).

The ancient sites, temples and images have been in some cases preserved and restored as vivid visual relics of the religious past. For a more living and continuing influence, even in distorted forms, we may turn to the arts of poetry, music and dance which have a powerful appeal. Traditionally these arts served together to honour those of high rank and genealogy, using the heightened speech of poetic chanting and storytelling. Music was mainly vocal and in the form of chanted songs. Dancing used movements mainly of the hands and arms to interpret a story. It is within this background that the Hawaiian *hula* should be understood. Although it has become commercialized in modern times as a sensuous hip-swaying dance, traditionally the *hula kahiko* could be performed only by men at a temple service. It was part of a religious rite requiring serious dedication to learning at the *hula* dance school. The men would wear leaf decorations and engage in poetic and narrative chanting to the accompaniment of percussive instruments such as gourds and bamboo rattles (Lewis 1990). For this purpose there was the *pahu hula* drum, beaten on its sharkskin drumhead; some splendid examples of these drums, about 50cm in height, have a wooden base consisting of many small carved human figures with supporting arms (Gathercole et al. 1979: 114). In recent years there has been some native Hawaiian revival of the ancient *hula* as part of a recovery of pride in the Polynesian heritage and ancient ritual (Kanahele 1986: 128–34).

What then of the future? Although indigenous Hawaiians are now only a minority in the Hawaiian state of modern USA, the traditional culture, with its diffused cosmic religion of nature and the body, may still have a contribution to make to Western civilization. As John Charlot points out, the ancient religion was not so static and hierarchical as officially portrayed,

59.   'Bloxam image', deity, Hawaii. Replica in Otago Museum (photo).

but rather a dynamic mixture of diverse traditions existing prior to the 'classical' system. Polynesians generally have continued much of these traditions and values alongside Christianity. This is expressed more openly in the arts, with the emergence of new syntheses of Polynesian and Western art forms: 'Hawaiian religion is far from reaching its final chapter' (Charlot 1983: 148).

Micronesia

The 'small islands' of Micronesia, more than two thousand of them, are scattered over an area of the north-western Pacific as extensive as either Melanesia or central Polynesia. Because the islands are mainly small atolls, limited in resources such as wood and stone, life was hard and preoccupied with survival which depended on gardening and fishing. The population derives from a mixture of Polynesian, Melanesian and Indonesian elements from the adjacent regions. The languages are Malayo-Polynesian, belonging to the Austronesian family covering the Pacific; the westernmost islands nearest to the Philippines belong to the Western Austronesian language group. Covered by the label 'Micronesia', there are at least four main cultural areas based on the island groups of the Marianas and the Carolines in the west to centre, and the Marshalls and Gilberts to the east. Their differences result from the geographical isolation of these island groups and the influences over the centuries from adjacent regions surrounding Micronesia. The boundary lines which we may draw on our map of the Pacific are blurred in practice. For instance, in the middle area of Micronesia are two Polynesian 'outliers', Nukuoro and Kapingamarangi. The Gilbert Islands are Micronesian as distinct from the adjacent Ellice Islands (Tuvalu) which are Polynesian; but when Kiribati was established in 1979 as an independent nation it included not only the Gilberts but the Phoenix and Line Islands reaching far into the Polynesian 'triangle'.

While for convenience this section on Micronesia is appended to the chapter on Polynesia, it can be stated that it is not pervaded by a homogeneous culture in the sense that we have noted for Polynesia with its unity-in-diversity. In his helpful overview of Micronesian religions William Lessa sets out several of its basic themes such as death, the soul, funerals, ancestor worship, rites of passage, sorcery and magic. But these do not represent a holistic system:

> Moreover, the religion is a mélange of many elements: celestial and terrestrial deities, nature spirits, demons and ancestral ghosts, with a strong infusion of magic, taboo and divination. No one trait dominates the system. (Lessa 1987: 498)

Micronesian religions did not have a hierarchy of deities for worship at sacred places focused on visual images and elaborate rituals of a priestly order. They appear to have used various themes and symbols in ways suitable to their local contexts.

Likewise in the arts there is no central tradition of visual arts related to religion. Artistic skill of a high order is to be seen in the decoration of objects of practical use such as plaited mats, and baskets, wooden bowls, shell ornaments, houses and outrigger canoes. The seafaring Micronesians would trade the products of their different art skills with neighbouring island groups. Designs were based mainly on angular and geometric figures. This was also the case with the once prevalent forms of body tattooing; motifs here could also include sharks and porpoises, while many designs had names relating to things which the people valued highly such as fish, birds, heavenly bodies and canoes (Leonard Mason, in *EWA* 1964: v. 9, 926–8). The art and craft of house-building also offered some scope for visual decoration, especially in the Palau group of the far western Carolines. There the men's club-houses (*bai*) served as a centre for the chief's council and for dancing and feasting; they were splendid constructions richly decorated on the gables with symbols of birds and natural creatures with a moral meaning. Stories from history, myth and legend made these a form of visual narrative. With the decline of the *bai* in modern Palau, the carving of these stories continues through the low-relief form of the story-board; this is reminiscent of the story-board developed in Papua New Guinea, but it was stimulated in Palau by a Japanese anthropologist and artist in the 1930s (D. Robinson, in Mead and Kernot 1983: 162–78).

Some exceptions do occur to offset the lack of images and anthropomorphic representation in religion. One is found in the admittedly atypical Polynesian outlier island of Nukuoro, an atoll in the Carolines. Illustrated here (figure 60) is the wooden goddess figure called Kawe de Hine Ali'gi which came from a 'god-house', *amalau,* and was reputed to be the object of human sacrifices. While similar figures preserved from this island have been mostly quite small, this one stands 220cm tall. These *tino* may be connected with Micronesian traditions in the Carolines known only through simple weather fetishes with a knob head. Here the *tino* figure has an egg-shaped head without features and the body also is simplified to combine abstraction and expressiveness in a way that modern Westerners find appealing. Restraint and simple stylization are also the marks of wooden face masks from Mortlock Island in the Carolines – apparently the only masks known in Micronesia. They represent a benevolent spirit in order to ward off dangerous typhoons (A. Bühler et al. 1962: 177, 180). Used for a similar purpose in the western Carolines from Yap to Pulawat were wooden doll-like fetishes wrapped in coconut leaves; canoe captains sailing between the atolls would

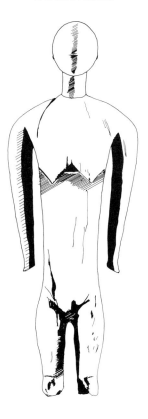

60. Goddess image, wood.
Nukuoro, Caroline Is.

brandish them in the face of oncoming storm clouds (L. Mason in *EWA* 1964: v. 9, 923–4). No doubt there were various cult objects used throughout Micronesia to represent clan deities, perhaps as receivers of food offerings (Linton and Wingert 1946: 71).

These are sparse examples and may reinforce the impression that Micronesian arts were limited in variety by local resources and were not widely related to religion. Certainly they do not equal the scope of arts in the religions of Polynesia and Melanesia. But we should not too readily assume the lack of religious significance of the arts mentioned for Micronesia. First, it may well be that the designs used to ornament objects of practical use had a religious significance over and above their decorative quality, as noted in other Pacific areas; the problem is to unearth the often forgotten symbolism. Secondly, in addition to visual and performing arts there is the literary art of story-telling; throughout Micronesia there is a strong tradition of mythology relating to the ancestors, the land, cosmogony, culture heroes, tricksters and death (Luomala 1987; Poignant 1967: 70–82). Within local traditions, researches into island cultures could well find further connections between religions and arts.

Traditional Micronesia has now been altered by the recent centuries of exposure to influences from Europeans, Japanese and Americans in the different island groups. The example of ancient Gilbertese society shows the 19th-century impact of whalers and then of missionaries of Protestant Christianity, leading to British colonization and finally independence (Kiribati 1979). The classic art forms were music, dancing and poetry, with the arts of sailing also being regarded as gifts of the gods. The Gilbertese passion for outrigger canoes still sees these as works of art. Traditionally the building of a canoe was preceded by invocations to ancestral gods such as Na Areau, 'the first-of-things'. Tufted crests and pennants were attached above the peak of the sail of the canoe to display the family totem and to recall the stories of how the ancestor had been deified (Grimble 1972: ch. 7). Ancestral beliefs often continue alongside Christianity. Recent years have seen some incorporation of Gilbertese culture, music and costume into Christian worship. At the more general level of cultural change, although tourism is not dominant, modern Western influences have some effect: 'Today the dance is still the major form of aesthetic expression, even though performances are put on for commercial purposes' (P. Dark, in Hanson 1990: 262, 248–56). Gilbertese entertainers living in other parts of the Pacific, such as Honiara in the Solomons, perform enthusiastically in their costume but also incorporate pan-Pacific music and dance such as Hawaiian guitar music and the Maori *haka*.

Tikopia

As a conclusion to this chapter we return to Tikopia (R. Firth 1970), the Polynesian outlier in the Melanesian Solomons which was mentioned briefly early in the chapter. It offers some parallel to the small islands of Micronesia with its limited resources, isolation and lack of visual images of religion. In Tikopia the emphasis is on songs, combining music and poetic imagery related to social life in its various aspects. For religious purposes the songs went traditionally with dances and ritual occasions for the 'work of the gods', such as funerals and celebrations of chiefs and pagan deities. The importance of song can be matched in Samoa (Moyle 1988) – probably the original parent culture of Tikopia. Since the conversion of Tikopia to Christianity in the decades from 1923, the old religious songs have been replaced by Christian hymns. In the case of dancing, comparable Christian dances did not replace traditional dances; but the Melanesian Mission of the Anglican church has given its blessing to some secular dance festivals by associating them with saints' days and the church year (Firth 1990: 71–5).

CHAPTER 5

AOTEAROA NEW ZEALAND

The story of man in these islands begins with a picture of brown men sailing. (Oliver 1960: 21)

At the south-west corner of the Polynesian triangle lie the islands named New Zealand from the discovery by the Dutch explorer Tasman in 1642 but discovered by Polynesian Maori settlers centuries earlier. Just how many centuries earlier is not certain. The first Polynesian landfall in Aotearoa may have been made around 800 CE with successive migrations consolidating the settlement of the country by 1000 CE. Oral traditions and genealogies of the Maori were memorized to recall the canoes and ancestral leaders who had come from the homeland of 'Hawaiki'. This is similar to the memories of other Polynesian peoples who looked back to the island home from which their voyaging ancestors had once set out. Hawaiki became pictured in myth as a paradisal beginning and also as the ancestral home to which souls returned at death (Orbell 1991: 3, 66).

While the historical dating and the forms taken by the settlement are matters of ongoing research and some debate, it appears that Aotearoa New Zealand was the last major area to be settled. Into an uninhabited land these Polynesians brought a common heritage of language, religion and social organization linking them with other parts of Polynesia. In the arts of carving some early examples of bone and wood-carving show links with central and eastern Polynesia such as the Marquesas and Austral Islands. For instance, from the far south of NZ, a necklace carved from bone of the NZ giant *moa* bird in the 'archaic' period (900–1200 CE) follows a style of imitation whale-tooth pendants very similar to ones excavated in the Society and Marquesas Islands (Mead 1984: 180, item 15). The wood-carving illustrated here (figure 61), from perhaps 12th–13th century CE and over 2 metres long, was found buried in a swamp at Kaitaia, Northland (the far north of NZ). It shows a squat figure at the centre with beaked monsters at the ends; this central figure has a large head and posture similar to figures on a carving which Captain Cook collected at the Australs in 1768–71 (see Barrow 1972: 49; Hanson 1990: 194–5). With this and other evidence in mind, it is likely that the Polynesians came from the Society and Austral Islands, then through the Cook Islands, to reach Aotearoa New Zealand.

61.   Kaitaia carving, wood, archaic Maori, Northland. Auckland Museum.

The Polynesian heritage was transplanted into a very different setting and here lies the distinctiveness of the New Zealand Maori. First, the islands were large in scope and resources, offering a land area larger than all the other Polynesian Islands put together (see map, figure 62). This shifted the cultural emphasis from that of an ocean-going people of small islands to a land-based people traversing the land rather than the sea. The Maori tribes wove their traditions into the remarkable natural features of the new land with its mountains, volcanoes, lakes and rivers (Orbell 1985). Secondly, the Maori had to acclimatize themselves to the temperate zone, half-way between the tropics and the Antarctic. This led to changes in food patterns, protective clothing, using flax, and different types of housing. Because the climate grew colder in the 14th century CE the majority of the population became concentrated in the northern half of the North Island (Bellwood 1978b: 139). Thirdly, the new country offered an abundance of wood for carving and for elaborate canoes; some of the largest canoes in the world have been those made by Maori carvers from giant trees. Also weapons for tribal warriors were carved from wood, stone and whalebone, while the native 'greenstone' was much sought after in the South Island for treasured ornaments.

Isolated from the Oceanic setting, Polynesian traditions were expressed in new forms by the various Maori tribal groups; especially in the so-called 'classical' Maori period of the 15th–18th century CE, wood-carving and other arts were brought to a high level. Thereafter contact with European civilization and Christianity brought changes in religion and the arts. The population of New Zealand has now become urbanized, as shown in the major cities today on the map; out of approximately 3.5 million people one tenth are Maori and the majority are non-Maori whites (Pakeha). In the latter half of the 20th century there has been a revival of Maori language, arts and culture (Maoritanga). As a result there is a greater sense of continuity with the Maori heritage and an emphasis on 'bi-culturalism' affecting religion, education and the arts. Fortunately it is possible to trace these patterns of change between tradition and modernity in the past two centuries of Aotearoa New Zealand. This chapter provides an opportunity to focus on some of these issues with selected examples.

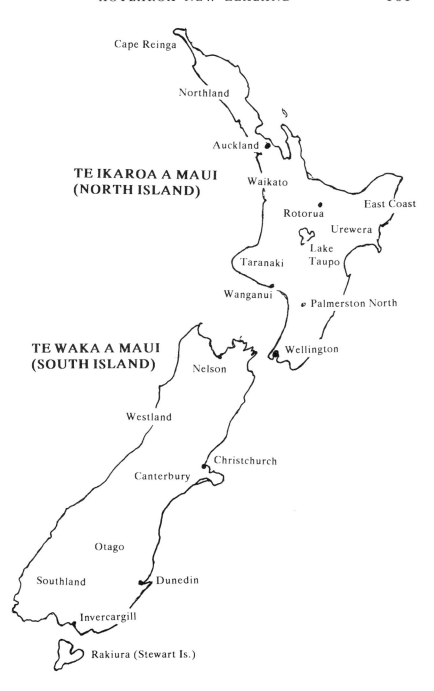

Cape Reinga

Northland

Auckland

**TE IKAROA A MAUI
(NORTH ISLAND)**

Waikato

Rotorua

East Coast

Urewera

Lake
Taupo

Taranaki

Wanganui

Palmerston North

**TE WAKA A MAUI
(SOUTH ISLAND)**

Nelson

Wellington

Westland

Christchurch

Canterbury

Otago

Southland

Dunedin

Invercargill

Rakiura (Stewart Is.)

62.   Map of Aotearoa New Zealand.

Maori ancestral religion

The traditional religion of the Maori people reflects the basic characteristics of primal religions as seen in other religions of the Pacific. The elemental experiences of human life and the natural world are woven into a spiritual conception of the universe. For the Maori world-view the realm of the human was adjacent to the realm of the sacred powers and the realm of the dead; within a holistic cosmology they are not closed systems but realms which interpenetrate one another (Irwin 1984: 16−17). The Polynesian emphasis on hierarchy and descent from the ancestors was developed by Maori oral tradition; long genealogies were memorized, tracing one's line of ancestry back to the primeval beginnings. There was a genealogy of the gods or sacred powers. According to teachings disclosed in the late-19th century this was traced back further to a supreme creator in the highest heaven, the high god Io, known only to those initiated in a secret cult. It is not known whether this was a pre-contact Maori belief or a response of Maori thinkers to Christian teachings of the one God of the Bible (Buck 1949: 531−6; Irwin 1984: 33−5; Alpers 1970: 395−6).

There is, however, no doubt about the pervasive importance of the myth of Rangi and Papa as a foundation story for Maori life and religious world-view (recounted by Grey in 1855). This is not a story of gods creating the world but of the emergence of the world from the primeval parents representing heaven or the sky father (the male Ranginui) and the earth mother (the female Papatuanuku). They were themselves the product of long cycles of emergence from the night. They mated and produced sons but remained locked in sexual embrace in the darkness. The sons rebelled, wanting to escape from the dark by forcing the parents apart to let light in. Eventually one of the sons (Tane, who was to be lord of the forests) standing with his hands like roots on mother earth and his legs upwards, forked like branches, forced Rangi upwards to the heavens. Finally sundered, Rangi and Papa showed their sorrow, like tears, in the falling rain and the rising mists. But light was now let into the world, so that the sons became departmental gods of the sea (Tangaroa), the winds (Tawhiri), food-gathering (Haumia), agriculture (Rongo) and war (Tu). When the brothers fell into strife it was Tu who eventually subdued the others in the service of human power. However the creation of woman and the founding of the human race was attributed to Tane who also obtained essential baskets of knowledge from the heavens. A figure called Tiki appears to be an alternative to Tane as the creative first man.

The importance of this cycle of myths is evident to this day in Maori oratory and arts. As with all myths there can be different versions and applications. For instance, the theme of Rangi and Papa is implied in the figures on the central post of a carved house, shown here (figure 63). The couple in sexual embrace are ancestors of a tribe who are 're-telling by re-living' the ancient story. Similar carvings are found on the storehouse (*pataka*) of a village to enhance the fertility and abundance of food by relating it to the original myth of fertile power in the primeval parents. Otherwise the figures of Rangi and Papa and their sons are not normally depicted in Maori carving, the subject of which is mostly human ancestors.

The several sons became 'gods' (*atua*, spiritual beings) in the sense of sacred powers expressed in their respective departments of the world around. Religious rituals of sacrifice and incantations to them were usually performed at the relevant place — for instance, on the battlefield, where the heart of the first victim would be offered to Tu as god of war. For success in agriculture a freshly dug sweet potato (*kumara*) would be offered to Rongo. Roughly hewn stone images or 'crop gods' were used in some areas such as Taranaki to protect the crop. But if images were used in the open-air rituals they usually were limited to portable 'god-sticks' (*tiki-wananga*); these were about 30cm—40cm long with a sharpened peg for thrusting in the ground, and with a carved head. The example from Wanganui (figure 64) is said to represent Tangaroa with its double face. However, it was not an object of worship in itself but only a temporary abode for the god to occupy with his presence. It was the responsibility of the priestly expert (*tohunga*) to name the identity of the god and to prepare the god-stick with flax fibre cord bound round the peg and the use of red clay and red feathers which symbolized the gods. Similar sticks used in Hawaii show the Polynesian origin. The *tohunga* could hold the stick in his hand or plant it in the ground, attach a string and jerk it a little before each chant to arrest the attention of the god (Barrow 1978: 46; 1969: 104—6).

In the Maori pantheon there were many other gods or sacred powers of various grades such as tribal war gods, family gods and local spirits, sometimes embodied in material objects (Best 1924, 1976: IV—V). There were also evil figures, demons and monsters. Among the latter were the *taniwha*, the water-spirits like dragons or giant lizards which were imagined to be waiting for human prey. An example of this belief is seen in the charcoal drawings on the ceiling of a limestone shelter in South Canterbury (see figure 65). The left figure is over 2 metres long and seems to depict a *taniwha* which has swallowed a man. Other rock-art sites are also found, mainly in the South Island prior to 1500 CE, and include humans, animals and birds as well as mythical creatures (Trotter and McCulloch 1981). Another related figure to be depicted in later wood carvings is the *marakihau*, the merman of fish and human form whose long tongue could drag people down into the water's depths. But some combinations could be beneficent, reflecting the primal picturing of the links between the animal and human. Guardian figures such

63.   Rangi and Papa embracing; wood-carved
house post. Otago Museum (photo).

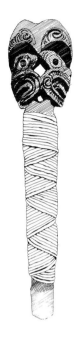

65. Taniwha monster, rock art.
South Canterbury.

64. God-stick (of
Tangaroa?) with
double face.

as the owl (*ruru*) became popular as totemic forms of ancestors who gave warnings through omens.

Turning now to the human ancestors, we have indicated already their central importance in Maori religion and art. One mythical figure combining human and divine as a culture-hero is Maui, famous throughout Polynesia for his trickster activities (Luomala 1949) and for his adventures both creative and fateful. Prometheus-like, he secured fire for humankind, snared the sun to prolong daylight and fished up islands from the sea. However his bold attempt to win immortality by entering the body of the goddess Hine led to his own death and the fate of death thereafter for humanity. These supernatural feats of Maui have been perennially recounted but little depicted in art until post-contact times. The 19th-century house panel carving (figure 66) shows the influence of European realistic representation in depicting Maui hauling up a fish. This alludes to stories of his fishing up what is now called the North Island of Aotearoa New Zealand, the Maori name being *Te Ikaroa-a-Maui*, the long fish of Maui. The South Island was his canoe (*waka*) and Stewart Island at its foot was the anchor (*punga*).

In the case of human ancestors, these have long been depicted in significant places of Maori tribal life. The tribes were warlike and became skilled at

66.   Maui
fishing, house
panel carving.

67.   Gateway image of
ancestor, wood.
Ohinemutu.

building elaborate stockades and fortified villages (*pa*). The gateway and
selected stockade posts round the village would be surmounted by ancestral
images such as the large one here (figure 67) from a village on the shore of
Lake Rotorua. Now in the Auckland museum, it stands 2 metres high, but
originally it was raised 3 metres higher at the gateway to serve as a constant
and impressive reminder of the ever-present ancestor who in this case was a
famous Arawa tribal chief, Pukaki. The small figures of his children set on the
torso also suggest the embracing fertility figures referred to previously; this in
turn relates to the power and fertility of the tribe manifest in the ancestor and
his descendants. The image was not intended as decoration but as a powerful
medium of the protection given by the ancestor's presence. It served to inspire
the people within the village and it was the aim of attacking warriors to
demolish such a defiant and powerful figure in order to capture the *pa*.

   The ancestors are also closely identified with the land. Descent from them
and ownership of the land make local people *tangata whenua,* 'people of the
land' (Metge 1976: ch. 8). Tribal lands remain to this day a basic part of the

Maori sense of identity and a religious symbol (Moore 1989b). To feel one's feet on the land is to have 'a place to stand' (*turanga-waewae*). This is conveyed especially on the village *marae* which is for the Maori the village green or courtyard for people to gather on. In Aotearoa the Maori did not develop the stone platform type of *marae* seen in central and eastern Polynesia, much less the elaborate *heiau* temple-complex which developed late in the Hawaiian Islands. There were indeed some Maori sacred sites called *tuaahu*, such as sacred pools outside the village for rituals of purification and the dedication of children, but otherwise, as in the use of god-sticks, sacred rituals took place on the scene of everyday activity. The village *marae* was not in any way a priestly enclosure or temple site but a ceremonial centre for social, military and political concerns of the gathered people. Religion was expressed, not as something separate but as interwoven with the diffused sacredness of the land and the tribal traditions from the ancestors. Here the notions of *mana* and *tapu* continue to be crucial. In the sense of sacred power and powerful action, *mana* is a spiritual power coming through the chain of ancestors and manifested in the prestige of chiefs and orators. All the tribe depends on this *mana*; but because it can be dangerous as well as beneficent (like high-voltage electricity) it needs to be surrounded by sacred restrictions, *tapu*. These restrictions apply to parts of the body, such as the head; to persons, such as the chief or *tohunga*; to occasions of crisis, such as death; and to places, such as a carved house under construction.

The impressive Maori carved house (*whare whakairo*) should be understood in this light. Its large modern form is a post-contact development; before European influence the central house was that of the chief, who was the focus of the ancestral tradition. The ancestor is the focus and the modern meeting house is still named after an important ancestor; indeed it embodies the ancestor and is symbolically his or her body (Metge 1976: 230). In speeches on the *marae* visitors will address the house along with the people: 'O house! O *marae* of the fathers! O people gathered!'

The great carved house 'Mataatua', originally built in 1872 at Whakatane in the Bay of Plenty, North Island, and now preserved in the Otago Museum (see figure 68), exemplifies this symbolism of the ancestor's body. The facade can be read as a body. At the apex is the *koruru*, the mask-head of the ancestor. (Often this is surmounted by a small image of a warrior.) From the head, the arms slope down as the barge-boards (*maihi*) and these end in parallel markings of the 'fingers'. Pairs of twins are carved on the upright supports on each side – boys on the left, warriors on the right. At the porch the door represents the mouth of the ancestor and the window his eye. Along the roof, the ridge-pole is his backbone and this is supported inside by the central pillar or heart-post (*poutokomanawa*). In front of this stands the image of another warrior chief with large tattooed head and holding his ceremonial club. The

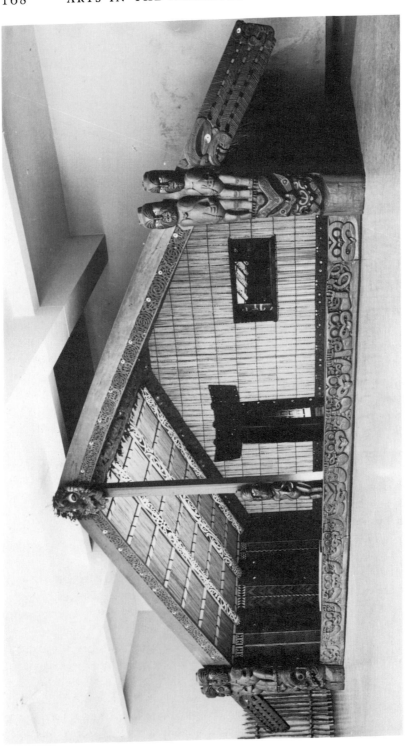

68. *Whare whakairo* (carved house), 'Mataatua'. Exterior, front. Otago Museum (photo).

rafters are the ribs of the ancestor, leading down in the interior to carvings of many ancestral figures with designs referring to genealogies. To be inside the house (figure 69) is to be in the bosom or chest (*poho*) of the ancestor.

Maori art: carving and tattooing

Maori carving has been praised as the highest achievement of Maori art, and the changing attitudes to the post-contact study of it makes an interesting story (Gathercole, in Mead 1979: ch. 11). Although it aroused interest in the early colonial period it was still seen as the art of warlike savages. By the end of the 19th century, when the Maori were often cited as a dying race and culture, efforts were made to record and restore their arts. A large compilation based on photographs of the varieties of arts in social life, ceremonial activities, war and everyday life, with extensive glossaries of Maori words, was published in 1896 by Augustus Hamilton, who was then registrar of the University of Otago in Dunedin and later became director of the Colonial Museum in Wellington. He characterized Maori art as all coming 'under the head of ornament' (Hamilton 1896: 6). One result was the establishment of pseudo-traditional Maori art centred at Rotorua under the 'veil of orthodoxy' (R. Neich, in Mead and Kernot 1983: ch. 16). A half-century later saw carving described as the iconographic expression of Maori conceptions of ancestors, family and human experiences and values: 'Maori carving is the writing of a people who never learned to write' (Phillipps 1955: 3). More recently there have been structuralist interpretations (Jackson 1972; A. Hanson, in Mead and Kernot 1983: ch. 14), seeking to discern a code of meanings and the construction of reality in the visual art. The designs express relationships between human beings, gods and ancestors. In pointing this out, Gathercole remarks that Maori carvers responded to the traumatic changes of the colonial period by producing imposing carved houses. Their efforts were marked by both persistence and inventiveness in incorporating new themes from religion and culture (Gathercole, in Mead 1979: 222–6). Eclecticism was already at work in the 19th century.

Considering the whole range of a thousand years of Maori carving, changes of style are evident from the earliest 'archaic' period coming out of Polynesia, to the 'classical' pre-contact period and to the modern period where steel chisels and new influences arrived. From our knowledge of classical carving traditions, it was believed to be derived from the gods and to be safeguarded by careful training of the experts (*tohunga*) in carving and the related arts of house and canoe construction. For this reason carving was surrounded by *tapu* restrictions, being confined to male carvers, and preceded by rituals at every stage; for instance, incantations (*karakia*) were offered to the god Tane in the forest before the cutting down of trees for carving. Various stories were told

69.   Interior view of 'Mataatua'. Otago Museum (photo).

about an ancestor, Rua, who started the art of carving after seeing images in the carved house of the sea god Tangaroa. Carving had thus an ancient source in a Polynesian god; but Rua's skill was able to improve on this with his lifelike images, so that a proverb asserts: 'The art of carving is the art of Rua'. Wood-carving, as in the case of a war canoe, was painted with red ochre and shark-liver oil, probably because of the preservative qualities of the mixture and the ritual function of the colour red to give spiritual protection. This was attributed to the spilling of the two bloods of Rangi and Papa when they were forced apart at the origin of the world (Neich 1993: vii, 25).

The subsequent development of the techniques, themes and styles of Maori carving have been well described by modern anthropologists and practitioners (Barrow 1969; Mead 1961). Different local styles of carving developed in the tribal-based culture areas of New Zealand (McEwen 1966). It is predominantly a frontal art and because of the importance and sacredness of the human head, displays the typically tattooed face in an enlarged form. The first feature then is the emphasis on the human figure (*tiki*). But secondly, this is depicted with non-human forms such as staring owl-like eyes and huge mouth. Such bird forms suggest an avian element of hybridization (Barrow 1969: 56). Linked with this is the recurring form of the *manaia*, a curious and unexplained creature combining the features of bird, lizard and human – it may be shown with its beak biting the ears or other parts of the body of an ancestor. A third feature of Maori carving is the elaborate use of curvilinear forms, in contrast to earlier rectilinear designs from Polynesia. The spiral was developed into a dominant motif, often as a double spiral with two threads linked at the centre winding outwards. Another recurring motif is the *koru*, a small, curling form suggested by a stalk or fern frond; this is used for many types of surface decoration, including the painted patterns on rafters of a meeting-house.

These features of carving are well displayed on the great canoes (*waka*) which could equal the carved house in quality of workmanship. The prow of the canoe in the Otago Museum has a carved head (figure 70) taken from a war canoe; its out-thrust tongue is a gesture of defiance used in human behaviour and in the war-dance, and here it may well have the further magical function of warding off malignant spirits (Barrow 1978: 51). Further carving using open spiral work was usually featured on the prow, and the stern of the canoe could be even more splendid with large sweeping patterns in wood and drapes of hawk feathers.

A further application of these designs is seen in Maori tattooing (*moko*). Like other forms of 'personal art' such as body-painting in Australia and the PNG Highlands or the elaborate body tattoo of Samoa and the Marquesas, it imprints patterns on the perishable human body. However, they could continue to be preserved after death if families dried the heads, examples of

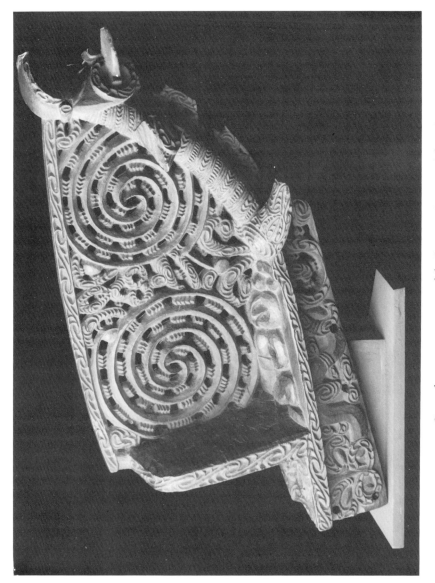

70.   Carved canoe prow, model. Otago Museum (photo).

which are still to be seen in some museums. Europeans in the early 19th century regarded *moko* as 'barbarous' and 'hideous' and with the ending of the old warrior lifestyle Maori men ceased to be tattooed after 1865 (Simmons 1986: 150). Fortunately there are many living examples of *moko* in the 19th century recorded in photographs, in drawings by Major General Horatio Robley and paintings by artists such as Angas, Lindauer and Goldie (Te Riria and Simmons 1989; Simmons 1986). They show a great variety of designs, yet all based on the ancestral patterns (including spirals and *koru*) seen in wood-carved panels and canoes. For men, the patterns covered the face, thighs and buttocks; these are rendered faithfully in the wood-carving of a tattooed ancestor shown in figure 71 which was the central post of a meeting-house. For women, tattoo was confined mainly to the chin and lips. Styles and practices differed according to tribes and family traditions; but the end result was a unique *moko* pattern for each individual, recognizable to others as that person's history and identity. In the early days of European contact, Maori chiefs would draw their *moko* on documents as their personal equivalent of a signature.

Tattooing can be understood as a form of carving on the body. It was a long and painful operation performed by an expert (*tohunga*) with a small chisel and blue-black dye. What induced people to undergo this ordeal? In a fierce warrior society *moko* was one of the marks which a self-respecting member would want to display. But it was more than just socially-imposed fashion or decoration. It had sacred connotations which made the person's body *tapu* while being tattooed; therefore he was fed through a funnel. At the individual level this emphasized the sacredness of the head. Here it is worth noting that Maori culture did not use masks as 'sacred faces' to be worn in rituals; the Maori already had his mask in his *moko* which needed no addition. This was no concealment: 'a Maori of rank did not get his real face until he was tattooed; henceforth the tribal self engraved upon him became his permanent mask' (Schwimmer 1966: 93). At the level of the religious cosmos, the world order is also symbolized in the almost symmetrical designs on either side of the face separated by the split down the middle; as Schwimmer points out, left and right reflect the cosmic dualism of earth and sky. Here then tattooing serves to link the individual to the tribal, ancestral and spiritual dimensions within a sacred cosmos.

The predominance of ancestor figures is seen in the carved panels (*poupou*) lining the interior of a meeting-house (figure 72). A fine example in the late classical style, 1.5m high, it was carved in the mid-19th century at Taupo, in the centre of the North Island. The face shows the typical 'avian' features, with slanted staring eyes made of iridescent *paua* shell and large mouth, with tongue thrust out; a *manaia* figure appears to be linked to one ear. Double spiral designs are carved on the cheeks and lower sides of the body. One

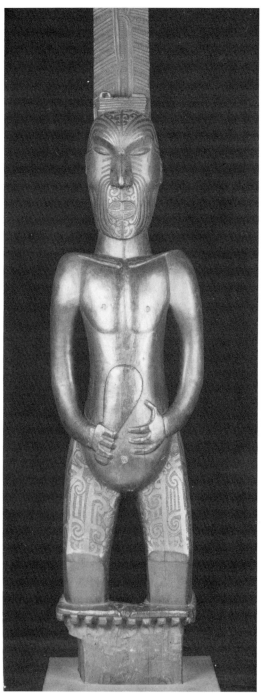

71.   Ancestor, exemplifying tattoo, wood-carving from
meeting-house. Otago Museum (photo).

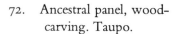

72.   Ancestral panel, wood-   73.   Uenuku, war-god,
      carving. Taupo.   image in wood.
                                          Waikato.

recurring feature of Maori sculpture seen here is the three-fingered hand. This may well derive from the bird-claw incorporated into hybrid forms. Various other explanations have been offered through stories and symbolism read into the number three; but it is likely that artists perpetuated this convention because three fingers were easier to carve and aesthetically pleasing (Mead 1961: 49–50).

Although there are comparatively few carvings depicting the 'gods' of the pantheon, a striking early post-carving from the period 1200–1500 CE was found at a lake in the Waikato district of the North Island in 1906 (see figure 73). This wooden post, overall 267 cm in height, represents Uenuku, the war god of the Waikato tribes. He originated as the rainbow god, a descendant of the great Tu, the warlike son of Rangi and Papa, and was said to have been brought out from Polynesia on the Tainui canoe ancestral to the Waikato. This post was made later and Uenuku's presence was invoked to talk with chief and priest. 'When the Waikato tribes went to war, Uenuku went with them. He was asked to inhabit a small carving which was then carried by the priest into battle' (Simmons, in Mead 1984: 183). This illustrates the reverence for images as means of power, to be guarded carefully by custodians who keep their presence alive in the tribe, and to be called upon for potency and

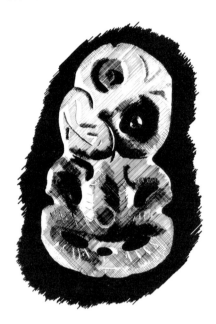

74.   *Hei-tiki,* greenstone pendant.

protection. This accords with the magical protective power expected from the exact recitation of ritual chants.

A final example of types of carving is taken from the greenstone *hei-tiki* (illustrated in figure 74). As already noted, the term *tiki* was the Polynesian term for any carved human figure, including large stone sculptures or Maori ancestral wood-carvings. The *hei-tiki,* however, is a small breast-pendant or neck-ornament in which the compact female figure typically has a large head tilted to one side. It is made of *pounamu,* the distinctive NZ jade or nephrite in varying shades of green. Maori expeditions would journey for long distances to obtain this valued material from remote areas of Otago and the West Coast of the South Island. From the classic age of around the 16th century the stone was used for ornaments which were regarded as precious treasures and heirlooms within a family. Because they have been associated with childbirth and worn by women, it has been suggested that they represented the human embryo as fertility charms; but men wore the *hei-tiki* in the 18th century (Buck 1949: 296). They are to be seen as stylized images of ancestors, and as such they are often valued for their *mana* and called by a personal name, even greeted as people on the *marae*. Here again the ancestors are a continuing presence.

It is especially through carving, including tattooing, that Maori art bridges the unseen world of ancestral spirits and the visible world of human faces and tribal life. As Schwimmer points out, it expresses the unifying world-order:

To the abstract patterns of these carvings the Maori artist brought his consciousness of the tight genealogical interlinking of all parts of the universe – the opulence and denseness of the spirals, showing how in his view the world was a potent, convoluted unity. (Schwimmer 1966: 97)

Other arts: decorative, ritual, performance

The arts of carving were prestigious and their *mana* confined their production to male artists. Yet they were surrounded and complemented by other art forms, including those allotted to women. The role of women is indicated in the carved lintel placed over the entrance to a meeting-house (figure 75). Here is a place with sacred associations and *tapu* restrictions surrounding *mana*. But there are occasions for lifting these restrictions and making life normal without being subject to dangers. The power of women to make things *noa*, or ordinary, has often been attributed to women as lacking *mana* and thereby 'neutralizing' *tapu*. But, as Bronwyn Elsmore has pointed out, examples of Maori highborn women in leadership show that they are not excluded from having *mana*. Rather, they have inherent power to bridge the temporal and the spiritual and thereby are able to channel *tapu* into the world of the spirit. Here, then, the female is complementary to the male in making life regular and everyday once again. When this principle is applied to the arts, males have charge of those related to the ancestral and supernatural world; women have charge of those related to the earth and domestic life. Instead of carving in the hard materials of wood, stone and bone, women use the soft materials such as flax to weave mats, baskets and cloaks. Instead of curvilinear designs they use rectilinear ones, as seen in the decorative latticework (*tukutuku*) where the stitches make patterns; these are placed in meeting-houses as sections between the ancestral carved panels.

Besides these more domestic arts of decoration, there are other arts involved in the ancestral rituals and carved treasures. Of first importance is the spoken word, a necessary companion to the iconography of visual images. In introducing the traditional treasures (*taonga*) of Maori art for the great Te Maori exhibition, S.M. Mead explains that these are not just 'art objects' but highly prized possessions to which is attached *korero*, meaning text or story. For instance, a genealogy staff has been the occasion of incantations during its making, then ritual ceremonies and speeches which all add to its *mana* through the personalities of the artists and orators (Mead 1984: 22). Maori oratory was an important part of an oral culture with a sophisticated use of language as an art form, full of vivid metaphors, proverbs and allusions to ancestral tradition. Story-telling and poetry likewise shared in these.

An important occasion which involved these arts was the *tangihanga*, the funerary rites which commenced with loud wailing and weeping and

75.   Lintel, wood-carved, featuring woman over entrance to house. Otago Museum (photo).

76. Carved coffin-box for bones of
child, 16th cent. Northland.

proceeded for several days with much oratory. The *tangi* continues into
modern times, with some modifications, as the most distinctive expression of
Maori religious life (D. Turner 1975). In pre-Christian times persons of chiefly
rank could be buried in a special wood-carved tomb. In any case, two years
later the body was exhumed and the bones scraped for a second burial in the
final, hidden, resting-place. For this a coffin-box could contain the bones, as in
the case of the illustrated carved box (figure 76) found in a cave in the North
Auckland district, possibly dating from the 16th century. With its curious
carved face, the small box was for the skull and bones of a child whose spirit
(*wairua*) would join the ancestors in the spirit land of Hawaiki at Te Reinga in
the far north.

The arts of music accompanied many social and ritual occasions, mainly in
vocal form. Since many of these dealt with ancestral names they were
regarded as *tapu* and guarded within the tribe; a parallel is seen here to the
Australian Aboriginal songs. In the case of the Maori, songs of this more ritual
type were recited – for instance, the mythical chants recounting cosmogonic
beginnings, religious incantations and spells (*karakia*) and songs for *haka* or
dances. As in other parts of Polynesia, recitation was in a rhythmical
monotone and had to be sustained in one breath by a group's continuous
sound. Those songs actually sung to music were *waiata*, covering mainly
laments for the dead with some lullabies, love-songs and occasional pieces for

entertainment. Many of these traditional songs have been studied and revived (McLean and Orbell 1990). In the case of traditional Maori musical instruments, however, such as types of bugle and flute, these are no longer played. Maori choirs and popular musical entertainers employ modern instruments such as guitars.

Song-and-dance performances are among the most popular forms used by modern Maori concert parties – notably the female *poi*-dance, twirling decorated balls on string, and the male *haka* or posture-dance. In particular the fierce war-dance (*peruperu*) attracts attention with the rhythm of feet stamping in unison, rolling eyes, out-thrust tongue and grimacing face. This was designed to terrify the enemy with verbal threats and the brandishing of weapons. In the various types of *haka*, whether war-like or gentle in purpose, there is much use of body-shuddering and quivering arms and hands. The origin of this is accounted for in a myth of the sun, Ra, whose two wives included the Summer Maid and her daughter Tanerore whose dancing is seen in the summer months: 'Now Tanerore is the name applied to the quivering appearance of the atmosphere as seen on hot summer days. From that origin sprang all the haka of the world' (Schwimmer 1966: 88–9). Modern entertainment has continuity here with traditional arts and the complementary roles of male and female.

Maori tradition and religious change

Maori culture had already been affected by European contact for several decades when Maori chiefs signed the Treaty of Waitangi in 1840 and Britain assumed sovereignty of New Zealand. The Maori people were quick and adaptable in responding to innovations in technology, weapons, trade and new lifestyles. Through Christian missions they became literate and were progressively converted to Christianity. At the same time much of the traditional culture was eroded, such as *tapu* observance and tattooing, as we have noted. The arrival of many white settlers and the resulting land wars of the 1860s led to antagonism and the decline of Maori confidence as they were reduced to a minority culture; yet the Maori people survived and Maori religious life and the arts continued in new forms.

An early example of successful integration of Christianity and Maori art is the Maori church named 'Rangiatea' at Otaki, north of Wellington. The Anglican missionary Octavius Hadfield had won the trust of the people through his mastery of the Maori language and also gained the support of the famous and much feared chief Te Rauparaha who was interested in Christianity. While the name 'Rangiatea (Abode of the Absolute)' referred to the ancestral Hawaiki, the symbolism of the church was planned to signify not the ancestors but the new faith. The great totara logs were hauled to the

77.   Virgin Mary and Christ child; wood-carving 1845 by Patoromu
Tamatea. Auckland Museum.

site to provide three central pillars symbolizing the Trinity (Shaw 1991: 22).
The impressive church was constructed in 1848–51.

From the same period in another area, lack of understanding led to failure.
At Maketu in the Bay of Plenty a Maori carver in 1845 offered his version of
the Virgin and Child to the Catholic chapel (figure 77). It combined the
typical postures of European religious art with traditional Maori features – the
large head, three fingers and tattooing on the faces and bodies. The latter led
to it being rejected by the European priest who saw only its associations with
war which would denigrate the Virgin Mary and the saviour Jesus. But the
artist's intention was to elevate the Virgin by giving her the full facial tattoo
which made the female completely *tapu*. The three diamonds on the fingers
signified the Trinity and the child was marked as the supreme *ariki* (lord or
chief): 'The carving itself expresses the new unity of the old Maori religion
and the new' (Simmons 1986: 128).

These examples illustrate the readiness for innovation in Maori art, given
favourable circumstances. Out of the following traumatic years of the land

wars some further efforts at innovation emerged. When the wars ended in 1872 the militant leader Te Kooti implemented his prophetic vision of the Maori as Israelites in a new and peaceful religious movement, the Ringatu Church. As seen elsewhere in the Pacific, such movements emerge from the tension between a primal religious culture and a world religion such as Christianity. Not only is there a new mixture from the two traditions, but prophet leaders bring new teachings to answer contemporary needs in the changing society. This can be seen in three important movements based on Maori prophets in the later-19th and early-20th centuries (Colless and Donovan 1985; Greschat 1980; Elsmore 1985). The expression of religion in art forms varies with each movement. In the case of Ringatu, Te Kooti encouraged innovative art in meeting-houses such as Rongopai (in the Poverty Bay area of the East Coast) which served as a Ringatu church. Whereas traditional carving had always been the sacred norm from the ancestors, now painting was admitted, drawing on representations of the land and nature and also on events of local and national history, indicating a linear view of historical time (R. Neich, in Hanson 1990: 164–83; Neich 1993: chs 5, 7). Such innovations tended to be ignored by the official revival of traditional Maori art; or they were regarded as interesting examples of 'folk art' (Taylor 1988).

Innovation of a different sort again was introduced by the prophet Rua for his 'New Jerusalem' in the remote Urewera country. In 1908 he built a circular meeting-house with an outdoor pulpit; the exterior decoration used red and black designs from playing-cards which were given symbolic meaning; the King of Clubs was the coming King, Rua the Messiah, *Mihaia* (Binney et al. 1979: 47–9). The much more influential Ratana movement which began near Wanganui in 1918 built a temple and churches with little concern for traditional Maori art because that belonged, along with many customs and tribal divisions, to the old and passing order. Instead, Ratana offered a form of Christianity for Maori people across the nation, expressed in political and social action as well as in church rallies using band music and uniforms as expressions of the church in the modern world (see figure 78).

More recently there have been efforts to renew and develop the links between Christianity and Maori art first explored in the mid-19th century. A striking example is the modern Maori church, St. Michael's, built in 1981–2 at Palmerston North (figure 79). The carver and director was a Maori pastor of the Anglican communion whose wife supervised the *tukutuku* work; various groups assisting with the construction and working-bees made it an ecumenical and cooperative venture. The pattern of the church is that of the traditional Maori meeting-house on a *marae* with its functions relating to teaching, life and death. But as a Christian house of worship it is not limited to the basis of tribal kinship. Therefore the apex of the facade does not feature

78. Ratana Temple, built 1928, Wanganui district. Sunday service, band parade, 1964. (Photo, A.C. Moore.)

79. St. Michael's church exterior. Palmerston North. (Photo, A.C. Moore.)

a warrior figure but a cross. Beneath it, instead of the head of the ancestor is a canoe prow to signify the Church as a ship captained by Christ, with the sternpost as the spire above the sanctuary at the other end of the church. Further use of traditional designs such as *koru* shapes, in the porch and interior panels, is intended to symbolize Christian faith and life and to include both Maori and Pakeha under the covering embrace of Christ. Innovation and adaptation go along with tradition here.

These are mainly instances of Maori efforts to retain their spiritual and cultural identity while adapting to changes introduced and accepted largely from Western culture and Christianity. But the process is not entirely one-way. At first, of course, the European perception of the Maori was that of the 'civilized' looking down on the 'savage', whether as a noble savage or fascinating curiosity. This colours the depictions of the Maori in European art, with gradual changes developing from the 19th to the 20th century (Bell 1980; Dittmer 1907). In recent years leading Pakeha artists such as Colin McCahon and the abstract artist Gordon Walters (Ross and Simmons 1989) have drawn inspiration from Maori tradition and art, not just for *genre* studies of Maori life but for sharing in and learning from the culture.

In relation to the Maori sense of identity between these 'two worlds', Michael King, as a Pakeha, cites with admiration the words of a remarkable Maori woman leader, Te Puea Herangi, who said in 1949:

> The language, history, crafts and traditions of the Maori should be an essential part of the curriculum throughout the country . . . . Unity of Maori and Pakeha can only grow from each sharing the worthwhile elements in the other's culture. (cited in Oliver 1981: 301; see King 1985: ch. 6)

This vision is a fitting preface to the emergence of modern Maori artists in the later 20th century.

Modern Maori artists and biculturalism

Traditional carving can be a spring of inspiration for moving forward into a distinctive New Zealand style. This has been boldly affirmed by Sidney Mead, for whom the revival of Maori carving should have two main functions: 'Firstly, the satisfaction of the Maori spirit and secondly the creation of a new New Zealand carving tradition, to which both Maori and Pakeha contribute and from which both derive aesthetic and spiritual satisfaction' (Mead 1961: 8). Developments in the following three decades have not produced any one distinctive NZ style, yet they have fulfilled something of the spirit of the proposal both in the Maori cultural renaissance and in the bicultural impact of modern Maori artists.

'Biculturalism implies the public recognition of two indigenous cultures, Maori and Pakeha, as being of central importance to the national life of Aotearoa-New Zealand' (Mulgan 1989: 149). It might be objected that most societies today are increasingly multicultural. But in NZ the term 'bicultural' signifies not so much cultures as the two peoples living in one country, with equal rights for Maori and Pakeha as rooted in the historic Treaty of Waitangi, 1840. Modern Pakeha writers who have worked with Maori people stress the need for mutual understanding and the sharing of perspectives in order for Maori and Pakeha to live together (King 1985: 172). The Pakeha needs to make the effort to appreciate the importance of the land, tribal traditions and spirituality for the Maori (Ritchie 1992: ch. 5). These differences can be accepted within one society if there are shared social and political institutions for life together. But also there must be shared symbols, in addition to the distinctive symbols, and here lies the significance of artists who draw on the cultural and religious resources of both Maori and Pakeha.

Modern Maori artists have broken through the barriers which relegated Maori art to the traditional ethnic domain of anthropologists and museums. For 'fine art' in the accepted European sense of progressive international art, one went to the art gallery institutions. This compartmentalization was changed by the growing sense of Maori identity and aspirations after World War II. Revised teaching of Maori 'arts and crafts' led on to new and innovative work by encouraging young artists in several fields, so that by the 1960s a survey could describe 'Modern trends in Maori art forms' (in Schwimmer 1968: 205–16). In a few years these artists had become public figures with substantial achievements covered in art books and exhibitions (Mataira 1984; Nicholas and Kaa 1986; Bett 1986: ch. 15). An important catalyst was the leading NZ painter Colin McCahon who used Christian symbols and Biblical words in his paintings, with major works in 1970 and 1975 on Parihaka and the Urewera, the places of famous Maori prophets (Brown 1984; Johnston 1992). McCahon, as a Pakeha painter, thus gave legitimation to religious and Maori material in the established art world. The travelling *Te Maori* exhibition of 1984–86 heightened consciousness of the traditional art as living spiritual possessions of the Maori (Mead 1984).

Among the modern Maori artists, Cliff Whiting is a notable influence. He himself acknowledges his bicultural heritage; Pakeha art education at the Dunedin Teachers College in the 1950s had broken through the restrictions of traditional rural-based art and encouraged him to experiment with modern art. As an art teacher he has explored new techniques such as multi-media works and teamwork associating women's *tukutuku* panel work along with the male arts of carving to give harmony (Nicholas and Kaa 1986: 14; Whiting 1992). He also appreciates the interchange between the two value-

80.   Cliff Whiting, *Te Wehenga*, mural 1969–75. Now in National Library,
Wellington. (Photo, A.C. Moore.)

systems of traditional Maori religion and Western Christianity. Maori are
masters of such dualities and can move in and out freely, doing a 'Christian
thing' then a 'Maori thing'. For instance the Rangi and Papa story represents
Maori cosmology and genealogy through a map of order of the natural
world, not for worshipping the 'gods'. Whiting has depicted this in a splendid
mural (figure 80) produced by a team under his leadership for a large *marae* in
1969–75; it is now available to a wider public in the reading room of the
National Library, Wellington. Rangi and Papa are not shown, since they are
pushed apart by Tane, standing on his head, to achieve the dividing of heaven
from earth ('Te Wehenga'). He and his brothers give order to the world.

The Maori myths of origins again provide the theme for a major
commission by Whiting at the Meteorological Service building in Wellington (see figure 81). For this secular Government office, the richly coloured
mural at the entrance depicts the weather in the figure of one of Tane's
brothers, the sacred power of the winds, 'Tawhiri-Matea'. Here he is the
centre figure carved in kauri wood, wrestling with his 'turbulent offspring',
the four winds shown as blue spiral forms. Through this, Whiting relates the
scientific task of weather recording and forecasting to the forces of nature as
experienced by humans in the living cosmos. Whiting also expresses his Maori
sense of lineage from the ancestral powers by identifying himself with

81.   Cliff Whiting, line drawing of *Tawhiri Matea*, 1984.

Tawhiri through a symbolic signature on the body: 'You look at this mural and you look at who I am' (Pannett 1984).

In the following years, Whiting has returned increasingly to his Maori roots, for instance in commissioned works showing more traditional wood sculptures of tattooed men. For the reconstructed Maori wing of the Otago Museum in Dunedin he guided the work of local groups of carvers in 1990 to produce an archway entrance called *Nga Waka Tipuna*. This features three ancestral canoes, with their captains, which brought the first Maori settlers to the Otago district. Whiting's work illustrates well the mixing of modern with traditional art forms as well as the bicultural realities of life for Maori people today.

In addition to such male artists working in this way, Maori women artists have increasingly come to the fore, by-passing restrictions from the past. Robyn Kahukiwa has painted the forms of the ancestors to express her re-discovered Maori identity through the ancestors, the land and the people (Nicholas and Kaa 1986: 37). An exhibition of her paintings of 'women of strength' from the past, 'Wahine Toa', has been reproduced in book form with the well-known Maori writer, Patricia Grace (Kahukiwa and Grace 1984). Some women artists have developed the traditional arts of women's work by weaving and creating innovative installations. Others, such as Emily Karaka, have developed artworks as political protests for Maori rights (Ihimaera 1991).

What is the significance of these modern bicultural artists? They unite a Maori heritage with Western culture and art forms. Often they expose the tensions felt by Maori people in a Pakeha society. These tensions between Maori spirituality and ancestral identity, on the one hand, and Western values both Christian and secular on the other hand, do pose problems (Moore 1987:

40–3). What then do these artists achieve? First, it can be said that by expressing these feelings and tensions in art they bring them powerfully to the awareness of both Maori and Pakeha. This does not solve the problems but instead transposes the conflicts and literal oppositions on to a new plane of the artistic imagination and symbolism; there the viewer has the chance of gaining a fresh view of the issues and empathy with what was previously unacceptable or incomprehensible. Secondly, these bicultural artists, by acknowledging their roots in two worlds, help to bridge the gap and to serve as role-models for those seeking new paths for the future. Thirdly, their use of primal traditions of art and religion provides roots and a sense of identity for people threatened by the rootlessness of a bland consumer culture. Their art often has an appeal for Westerners because of the rich use it makes of the mythical imagination. Fourthly, their work resonates with the emphasis on bicultural approaches which many museums are seeking to implement. These were discussed by Whiting, Kaeppler and Ames at the 1990 Taonga Maori conference (Cultural Conservation 1990).

Finally, it is important that these issues of biculturalism be viewed in the wider context of the whole Pacific area. The human settlement of Aotearoa New Zealand began with the Polynesian landfall. In the 20th century there has been a 'rediscovery' of Polynesia both by Pakeha and by Maori through cultural renaissance. This wider involvement in the Pacific offers a more comprehensive and challenging setting than parochialism can supply. Where this leads must remain open for the future. As Allen Curnow's poem *The Unhistoric Story* reminds us:

And whatever islands may be
Under or over the sea,
It is something different, something
Nobody counted on. (Curnow 1960: 203–4)

CHAPTER 6

CONCLUSION: THE FUTURE OF ARTS IN RELIGIONS OF THE PACIFIC

One must hope that, increasingly, the Polynesians become the makers of their own future. (Gathercole et al. 1979: 74)

Indeed, one is moved to affirm the hope of this writer after his summary of the impact of the Western world on Polynesia with its debilitating effect on cultural continuity and many art forms. In covering the major regions of the Pacific in this book we have sought to appreciate both the traditional art forms of religions in their life-setting and also the changes which have led to decline and innovation in these arts. By way of conclusion we now ask 'What of the future?' In attempting to find some answers we are not seeking to compress the variety of arts and religions in the Pacific into some homogenized blend or into a few theoretical principles. Nor do we seek to idealize the effects of these arts either in their traditional or in their modern forms. We do well to start with some negative thinking. What are the problems and tensions which are of concern now and are likely to cloud the future?

First, the traditional basis of arts in the Pacific has been religious and connected with the whole life of the culture concerned, as was noted in the first chapter. But this basis has been undermined by Western contact, bringing not only Christianity but also secular values which marginalize traditional standards in religion and the arts. The arts may be further debased by production for outsiders and commercial gain, even though there are some more positive results from tourism. The pressure is then to present a bland form of entertainment which purports to represent the 'happy Pacific way' but which in reality has lost the integral connections with both traditional arts and modern experiences of Pacific peoples.

This leads, secondly, to a tension between the pleasing front presented to tourists and the underlying realities of life. As Trompf points out (1991: 271) the name 'Pacific' means 'peaceful', but the realities are full of problems and conflicts. Racist attitudes, inter-tribal feuds, forms of religious fanaticism, crime and violence in society and political corruption raise their heads in 'the happy isles of Oceania' as well as in other parts of the world. A short-term traveller such as Paul Theroux (1992) can observe this and write shrewdly and entertainingly of the realities he encounters. More searching in the long run, however, are the reports of people who know the Pacific from the inside as indigenous citizens or as expatriates who have dedicated years of their lives to work such as teaching, administration, industry and religious ministry. 'How many sources of truth?' 'How many cultures?' These questions about religion and culture, and others, are well introduced by Ron Crocombe (1973; 1992) of the University of the South Pacific and after 20 years are still important questions to work at. Related to these is a further source of tension, within the field of religious changes in the mainly Christian tradition. Amid increasing social changes, 'new religious groups' come promising salvation with an apocalyptic emphasis. Usually opposed to traditional cultures with their arts and also rejecting ecumenical cooperation with the mainline Christian churches, these formerly 'fringe' groups have grown rapidly in the last 30 years to reach an average of 18 per cent in the population of the Pacific Islands (Ernst 1994).

Thirdly, there is a tension between the ideals of educational development in the Pacific and frequent failure to fill the void left by modernity in the enduring areas of the arts, religious values and cultural life. Education systems tend to develop a life of their own, especially if based on imported models; in the competition for success through examination results the majority may be deprived of valuable traditions from their own cultures. Here, knowledge of the arts and religion should be inculcated 'for life's sake' and related to the problems to be faced in the world of today. Otherwise they become mere marginal frills for leisure time.

These problems and tensions are deep-seated and no easy solutions are to be expected. Yet there are more positive signs and resources which may lead towards the renewal of traditional arts and their religious inspiration. Foremost is the presence of a number of creative artists who are themselves deeply concerned with this renewal and have already achieved some recognition in their work for churches, public institutions and art education. We have mentioned some examples of such artists' work in the preceding chapters. Here the name of Frank Haikiu (see figure 83) also deserves mention as a sculptor in the Solomon Islands, originally from the island of Bellona and now based in Honiara. He has done fine artwork for the Roman Catholic cathedral in Honiara, combining a representational style with the Solomons skill in wood and decoration. More recently he has developed modern stylized forms of traditional Solomons figures such as the shark spirit. He has during the last 20 years visited the other major areas of the Pacific, as well as Canada, thus extending his own vision and skill in wood sculpture. He thus exemplifies the artist who is 'pan-Pacific' in his understanding while rooted

82.   Frank Haikiu, artist, at his gallery in Honiara, Solomon Is. (Photo, A.C. Moore).

in his own traditions of the Solomons; he is able to go beyond the conventionalized tourist market and provide opportunities for creative art.

Support for such artwork has come from churches and institutions of education and business (such as banks) from time to time. It is important that such support be continued in new ways, to supplement the emphasis on traditional art which must be the concern of the museums. Encouragement also comes from 'overseas', both through purchasers of artworks and through members of organizations such as the Pacific Arts Association who are scattered over the rest of the world as well as over the Pacific area. Important centres for 'pan-Pacific' resources and education are Honolulu and Suva. For instance, Suva is a convenient centre of communications for travel in the south and central Pacific; its University of the South Pacific has branches in other regions of the Pacific; it has significant centres for theological study at the Pacific Theological College and Pacific Regional Seminary. At these institutions there is a growing concern to draw on the arts of the various Pacific regions from which students are drawn and to further religious cooperation in the Pacific (Afeaki et al. 1983; Johnson-Hill 1993). At the more general level of sharing in the arts and performances of the various cultures, the Pacific Arts Festival has been held since 1972 in Suva and then in other Pacific centres at about four-yearly intervals, the most recent being in Rarotonga 1992 (*PAJ* 1993, 7: 67–71). Thousands of performers and spectators participate in the offering of distinctive regional art forms within a welcoming framework based on a pan-Pacific consciousness (Tausie 1979: ch. 5).

In this book it is appropriate to point out the positive contribution of the academic study of the world's religions. The 'subject-field' of Religious Studies is concerned to view the whole field of religions by the careful use of historical, comparative and other research methods in order to understand religions as a universal human phenomenon. As we have observed in the first chapter, the primal religions of the Pacific have been a significant area of study as well as the great inter-continental religions. In this book we have sought to study these religions in relation to the human response and life-situation of the Pacific peoples, our focus being especially on the response through their arts. If the creative arts are the 'soul of a people' (Crocombe 1973: ch. 15), it is important to make an effort to understand them and to empathize with them as far as possible. It is hoped that the approach used in this book will serve these ends.

Education has become a significant part of modernization and 'development' in the Pacific (Garrett, in Afeaki et al. 1983: 192–3). What could be the effect of Religious Studies as outlined here? I suggest two valuable contributions to education for the future. For a world where increasingly different religions and world-views meet, a study which encourages understanding and empathy can reduce the danger of fanaticism and encourage a positive tolerance of other views. Of course there can be no guarantee of this result, any more than an academic subject can prescribe moral goals for its students; but education has the opportunity of widening our human sympathies in all directions, including religion, without requiring a narrow exclusivist stance. Secondly, a wider study of the world's religions will enrich the local cultures and religions by taking them out of parochial isolation and providing a global context. This may be viewed by some as a threat which relativizes one's own religion by swamping it with a host of other views. But comparison need not have this result; it may be accepted in terms of understanding the wider links which illuminate and extend one's present vision. As we have sought to show, the arts of primal religions may be valued as vital forms of expression in the changed modern setting. Whatever one's view of religion may be, there is something to be learned from this approach to the religions of the Pacific area and the global context in which we now live.

It has been a central thrust of this book to relate the arts and religions of the Pacific to the life-experiences of the peoples concerned. We recall the Australian Aboriginal arts relating to the land and the Dreaming, Melanesian masks and celebrations of biocosmic fertility, Polynesian tattooing and carvings related to the ancestral powers of the departments of life. These are to be seen as 'symbols of life' — to use the evocative phrase of Mary MacDonald (in Mantovani 1984). Primal religions the world over have used symbolism from the natural world on which human life depends: sky, sun, moon, waters, stone, earth, blood, vegetation and agriculture (Eliade 1958; Dillistone 1986). Such symbols continue to be potent sources of energy in religious life and to enrich the imaginative forms of the arts. The enrichment applies not only to the Pacific peoples themselves but also to newcomers to their symbolic worlds who find a new awareness of symbolism deepened in their own religion and cultural world-view. To share in these symbols of life can place one's rituals, sacred places and arts in a 'larger universe of meaning' (D. Cave 1993: 123; chaps 3 and 5). Religious symbols are thereby a means of relating individuals and groups to a living cosmos, the microcosm to the macrocosm. They also relate isolated local cultures to the extended Pacific and wider world.

Academic study alone does not change attitudes or solve the world's problems. Nor will the study of the arts of religions directly provide solutions to the tensions outlined above. Yet the example of modern Maori artists suggests that art can provide a fresh view of the tensions and help to bridge the gap between literally opposed positions and concepts. The artist finds ways to probe and to energize.

We choose a final example for this book from a young artist of Samoan family origin living in Invercargill in the far south of NZ. Lyle Penisula elsewhere has painted an impressive stylized Crucifixion which incorporates Samoan tattoo patterns along with the crown of thorns as marks of Christ's suffering. In the painting shown here (figure 84) entitled *Christ, it ain't easy* (1990) he turns his focus on suffering as a social problem. Here is a youth, probably a Samoan with whose figure the artist identifies, sitting despondently on a street pavement. He has a beer bottle beside him and looks dejected and lonely, with the alienation felt by many unemployed young people. Maybe he could be helped out of this to find some direction. But the church at the right seems dark, distant and judgemental; it is separated from the youth by the wall where he sits. It is then that we begin to see that words are written on the wall and the pavement, but the words are indistinct. At last we come to decipher his message:

> How can I go forward if I don't know
> which way I'm facing?

Viewers are left to think on this human question.

The words have continued to fascinate and even to haunt the writer while viewing the painting over the past four years at the Otago University Library. Readers are invited to ponder them in relation to the arts of the religions of Oceania.

83. Lyle Penisula, *Christ, it ain't easy*, painting 1990. c.80×160cm. University of Otago Library (photo).

84.   Pacific seafarers: display window, Otago Museum.

REFERENCES

Adam, Leonhard. 1948. *Primitive Art*. Penguin Books, Melbourne.

Aerts, Theo. 1984. 'Christian Art from Melanesia', in *Bikmaus: A Journal of Papua New Guinea Affairs, Ideas and the Arts*, vol. V, pp. 47–83. Institute of PNG Studies, Port Moresby.

Afeaki, Emiliana, Crocombe, Ron and McClaren, John (eds). 1983. *Religious Cooperation in the Pacific Islands*. University of the South Pacific, Suva.

Alpers, Antony. 1970. *Legends of the South Sea: the world of the Polynesians seen through their myths and legends, poetry and art*. Whitcombe and Tombs, Wellington.

Amishai-Maisels, Ziva. 1985. *Gauguin's Religious Themes*. Garland, New York.

Andersen, Johannes C. 1969 (1928). *Myths and Legends of the Polynesians*. C.E. Tuttle, Tokyo.

Archey, Gilbert. 1965. *The Art Forms of Polynesia*. Bulletin of the Auckland Institute and Museum, No. 4, Auckland.

Archey, Gilbert. 1966. 'Polynesia', 'Polynesian Cultures', in *EWA*, vol. XI, 438–66.

Armstrong, Robert Plant. 1971. *The Affecting Presence: an essay in humanistic anthropology*. University of Illinois Press, Urbana.

Atlas of the South Pacific. 1986. NZ Government Printing Office, Wellington.

Attenborough, David. 1976. *The Tribal Eye*. British Broadcasting Corporation, London.

Baaren, Th. P. van. 1968. *Korwars and Korwar Style: Art and ancestor worship in North-West New Guinea*. Mouton, The Hague.

Badger, Geoffrey. 1988. *The Explorers of the Pacific*. Kangaroo Press, Kenthurst.

Bahn, Paul G. and Flenley, John. 1992. *Easter Island: Earth Island*. Thames & Hudson, London.

Barber, Laurie. 1989. *New Zealand: A Short History*. Century Hutchinson, Auckland.

Barbier, Jean Paul and Newton, Douglas. 1988. *Islands and Ancestors: Indigenous Styles of Southeast Asia*. Prestel Verlag, München.

Barrow, Terence. 1969. *Maori Wood Sculpture of New Zealand*. A.H. & A.W. Reed, Wellington.

Barrow, Terence. 1972. *Art and Life in Polynesia*. Reed, Wellington.

Barrow, Terence. 1978 (1982). *Maori Art of New Zealand*. A.H. & A.W. Reed, Wellington; UNESCO Press, Paris.

Barrow, Terence. 1979. *The Art of Tahiti and the Neighbouring Society, Austral and Cook Islands*. Thames and Hudson, London.

Beckwith, Martha W. 1970 (1940). *Hawaiian Mythology*. University of Hawaii Press, Honolulu.

Beckwith, Martha W. 1972 (1951). *The Kumulipo: A Hawaiian Creation Chant*. University Press of Hawaii, Honolulu.

Beier, Ulli and Kiki, Albert M. 1970. *Hohao: The uneasy survival of an art form in the Papuan Gulf*. Nelson, London.

Beit-Hallahmi, Benjamin. 1989. *Prolegomena to the Psychological Study of Religion.* Bucknell University Press, Lewisburg.

Bell, Leonard. 1980. *The Maori in European Art.* A.H. & A.W. Reed, Wellington.

Bellwood, Peter. 1978a. *Man's Conquest of the Pacific: The Prehistory of Southeast Asia and Oceania.* Collins, Auckland

Bellwood, Peter. 1978b. *The Polynesians: Prehistory of an island people.* Thames and Hudson, London.

Berger, Peter L. 1967. 'Religious Institutions', 329–79, in *Sociology: an introduction.* Ed. N.J. Smelser, Wiley, New York.

Berger, Peter L., Berger, Brigitte and Kellner, Hansfried. 1974. *The Homeless Mind: Modernization and Consciousness.* Penguin Books, Harmondsworth.

Berger, Peter L. and Luckmann, Thomas. 1966. *The Social Construction of Reality.* Doubleday, Garden City.

Berndt, R.M. 1974. *Australian Aboriginal Religion.* E.J. Brill, Leiden.

Berndt, R.M. and C.H. 1964 (1985). *The World of the First Australians.* Ure Smith, Sydney.

Berndt, Ronald M. and Catherine H. with Stanton, John E. 1982. *Aboriginal Australian Art: A visual perspective.* Methuen Australia, Sydney.

Berndt, R.M. and Phillips, E.S. 1973. *The Australian Aboriginal Heritage: An Introduction through the Arts.* Ure Smith, Sydney. (With LP recordings of didjeridu and songs.)

Best, Elsdon. 1976 (1924); 1982. *Maori Religion and Mythology*, parts 1 and 2. Government Printer, Wellington.

Bett, Elva. 1986. *New Zealand Art: A Modern Perspective.* Reed Methuen, Auckland.

Binney, Judith, Chaplin, G. and Wallace, C. 1979. *Mihaia: The Prophet Rua Kenana and His Community at Maungapohatu.* Oxford University Press, Wellington.

Bodrogi, Tibor. 1959. *Oceanic Art.* Corvina, Budapest.

Bowra, C.M. 1963. *Primitive Song.* New American Library, New York.

Brake, Brian, McNeish, James and Simmons, David. 1979. *Art of the Pacific.* Oxford University Press.

Brown, Gordon H. 1984. *Colin McCahon: Artist.* A.H. & A.W. Reed, Wellington.

Buck, Peter H. 1959 (1938). *Vikings of the Pacific.* University of Chicago Press, Chicago.

Buck, Sir Peter (Te Rangi Hiroa). 1949. *The Coming of the Maori.* Whitcombe & Tombs, Wellington.

Buck, Peter H. (Te Rangi Hiroa). 1964 (1957). *Arts and Crafts of Hawaii: Section XI, Religion*, 465–532. Bishop Museum Press, Honolulu.

Bühler, Alfred, Barrow, T. and Mountford, C.P. 1962. *Oceania and Australia: The Art of the South Seas.* Methuen, London.

Caruana, Wally. 1993. *Aboriginal Art.* Thames & Hudson, London.

Cave, David. 1993. *Mircea Eliade's Vision for a New Humanism.* Oxford University Press, New York.

Charlesworth, Max, Kimber, Richard and Wallace, Noel. 1990. *Ancestor Spirits: Aspects of Australian Aboriginal Life and Spirituality.* Deakin University Press, Geelong.

Charlesworth, Max, Morphy, Howard, Bell, Diane and Maddock, Kenneth (eds). 1984. *Religion in Aboriginal Australia: An Anthology.* University of Queensland Press, St Lucia.

Charlot, John. 1983. *Chanting the Universe: Hawaiian Religious Culture*. Emphasis International, Honolulu.

Chick, John and Sue. 1978. *Grass Roots Art of the Solomons: Images and Islands*. Pacific Publications, Sydney.

Chidester, David. 1983. 'Aesthetic Strategies in Western Religious Thought', in *Journal of American Academy of Religion*. March 1983, Ii: 55–66.

Chisholm, A.H. (ed.) 1958. *The Australian Encyclopaedia*. Angus & Robertson, Sydney. (Articles on Aboriginal dance, sign-language.)

Chowning, Ann. 1973. *An Introduction to the Peoples and Cultures of Melanesia*, Module in Anthropology, no. 38. Addison-Wesley, Reading, Mass.

Chowning, Ann. 1987. 'Melanesian Religions: an overview', in *Encyclopedia of Religion*, ed. M. Eliade, vol. 9, pp. 349–59.

Clunie, Fergus. 1986. *Yalo i Viti: Shades of Viti: A Fiji Museum Catalogue*. Fiji Museum, Suva.

Cochrane, Glynn. 1970. *Big Men and Cargo Cults*. Clarendon Press, Oxford.

Codrington, R.H. 1891. *The Melanesians: Studies in their Anthropology and Folk-lore*. Clarendon Press, Oxford.

Colless, Brian and Donovan, Peter (eds). 1985 (1980). *Religion in New Zealand Society*. Dunmore Press, Palmerston North.

Cooper, Carol, Morphy, Howard, Mulvaney, J. and Peterson, N. 1981. *Aboriginal Australia*, exhibition catalogue. Australian Gallery Directors Council, Sydney.

Coote, Jeremy and Shelton, Anthony (eds). 1992. *Anthropology, Art and Aesthetics*. Clarendon Press, Oxford.

Crawford, A.L. 1981. *Aida: Life and ceremony of the Gogodala*. National Cultural Council of Papua New Guinea, in association with Robert Brown, Bathurst, Australia.

Crawford, Ian M. 1968. *The Art of the Wandjina: Aboriginal Cave Paintings in Kimberley, Western Australia*. Oxford University Press, London.

Crocombe, R.G. 1973. *The New South Pacific*. Reed Education, Wellington. (University of South Pacific).

Crocombe, Ron. 1992. *Pacific Neighbours: New Zealand's Relations with Other Pacific Islands*. Centre for Pacific Studies, University of Canterbury, Christchurch; Institute of Pacific Studies, University of the South Pacific, Suva.

Crumlin, Rosemary. 1988. *Images of Religion in Australian Art*. Bay Books, Kensington, NSW.

Crumlin, Rosemary (ed.). 1991. *Aboriginal Art and Spirituality*. Collins Dove, North Blackburn, Australia.

Cultural Conservation Advisory Council. 1990. *Taonga Maori Conference*. NZ Department of Internal Affairs, Wellington.

Curnow, Allen (ed.). 1960. *The Penguin Book of New Zealand Verse*. Penguin Books, Harmondsworth.

Danielsson, Bengt. 1965. *Gauguin in the South Seas*. Allen and Unwin, London.

Dark, Philip J.C. 1974. *Kilenge Art and Life: A look at a New Guinea people*. Academy Editions, London.

Dark, Philip J.C. (ed.) 1984. *Development of the Arts in the Pacific*. Occasional Papers No. 1 of the Pacific Arts Association. National Museum, Wellington.

Dark, Philip J.C. and Rose, Roger G. (eds). 1993. *Artistic Heritage in a Changing Pacific*. University of Hawaii Press, Honolulu.

Davis, Frank. 1976. 'Maori Art and Artists', 10 articles, in *Education*, vol. 25, nos. 1–10. Department of Education, Wellington.

Davis, Te Aue (compiler). 1990. *Place Names of the Ancestors: A Maori Oral History Atlas*. New Zealand Geographic Board, Wellington.

Daws, Gavan. 1980. *A Dream of Islands: Voyages of Self-Discovery in the South Seas*. Jacaranda Press, Queensland; W.W. Norton, New York.

Dennett, Helen. 1975. *Mak Bilong Sepik: A Selection of Designs and Paintings from the Sepik River*. Wirui Press, Wewak.

Dillistone, F.W. 1986. *The Power of Symbols*. SCM Press, London.

Dittmer, Wilhelm. 1907. *Te Tohunga: the ancient legends and traditions of the Maoris, orally collected and pictured*. Routledge, London.

Dodd, Edward. 1967. *Polynesian Art: The Ring of Fire*. Dodd, Mead and company, New York.

Donovan, Peter (ed.). 1990. *Religions of New Zealanders*. Dunmore Press, Palmerston North.

Duff, Roger (ed.). 1969. *No Sort of Iron: Culture of Cook's Polynesians*. Art Galleries and Museums' Association of New Zealand, Christchurch.

Duncan, Betty K. 1985. 'Some Traditional Symbols in Samoan Christianity'. Unpublished paper, foreshadowing research entitled 'A Hierarchy of Symbols', 1994. University of Otago, Dunedin.

Duncan, Betty K. 1990. 'Christianity: Pacific Island Traditions', in P. Donovan (ed.), *Religions of New Zealanders*, 128–41. Dunmore Press, Palmerston North.

Durkheim, Emile. 1915. *The Elementary Forms of Religious Life: A Study in Religious Sociology*. Allen and Unwin, London.

Eather, Michael and Hall, Marlene. 1990. *Balance 1990: Views, Visions, Influences*. Queensland Art Gallery, Brisbane.

Eliade, Mircea. 1958. *Patterns in Comparative Religion*. Sheed & Ward, London.

Eliade, Mircea. 1959. *The Sacred and the Profane: The Nature of Religion*. Harcourt, Brace. New York.

Eliade, Mircea. 1985. *Symbolism, the Sacred and the Arts* (ed. Diane Apostolos-Cappadona). Crossroad, New York.

Eliade, Mircea (ed.). 1987. *Encyclopedia of Religion*, 16 vols. Macmillan, New York. (Articles on: Oceanic Religions; Christianity in Australia and NZ/in Pacific Islands; Anthropology; Religion; Religion, Community and Society; Power; Magic; Taboo; Masks; Initiation; Rites of Passage; Death; Ritual; Myth; Sacred Space/Time; Aesthetics; Arts, Crafts and Religion; Architecture; Dance and Religion; Drama; Music and Religion; Iconography; Images, Veneration; Dreams; Visions.)

Eliade, Mircea (ed.). 1987. *Encyclopedia of Religion*, 16 vols. Macmillan, New York. (Articles on: Australian Religions; Djanggawal; Iconography: Australian Aboriginal; Mardudjara; Ngukurr; Tjurungas; Ungarinyim; Wandjina; Walbiri; Wawalag; Yulunggul Snake.)

Eliade, Mircea (ed.). 1987. *Encyclopedia of Religion*. 16 vols. Macmillan, New York. (Articles on: Melanesian Religions; New Guinea; New Caledonian Religion; Solomon Islands Religions; Vanuatu Religions; Cargo Cults.)

Eliade, Mircea (ed.). 1987. *Encyclopedia of Religion*. 16 vols. Macmillan, New York (Articles on: Polynesian religions; Hawaiian religion; Maori religion; Tikopia religion; Maui; Tangaroa; Micronesian religion.)

Elkin, A.P. 1938 (1964). *The Australian Aborigines: How to Understand Them*. Angus & Robertson, Sydney.

Ellis, Catherine J. 1985. *Aboriginal Music: Education for Living*. University of Queensland Press, St Lucia.

Ellwood, Robert S. 1983. *Introducing Religion: from inside and outside*. Prentice-Hall, Englewood Cliffs.

Elsmore, Bronwyn. 1985. *Like Them That Dream: The Maori and the Old Testament*. Tauranga Moana Press, Tauranga.

Encyclopaedia of World Art. 1959–68, 1983. McGraw-Hill, New York. (Articles on: Australia, Australian cultures; Melanesia; Micronesia; Polynesia.)

Ernst, Manfred. 1994. *Winds of Change: Rapidly growing religious groups in the Pacific Islands*. Pacific Conference of Churches, Suva.

Feuerbach, Ludwig. 1957 (Ger. 1841). *The Essence of Christianity*. Harper, New York.

Firth, Raymond. 1936. *Art and Life in New Guinea*. The Studio, London.

Firth, Raymond. 1970. *Rank and Religion in Tikopia*. Allen and Unwin, London.

Firth, Raymond. 1990. *Tikopia songs: Poetic and musical art of a Polynesian people of the Solomon Islands*. Cambridge University Press, Cambridge.

Fischer, Ernst 1963. *The Necessity of Art: A Marxist Approach*. Penguin Books, Harmondsworth.

Fischer, Hans. 1983 (Ger. 1958). *Sound-producing Instruments in Oceania: Construction and Playing-Technique – Distribution and Function*. Institute of Papua New Guinea Studies, Boroko, PNG.

Fischer, Steven R. (ed.). 1993. *Easter Island Studies*. Oxborow Monograph 32. Oxborow Books, Oxford.

Forge, Anthony (ed.). 1973. *Primitive Art and Society*. Oxford University Press, London; Wenner-Gren Foundation.

Forman, Charles W. 1982. *The Island Churches of the South Pacific: Emergence in the Twentieth Century*. Orbis Books, Maryknoll.

Fraser, Douglas. 1966. 'The Heraldic Woman: A Study in Diffusion', in Douglas Fraser (ed.) *The Many Faces of Primitive Art*, Prentice-Hall, Englewood Cliffs, N.J., pp. 36–99.

Freedberg, David. 1989. *The Power of Images: Studies in the History and Theory of Response*. University of Chicago Press, Chicago.

Gablik, Suzi. 1991. *The Reenchantment of Art*. Thames and Hudson, London.

Garrett, John. 1982. *To Live Among the Stars: Christian Origins in Oceania*. University of South Pacific, Suva.

Gathercole, Peter, Kaeppler, Adrienne L. and Newton, Douglas. 1979. *The Art of the Pacific Islands*. National Gallery of Art, Washington.

Gerbrands, Adrian A. 1967. *Wow-Ipits: Eight Asmat Woodcarvers of New Guinea*. Mouton, The Hague.

Gill, Sam D. 1982. *Beyond the 'Primitive': the religions of nonliterate peoples*. Prentice-Hall, Englewood Cliffs, N.J.

Gillman, Ian (ed.). 1988. *Many faiths, one nation: a guide to the major faiths and denominations in Australia*. Collins, Sydney.

Goldman, Irving. 1970. *Ancient Polynesian Society*. University of Chicago Press, Chicago.

Goldwater, Robert. 1986. *Primitivism in Modern Art*. Belknap, Harvard University Press. (1938; 1966 revised edn).

Gombrich, Ernst H. 1955. *The Story of Art*. Phaidon Press, London.

Gould, Richard A. 1976. 'Desert Rituals and the Sacred Life', in Richard Schechner and Mady Schuman (eds), *Ritual, Play and Performance*. Seabury Press, New York. (pp. 166–79).

Graburn, Nelson H.H. (ed.). 1976. *Ethnic and Tourist Arts*. University of California Press, Berkeley.

Greeley, Andrew M. 1981. *The Religious Imagination*. Sadlier, Los Angeles.

Green, Garrett. 1989. *Imagining God: Theology and the Religious Imagination*. Harper & Row, New York.

Green, R.C. and Kaye. 1968. 'Religious Structures (Marae) of the Windward Society Islands', in *New Zealand Journal of History*, vol. 2, 66–89.

Greenhalgh, Michael and Megaw, Vincent (eds). 1978. *Art in Society: Studies in style, culture and aesthetics*. Duckworth, London.

Greschat, Hans-Jürgen. 1980. *Mana und Tapu: Die Religion der Maori auf Neuseeland*. D. Reimer Verlag, Berlin.

Grey, Sir George. 1956 (1855). *Polynesian Mythology*. Whitcombe & Tombs, Wellington.

Grimble, Arthur. 1972. *Migrations, Myth and Magic from the Gilbert Islands*. Routledge and Kegan Paul, London.

Groger-Wurm, Helen M. 1973. *Australian Aboriginal Bark Paintings and their Mythological Interpretation: Vol. I, Eastern Arnhem Land*. Australian Institute of Aboriginal Studies, Canberra.

Guiart, Jean. 1963. *The Arts of the South Pacific*. Thames & Hudson, London.

Guiart, Jean, Kaeppler, Adrienne, L. and Christensen, Dieter. 1974. 'Oceanic Peoples, Arts of', in *Encyclopaedia Britannica*, vol. 13, 448–68.

Gunn, Michael. 1992. *Malagan Ritual Art on Tabar, New Ireland, Papua New Guinea*. University of Otago, Dunedin. (Unpublished PhD thesis)

Habel, N.C. (ed.) 1979. *Powers, Plumes and Piglets: Phenomena of Melanesian Religion*. Australian Association for the Study of Religions, Adelaide.

Habel, Normal C. (ed.) 1992. *Religion and Multiculturalism in Australia: Essays in honour of Victor C. Hayes*. Australian Association for the Study of Religion, Adelaide.

Hamilton, Augustus. 1896 (1972 reprint). *Maori Art: The Art Workmanship of the Maori Race in New Zealand*. New Zealand Institute, Wellington.

Handy, E.S. Craighill. 1927. *Polynesian Religion*. Bulletin 34. Bernice P. Bishop Museum, Honolulu.

Hanna, Judith Lynne. 1979. *To Dance is Human: A Theory of Nonverbal Communication*. Texas University Press, Austin.

Hannemann, E.F. 1969. *Grass Roots Art of New Guinea*. Pacific Publications, Sydney.

Hanson, Allan. 1983. 'Art and the Maori Construction of Reality', in Mead & Kernot (eds) *Art and Artists in Oceania*, ch. 14. Dunmore Press, Palmerston North.

Hanson, F. Allan. 1987. 'Polynesian Religions: An Overview', in M. Eliade (ed.) *ER*, vol. 11, 423–32.

Hanson, F.A. and L. 1983. *Counterpoint in Maori Culture*. Routledge and Kegan Paul, London.

Hanson, Allan and Louise (eds). 1990. *Art and Identity in Oceania*. University of Hawaii Press, Honolulu.

Hardy, Jane, Megaw, J.V.S. and Megaw, M. Ruth (eds). 1992. *The Heritage of Namatjira: The Watercolourists of Central Australia*. William Heinemann Australia, Port Melbourne.

Heermann, Ingrid (ed.). 1979. *Tingting bilong mi: Zeitgenössische Kunst aus Papua-Neuguinea.* Institut für Auslandbeziehungen, Stuttgart.

Henry, Teuira. 1928. *Ancient Tahiti.* Bulletin 48. Bishop Museum, Honolulu.

Herdt, Gilbert and Stephen, Michele. 1989. *The Religious Imagination in New Guinea.* Rutgers University Press, New Brunswick.

Hiller, Susan (ed.). 1991. *The Myth of Primitivism: Perspectives on Art.* Routledge, London.

Hinnells, John R. (ed.). 1985. *A Handbook of Living Religions.* Viking, Baltimore.

Holm, Jean and Bowker, John (eds). 1994. *Themes in Religious Studies,* 10 vols. Pinter Publishers, London.

Hooper, Antony and Huntsman, Judith. 1985. *Transformations of Polynesian Culture.* The Polynesian Society, Auckland.

Howard, Alan and Borovsky, Robert (eds). 1989. *Developments in Polynesian Ethnology.* University of Hawaii Press, Honolulu.

Howells, William. 1973. *The Pacific Islanders.* Weidenfeld and Nicolson, London.

Ihimaera, Witi. 1991. 'Karaka', in *Art New Zealand,* 60: 78–81, 109. Auckland.

Irwin, James. 1984. *An Introduction to Maori Religion.* Australian Association for the Study of Religions, Adelaide.

Isaacs, Jennifer. 1980. *Australian Dreaming: 40,000 Years of Aboriginal History.* Lansdowne Press, Sydney.

Isaacs, Jennifer. 1989. *Aboriginality: Contemporary Aboriginal Paintings & Prints.* University of Queensland Press, St Lucia.

Jackson, Michael. 1972. 'Aspects of Symbolism and Composition in Maori Art', in *Bijdragen tot de Taal-, Land-, en Volkenkunde,* 128: 33–80. Leiden.

Johansen, J. Prytz. 1954. *The Maori and His Religion in its Non-ritualistic Aspects.* Munksgaard, Copenhagen.

Johnson-Hill, Lydia (ed.). 1993. *Pacific Journal of Theology,* series II, no. 9, Issue on arts in Pacific worship. South Pacific Association of Theological Schools, Suva.

Johnston, Alexa M. 1992. 'Christianity in New Zealand Art', in *Headlands: Thinking through New Zealand Art,* exhibition catalogue, 99–111. Museum of Contemporary Art, Sydney.

Jones, Philip and Sutton, Peter. 1986. *Art and Land: Aboriginal Sculptures of the Lake Eyre Region.* South Australian Museum, Adelaide.

Jopling, Carol F. (ed.). 1971. *Art and Aesthetics in Primitive Societies: A Critical Anthology.* E.P. Dutton, New York.

Jupp, James (ed.). 1988. *The Australian People.* Angus & Robertson, Sydney. (pp. 135–259, Australian Aborigines).

Kaeppler, Adrienne L. 1987. 'Polynesian Religions: Mythic Themes', in M. Eliade (ed.) *ER,* vol. 11: 432–5.

Kahukiwa, Robyn and Grace, Patricia (text) 1984 (1991). *Wahine Toa: Women of Maori Myth.* Collins, Auckland; Viking Pacific.

Kanahele, George Hu'eu Sanford. 1986. *Ku Kanaka: Stand Tall: A Search for Hawaiian Values.* University of Hawaii Press, Honolulu.

Keesing, Roger M. 1982. *Kwaio Religion: The Living and the Dead in a Solomon Island Society.* Columbia University Press, New York.

Keesing, Roger M. 1984. 'Rethinking Mana', in *Journal of Anthropological Research,* vol. 40, pp. 137–156.

Kelm, Heinz. 1966, 1968. *Kunst vom Sepik,* 3 Bände. Museum für Völkerkunde, Berlin.

Kernot, Bernie. 1984. 'Kuai Maueha, 1933–1981'. Review of posthumous exhibition in Suva, in *Pacific Arts Newsletter*, No. 19 (June 1984), 11–13.

Kiki, Albert Maori. 1968. *Kiki: Ten Thousand Years in a Lifetime: A New Guinea Autobiography*. F.W. Cheshire, Melbourne.

King, Michael. 1985. *Being Pakeha: An Encounter with New Zealand and the Maori Renaissance*. Hodder & Stoughton, Auckland; London.

King, Winston L. 1968. *Introduction to Religion: A Phenomenological Approach*. Harper & Row, New York.

Kiribati Ministry of Education. 1979. *Kiribati: Aspects of History*. University of the South Pacific, Suva.

Kolig, Erich. 1981. *The Silent Revolution: The Effects of Modernization on Australian Aboriginal Religion*. Institute for the Study of Human Issues, Philadelphia.

Kooijman, Simon. 1964. 'Ancient Tahitian God-figures', in *Journal of the Polynesian Society*, vol. 73: 110–25. Wellington.

Kupka, Karel. 1965. *Dawn of Art: Painting and Sculpture of Australian Aborigines*. Angus & Robertson, Sydney.

Lakoff, George and Johnson, Mark. 1980. *Metaphors We Live By*. University of Chicago, Chicago.

Lang, Nikolaus. 1988. *Australian Imaginary Figurations 1986–1988*. Catalogue folder. Art Gallery of South Australia, Adelaide.

Lange, Nushka K. 1992. *To Carve New Paths: The Value of Visual Arts in Pacific Worship*. Pacific Theological College, Suva. (Unpublished B.D. Honours thesis)

Laracy, Hugh (ed.). 1989. *Ples Blong Iumi, Solomon Islands: The Past Four Thousand Years*. University of South Pacific, Suva and Honiara.

Lavine, Stephen D. and Karp, Ivan. 1991. *Exhibiting Cultures: The Poetics and Politics of Museum Display*. Smithsonian Institution Press, Washington DC.

Lawrence, P. and Meggitt, M.J. (eds). 1965. *Gods, Ghosts and Men in Melanesia*. Oxford University Press, Melbourne.

Layton, Robert. 1981. *The Anthropology of Art*. Elek Books, London.

Leeuw, Gerardus van der. 1938. *Religion in Essence and Manifestation: A Study in Phenomenology*. Allen and Unwin, London.

Leeuw, Gerardus van der. 1963 (Dutch 1932). *Sacred and Profane Beauty: The Holy in Art*. Weidenfeld and Nicolson, London.

Lerner, Daniel. 1958. *The Passing of Traditional Society*. Free Press, Glencoe.

Lessa, William A. 1987. 'Micronesian Religions: An Overview', in M. Eliade (ed.), *ER*, 9: 498–505. Macmillan, New York.

Levy, Robert I. 1973. *Tahitians: Mind and Experience in the Society Islands*. University of Chicago Press, Chicago.

Lewis, George H. 1990. 'A Soul Awakening: Social Identity in Hawaiian Music', in *The World and I*, vol. 5, 11: 618–29. Washington DC.

Linton, Ralph. 1923. *The Material Culture of the Marquesan Islands*. Memoirs 8, 5. Bernice P. Bishop Museum, Honolulu.

Linton, Ralph and Wingert, Paul S. 1946. *Arts of the South Seas*. Museum of Modern Art, New York.

Loeliger, Carl and Trompf, Garry (eds). 1985. *New Religious Movements in Melanesia*. University of the South Pacific, Suva; and Univ. PNG.

Luomala, Katherine. 1949. *Maui-of-a-thousand-tricks*. Bulletin 198. Bishop Museum, Honolulu.

Luomala, Katherine. 1987. 'Micronesian Religions: Mythic Themes', in M. Eliade (ed.), *ER*, 9: 505–9. Macmillan, New York.

Lutkehaus, Nancy, Kaufman, Christian et al. (eds). 1990. *Sepik Heritage: Tradition and Change in Papua New Guinea*. Crawford House Press, Bathurst; Wenner Gren Foundation.

Malinowski, Bronislaw. 1948 (1925). *Magic, Science and Religion; and other essays*. Doubleday Anchor Books, Garden City, NY.

Mané-Wheoki, Jonathan. 1990. 'Work of Maori Architects adds to our Heritage', in *New Zealand Historic Places*, no. 31: 29–37. NZ Historic Places Trust, Wellington.

Mantovani, Ennio (ed.). 1984. *An Introduction to Melanesian Religions*. Melanesian Institute, Goroka, PNG.

Mataira, Katerina. 1984. *Maori Artists of the South Pacific*. NZ Maori Artists & Writers Society, Raglan.

McCarthy, Frederick D. 1958. *Australian Aboriginal Rock Art*. Australian Museum, Sydney.

McEwen, J.M. 1966. 'Maori Art', in *An Encyclopaedia of New Zealand*, vol. 2, 408–29. Government Printer, Wellington.

McLean, Mervyn and Orbell, Margaret. (1975) 1990. *Traditional Songs of the Maori*. Auckland University Press, Auckland.

McLintock, A.H. (ed.). 1966. *An Encyclopaedia of New Zealand*. 3 vols. Government Printer, Wellington.

Mead, Sidney M. 1961. *The Art of Maori Carving*. A.H. & A.W. Reed, Wellington.

Mead, Sidney M. (ed.). 1979. *Exploring the Visual Art of Oceania: Australia, Melanesia, Micronesia, and Polynesia*. University Press of Hawaii, Honolulu.

Mead, Sidney Moko (ed.). 1984. *Te Maori: Maori Art from New Zealand Collections*. Heinemann, Auckland; American Federation of Arts, New York.

Mead, Sidney M. and Kernot, Bernie (eds). 1983. *Art and Artists of Oceania*. Dunmore Press, Palmerston North, NZ.

Metge, Joan. 1976 (1967). *The Maoris of New Zealand: Rautahi*. Routledge & Kegan Paul, London.

Mol, Hans J. 1976. *Identity and the Sacred: A sketch for a new social scientific theory of religion*. Blackwell, Oxford.

Moore, Albert C. 1977. *Iconography of Religions: An introduction*. SCM Press, London; Fortress Press, Philadelphia.

Moore, Albert C. 1983. 'The Transforming Vision of God in Religion and Art' in *The Scottish Journal of Religious Studies*, Stirling, iv: 107–120.

Moore, Albert C. 1987. 'The Religious Significance of Modern Maori Artists', in P. Matheson (ed.), *The Catholic Presbyterian: essays in honour of Frank Nichol*. Theological Hall, Knox College, Dunedin.

Moore, Albert C. 1989a. 'Windows to the Divine: A Theory of Religious Art, Traditional and Modern', in *Dialogue and Alliance* 3(2): 15–23.

Moore, Albert C. 1989b. 'The Land as Religious Symbol: a View from New Zealand', in Yeow Choo Lak and John C. England (eds), *Doing Theology with People's Symbols and Images*, 84–100. ATESEA Occasional Papers No. 8, Association for Theological Education in S.E. Asia, Singapore.

Moore, Albert C. 1990. 'Religion, the Arts and the "Tutored Imagination"', in *Australian Religion Studies Review*. (Sept. 1990), 3: 30–36.

Mountford, Charles P. 1965. *Ayers Rock*. Angus & Robertson, Sydney.

Moyle, Richard M. 1986. *Alyawarra Music: Songs and society in a central Australian community*. Australian Institute of Aboriginal Studies, Canberra.

Moyle, Richard. 1988. *Traditional Samoan Music*. Auckland University Press, Auckland.

Mulgan, Richard. 1989. *Maori, Pakeha and Democracy*. Oxford University Press, Oxford; Auckland.

Muller, Kal. 1974. 'Tanna awaits the coming of Jon Frum', in *National Geographic*, cxliv (May 1974), 706–15.

Munn, Nancy D. 1973. *Walbiri Iconography*. Cornell University Press, Ithaca.

Neich, Roger, 1982. 'A Semiological Analysis of Self-decoration in Mount Hagen, New Guinea', in Ino Rossi et al., *The Logic of Culture*: 214–230. Bergin, South Hadley, Mass.

Neich, Roger. 1984. 'Some Recent Developments in the Anthropology of the Visual Arts', in *Pacific Arts Newsletter*, no. 19, 24–42.

Neich, Roger. 1985. *Material Culture of Western Samoa: Persistence and Change*. Bulletin 23. National Museum of New Zealand, Wellington.

Neich, Roger. 1993. *Painted Histories: Early Maori Figurative Painting*. Auckland University Press, Auckland.

Newton, Douglas. 1961. *Art Styles of the Papuan Gulf*. Museum of Primitive Art, New York.

Newton, Douglas. 1967. *New Guinea Art in the Collection of the Museum of Primitive Art*. Museum of Primitive Art Handbooks, New York.

Newton, Douglas. 1971. *Crocodile and Cassowary: Religious Art of the Upper Sepik River, New Guinea*. Museum of Primitive Art, New York.

Newton, Douglas (text). 1978. *Masterpieces of Primitive Art*. Knopf, New York.

Nicholas, Darcy and Kaa, Keri (interviews). 1986. *Seven Maori Artists*. Government Printer, Wellington.

Niles, Don and Webb, Michael. 1987. *Papua New Guinea Music Collection*. Institute of Papua New Guinea Studies, Port Moresby.

Novitz, David. 1992. *The Boundaries of Art*. Temple University Press, Philadelphia.

O'Hanlon, Michael. 1989. *Reading the Skin: Adornment, Display and Society among the Wahgi*. British Museum, London; Crawford House, Bathurst.

O'Keefe, Daniel. 1982. *Stolen Lightning: The Social Theory of Magic*. Martin Robertson, Oxford.

Oliver, Douglas L. 1974. *Ancient Tahitian Society*, 3 vols. University Press of Hawaii, Honolulu.

Oliver, W.H. 1960. *The Story of New Zealand*. Faber, London.

Oliver, W.H. (ed.). 1981. *The Oxford History of New Zealand*. Clarendon Press, Oxford.

Orbell, Margaret. 1985. *The Natural World of the Maori*. David Bateman, Auckland.

Orbell, Margaret. 1991 (1985). *Hawaiki: A new approach to Maori tradition*. Canterbury University Press, Christchurch.

Osborne, Harold (ed.). 1970. *The Oxford Companion to Art*. Oxford University Press, London.

Otten, Charlotte M. (ed.). 1971. *Anthropology and Art: Readings in Cross Cultural Aesthetics*. Natural History Press, Garden City, NY.

Otto, Rudolf. 1923 (Ger. 1917). *The Idea of Holy*. Oxford University Press, London.

Pacific Arts Association. *Pacific Arts Newsletter*, (nos 1–27) 1975–89; *Pacific Arts*, Journal, 1990–. Honolulu.

Pannett, Ralph A. 1984. 'Tawhiri-Matea', notes in typed form. NZ Meteorological Service, Wellington.

Pernet, Henry. 1992 (Fr. 1988). *Ritual Masks: Deceptions and Revelations.* University of South Carolina Press, Columbia, S.C.

Petri, Helmut. 1960. 'Australian Cultures', in *Encyclopedia of World Art,* II, 126–139, McGraw-Hill, New York.

Phillipps, W.J. 1981 (1955). *Maori Carving Illustrated.* A.H. & A.W. Reed, Wellington.

Poignant, Roslyn. 1967. *Oceanic Mythology.* Paul Hamlyn, London (pp. 12–82, Polynesia and Micronesia).

Premont, Roslyn and Lennard, Mark. 1988. *Tjukurrpa: Desert Paintings of Central Australia.* Centre for Aboriginal Artists, Alice Springs.

Pritchard, Mary J. 1984. *Siapo: Bark Cloth Art of Samoa.* American Samoa Council on Culture, Arts and Humanities.

Pruyser, Paul. 1968. *A Dynamic Psychology of Religion.* Harper and Row, New York.

Pruyser, Paul. 1983. *The Play of the Imagination: Towards a Psychoanalysis of Culture.* International Universities Press, New York.

Pruyser, Paul (ed.). 1987. *Changing Views of the Human Condition.* Mercer, Atlanta. (ch. 7).

Renselaar, H.C. van. 1956. *Asmat: Art from Southwest New Guinea.* Royal Tropical Institute, no. 121, Amsterdam.

Rice, Edward. 1974. *Jon Frum He Come.* Doubleday, New York.

Ritchie, James. 1992. *Becoming Bicultural.* Huia Publishers, Wellington.

Rockefeller, M.C. and Gerbrands, Adrian A. 1967. *The Asmat of New Guinea: The Journal of Michael Clark Rockefeller* (ed. A.A. Gerbrands). Museum of Primitive Art, New York.

Rongokea, Lynnsay. 1992. *Tivaevae: Portraits of Cook Islands Quilting.* Daphne Brasell Associates, Auckland.

Ross, J. and Simmons, L. (eds). 1989. *Gordon Walters: Order and Intuition.* Walters Publications, Auckland.

Rouget, Gilbert. 1985. *Music and Trance: A Theory of the Relation between Music and Possession.* University of Chicago Press, Chicago.

Rubin, William (ed.). 1984. *'Primitivism' in 20th century art: affinity of the tribal and the modern.* Museum of Modern Art, New York.

Ryan, Judith. 1989. *Mythscapes: Aboriginal Art of the Desert.* National Gallery of Victoria, Melbourne.

Ryan, Judith. 1990. *Paint Up Big: Warlpiri Women's Art of Lajamanu.* National Gallery of Victoria, Melbourne.

Ryan, Peter (ed.). 1972. *Encyclopaedia of Papua and New Guinea.* Melbourne University Press.

Salisbury, Kevin B. 1984. 'Tradition and Change in the Music of Pukapuka, Cook Islands', in *Pacific Arts Newsletter,* No. 19: 42–55.

Schmitz, Carl A. 1963. *Wantoat: Art and Religion of the Northeast New Guinea Papuans.* Mouton, The Hague.

Schmitz, Carl A. 1971. *Oceanic Art: Myth, Man, and Image in the South Seas.* Harry N. Abrams, New York.

Schwimmer, E. 1966. *The World of the Maori.* A.H. & A.W. Reed, Wellington.

Schwimmer, Erik (ed.). 1968. *The Maori People in the Nineteen-Sixties.* Blackwood & Janet Paul, Auckland.

Segal, Gerald. 1990. *Rethinking the Pacific*. Clarendon Press, Oxford.

Sharpe, Eric J. 1983. *Understanding Religion*. Duckworth, London.

Shaw, Peter. 1991. *New Zealand Architecture, from Polynesian Beginnings to 1990*. Hodder & Stoughton, London.

Sierksma, Fokke. 1960. *The Gods as we Shape Them*. Routledge & Kegan Paul, London.

Simmons, David R. 1985. *Whakairo: Maori Tribal Art*. Reed Methuen, Auckland.

Simmons, David R. 1986. *Ta Moko: The Art of Maori Tattoo*. Reed Methuen, Auckland.

Simons, Susan C. and Stevenson, Hugh (eds). 1990. *Luk Luk Gen! Look Again! Contemporary Art from Papua New Guinea*. Perc Tucker Regional Gallery, Townsville.

Sinclair, James. 1985. *Papua New Guinea: The First 100 Years*. Robert Brown & Associates, Bathurst.

Smart, Ninian. 1983. *Worldviews: Crosscultural Explorations of Human Beliefs*. Scribners, New York.

Smart, Ninian. 1989. *The World's Religions: Old Traditions and Modern Transformations*. Cambridge University Press, Cambridge.

Smith, Bernard. 1985. *European Vision and the South Pacific*. Yale University Press, New Haven. (1st edn 1959).

Speiser, Felix. 1966 (Ger. 1941). 'Art Styles in the Pacific', in Douglas Fraser (ed.), *The Many Faces of Primitive Art*, Prentice-Hall, pp. 132–60.

Spencer, Paul (ed.). 1985. *Society and the Dance: The Social Anthropology of Process and performance*. Cambridge University Press, Cambridge.

Spencer, W.B. and Gillen, F.J. 1927 (1899). *The Native Tribes of Central Australia*. Macmillan, London.

Stanner, W.E.H. 1958. 'The Dreaming', in W.A. Lessa & E.Z. Vogt (eds), *Reader in Comparative Religion*. Harper & Row, New York (1958, 1965, 1972).

Stanner, W.E.H. 1965. 'Religion, Totemism and Symbolism', in R.M. and C.H. Berndt, eds, *Aboriginal Man in Australia*. Angus & Robertson, Sydney. (pp. 207–37).

Steinen, Karl von den. 1925–28. *Die Marquesaner und ihre Kunst: Primitive Südseeornamentik*. 3 Bände. Dietrich Reimer/Ernst Vohsen, Berlin.

Strathern, Andrew and Marilyn. 1971. *Self-decoration in Mount Hagen*. Duckworth, London.

Strehlow, T.G.H. 1971a. 'Religions of Illiterate People: Australia', in C.J. Bleeker and G. Widengren (eds), *Historia Religionum*. E.J. Brill, Leiden (vol. 2, 609–28).

Strehlow, T.G.H. 1971b. *Songs of Central Australia*, Angus and Robertson, Sydney.

Streng, Frederick J., Lloyd, Charles L. and Allen, Jay T. 1973. *Ways of Being Religious: readings for a new approach to religion*. Prentice-Hall, Englewood Cliffs.

Suggs, Robert C. 1960. *The Island Civilizations of Polynesia*. New American Library, New York.

Suggs, Robert C. 1965. *The Hidden Worlds of Polynesia*. New American Library, New York.

Sutton, Peter (ed.). 1988. *Dreamings: The Art of Aboriginal Australia*. Viking, New York; South Australian Museum.

Swain, Tony. 1985. *Interpreting Aboriginal Religion: An Historical Account*. Australian Association for the Study of Religions, Bedford Park S.A.

Swain, Tony and Rose, Deborah Bird (eds). 1988. *Aboriginal Australia and Christian Missions*. Australian Association for the Study of Religions, Adelaide.

Swain, Tony. 1992. 'Reinventing the Eternal: Aboriginal Spirituality and Modernity', in Habel 1992, 122–36.

Takenaka, Masao and O'Grady, Ron. 1991. *The Bible Through Asian Eyes*. Pace Publishing, Auckland/Asian Christian Art Association, Kyoto.

Tausie, Vilsoni. 1979. *Art in the New Pacific*. Institute of Pacific Studies, Suva, Fiji.

Taylor, Alan. 1988. *Maori Folk Art*. Century Hutchinson, Auckland.

Te Riria, Ko and Simmons, David. 1989. *Maori Tattoo*. Bush Press, Auckland.

Theroux, Paul. 1992. *The Happy Isles of Oceania*. Hamish Hamilton, London.

Thorogood, Bernard. 1960. *Not Quite Paradise*. London Missionary Society, London.

Tippett, Alan R. 1967. *Solomon Islands Christianity: A study in growth and obstruction*. Lutterworth.

Tonkinson, Robert. 1978. *The Mardudjara Aborigines: Living the Dream in Australia's Desert*. Holt, Rinehard and Winston, New York.

Torgovnick, Marianna. 1990. *Gone Primitive: Savage Intellects, Modern Lives*. University of Chicago Press, Chicago.

Trask, Willard R. (ed.). 1966–67. *The Unwritten Song: Poetry of the Primitive and Traditional Peoples of the World*. Macmillan, New York. (Vol. 1, 187–261, Melanesia, Australia. Vol. 2, 1–120, Micronesia, Polynesia).

Trompf, G.W. 1991. *Melanesian Religion*. Cambridge University Press, Cambridge, U.K. and Melbourne.

Trompf, Garry W. 1994. *Payback: The Logic of Retribution in Melanesian Religions*. Cambridge University Press, Oakleigh, Australia.

Trotter, M. and McCulloch, B. 1981 (1971). *Prehistoric Rock Art of New Zealand*. Longman Paul, Auckland.

Turner, Dennis. 1975 (1963). *Tangi*. A.H. & A.W. Reed, Wellington.

Turner, Harold W. 1977. 'Primal Religions of the World and their Study'; 'New Religious Movements in Primal Societies', in *Australian Essays in World Religions* (ed. Victor C. Hayes) 27–48. The Australian Association for the Study of Religions, Bedford Park, S.A.

Tuzin, Donald F. 1980. *The Voice of Tambaram: Truth and Illusion in Ilahita Arapesh Religion*. University of California Press, Berkeley.

Ucko, Peter J. (ed.). 1977. *Form in Indigenous Art*. Australian Institute of Aboriginal Studies, Canberra.

Wagner H. and Reiner H. (eds). 1986. *The Lutheran Church in Papua New Guinea, 1886–1986*. Lutheran Publishing House, Adelaide.

Waite, Deborah. 1983. *Art of the Solomon Islands: from the Collection of the Barbier-Müller Museum*. Geneva.

Warlukurlangu Artists. 1987. *Kuruwarri: Yuendumu Doors*. Australian Institute of Aboriginal Studies, Canberra.

Warnock, Mary. 1976. *Imagination*. Faber & Faber, London.

Webb, Michael H. 1987. *Paitim, Winim na Meknais: Construction And Uses Of Sound Producing Instruments of Papua New Guinea*. University of PNG – Goroka Teachers College.

Wendt, Albert. 1983. 'Contemporary Arts in Oceania: Trying to Stay Alive in Paradise as an Artist', in *Art and Artists in Oceania* (eds S.M. Mead and B. Kernot). Dunmore, Palmerston North.

West, Margie K.C. (ed.). 1988. *The Inspired Dream: Life as art in Aboriginal Australia.* Queensland Art Gallery, Brisbane.

Whiting, Cliff. 1992. 'Te Po, Te Whaio, Te Ao Marama', interview in *Headlands: Thinking Through New Zealand Art*, exhibition catalogue: 113–21. Museum of Contemporary Art, Sydney.

Williams, Francis E. 1940. *Drama of Orokolo: The Social and Ceremonial Life of the Elema.* Clarendon Press, Oxford.

Williamson, R.W. 1937. *Religion and Social Organization of Polynesia.* Cambridge University Press, Cambridge.

RECOMMENDED READING

(A) Books and Encyclopaedia Surveys

These are helpful introductions and in most cases are illustrated with colour and other plates.

Barrow, Terence. 1972. *Art and Life in Polynesia*. Reed, Wellington. [Polynesia].

Barrow, Terence. 1984. *An Illustrated Guide to Maori Art*. Reed and Octopus, Auckland. [Aotearoa NZ].

Birnbaum, Phil and Strathern, Andrew J. 1990. *Faces of Papua New Guinea*. Emperor Publishing, Darlinghurst, NSW, Australia. [Melanesia]

Brake, Brian, McNeish, James and Simmons, David. 1979. *Art of the Pacific*. Oxford University Press. [Pacific].

Crawford, Peter. 1993. *Nomads of the Wind: A Natural History of Polynesia*. BBC Books, London. [Polynesia]

Gathercole, Peter, Kaeppler, Adrienne L. and Newton, Douglas. 1979. *The Art of the Pacific Islands*. National Gallery of Art, Washington. [Pacific].

Guiart, Jean. 1963. *The Arts of the South Pacific*. Thames & Hudson, London. [Melanesia].

Guiart, Jean, Kaeppler, Adrienne L. and Christensen, Dieter. 1986. 'Oceanic Arts', in *Encyclopaedia Britannica*, vol. 25, 103–22. [Pacific].

Mead, Sidney Moko (ed.) 1984. *Te Maori: Maori Art from New Zealand Collections*. Heinemann, Auckland; American Federation of Arts, New York. [Aotearoa NZ].

Poignant, Roslyn. 1967. *Oceanic Mythology*. Hamlyn, London. [Polynesia and Melanesia].

Sutton, Peter (ed.). 1988. *Dreamings: The Art of Aboriginal Australia*. Viking, New York; South Australian Museum. [Australia].

Tausie, Vilsoni. 1979, 1981. *Art in the New Pacific*. Institute of Pacific Studies, Suva, Fiji. [Pacific].

Thorne, Alan and Raymond, Robert. 1989. *Man on the Rim: The Peopling of the Pacific*. Angus and Robertson, for Australian Broadcasting Corporation, Sydney. [Pacific]

Trompf, Garry W. 1991. *Melanesian Religion*. Cambridge University Press, Cambridge, UK and Melbourne. [Melanesia].

(B) Journals

Oceania. 1930—. Australian National Research Council, Melbourne & Sydney.
Journal of Polynesian Studies. 1892—. Wellington, NZ.
Journal of Pacific History. 1965—. Research School of Pacific Studies, Australian National University, Canberra.
Catalyst. 1971—. Melanesian Institute for Pastoral and Socio-Economic Service, Goroka, PNG.
Pacific Studies. 1977—. Institute for Polynesian Studies, Brigham Young University, Hawaii.
Pacific Arts. 1990—. Pacific Arts Association, Honolulu. (Preceded by *Pacific Arts Newsletter* 1975—89).

Valuable materials on Pacific religions and arts are to be found in many other journals in the Pacific area and in international journals of History, Anthropology, Social Sciences, Arts, Languages, Religion, Theology and Christian Missions.

Library resources on the Pacific area are available at university centres in Honolulu (Univ. of Hawaii; East-West Center), in Suva (Univ. of South Pacific) and Waigani, Port Moresby (Univ. of PNG), as well as in the universities of Australia and New Zealand.

GLOSSARY

Anthropomorphic:	in human form, as in images depicting gods as persons.
Atua, akua:	gods, in sense of sacred powers related to departments of life (Polynesia).
Big man:	Melanesian leader who achieves status by effort in his lifetime.
Biocosmic:	emphasizing abundant life as the union of the biological and spiritual.
Bullroarer:	thin board whirled round on a cord to produce an awesome roaring round.
Cargo-cult:	Melanesian movement combining primal traditions of ancestor with new expectations of imminent advent of wealth (cargo).
Corroboree:	celebration in singing and dancing of Australian Aboriginal.
Cosmogony:	account of how the cosmos or universe began.
Cosmos:	an ordered universe which includes all things, visible and invisible.
Didjeridu:	drone pipe of hollow wood, N. Australia.
Dreaming, Dreamtime:	Australian Aboriginal terms for time of ancestor heroes which is eternal and continues to shape the land, culture and individuals.
Ethnoaesthetics:	deals with art as perceived by the people who produce and use it.
Iconography:	literally 'writing in images'; the study of the meaning of patterns used in art, as in religious symbolism and narratives concerning deities.
Malagan/Malanggan:	intricate painted carvings associated with spirit-world and death and initiation ceremonies in New Ireland, Melanesia.
Mana:	power and efficacy in working; spiritual force, authority and prestige.
Marae:	ceremonial courtyard, in the form of a stone

	platform in central and eastern Polynesia; a green space in front of the meeting-house in NZ.
Moko:	facial tattoo of NZ Maori.
Myth:	founding story, regarded as true because it provides the pattern for living from gods and ancestors.
Personal art:	art applied to human body as in decoration, body-painting, tattoo.
Phenomenology of religion:	study of religion as a human phenomenon, seeking understanding of the experience and intention of the religious participants and comparing types of expression of the religion.
Pluralism:	coexistence of different religions within one society.
Pre-contact:	prior to coming of European influence by trade, conquest or religious missions.
Primal religions:	religions of tribal, non-literate cultures; elemental and basic (used in preference to 'primitive').
Religion:	(see definitions in section of ch. 1).
Sacred:	transcending the ordinary profane world; ultimate and beyond; de-limited from profane handling because of high power.
Shaman:	religious leader or healer who goes into ecstatic state to contact the spirit world.
Songline:	series of Aboriginal songs recounting one myth.
Taonga:	belongings, treasures (as in Maori art).
Tapa:	bark-cloth made from paper mulberry; imprinted with designs in W. Polynesia.
Tapu, taboo:	set apart; placed under restriction to maintain *mana* or sacred state and safeguard from danger.
Tiki:	image in human form (Polynesia), based on primeval first man; stylized as neck-pendant, *hei-tiki* in NZ.
Tjurunga:	flat board or stone, incised with symbols, regarded by Australian Aboriginals as sacred links with Dreaming.
Tohunga:	expert, including priestly expert (Maori, including cognate Polynesian terms).

Totem: thing or animal conferring bond of unity among people.

Wandjina: Aboriginal paintings in caves of N.W. Australia depicting rain-spirits.

Whare whakairo: house of carving; Maori meeting house decorated with ancestral carving.

Extensive glossaries are found in Jean Guiart, *The Arts of the South Pacific*, 1963: 405–16, and in S.M. Mead (ed.), *Te Maori* 1984: 236–39. Readers may find it helpful to compose a glossary of their own selection.

INDEX